# Logical
# Self-Defense

# Logical
# Self-Defense

**Ralph H. Johnson, Ph.D.**
Associate Professor of Philosophy
University of Windsor

**J. Anthony Blair, B.A.**
Assistant Professor of Philosophy
University of Windsor

**McGRAW-HILL RYERSON**
Toronto   Montreal   New York   St. Louis   San Francisco
Auckland   Bogotá   Düsseldorf   Johannesburg   London
Madrid   Mexico   New Delhi   Panama   Paris
São Paulo   Singapore   Sydney   Tokyo

Logical Self-Defense

1 2 3 4 5 6 7 8 9 10   AP   6 5 4 3 2 1 0 9 8 7

ISBN 0-07-082348-0

Printed and bound in Canada


Canadian Cataloguing in Publication Data

Johnson, Ralph Henry, 1940-
  Logical self-defense

Includes index.
ISBN 0-07-082348-0

1. Fallacies (Logic)  2. Reasoning. I. Blair,
J. Anthony, 1941-    II. Title.

BC175.J63          165        C77-001232-9

Credits

The authors thank the following copyright holders for granting permission to use their material. For permission to use excerpts from columns or articles we thank the following newspapers and magazines: *The Windsor Star;* the *Globe and Mail,* Toronto; the St. John's *Evening Telegram; The Detroit News; Maclean's; Canadian Tribune; Saturday Review.* For permission to use excerpts from their newspaper columns we thank Mr. Dalton Camp; Professor James Eayrs; Mr. Charles Lynch; and Ann Landers, Field Newspaper Syndicate, and *The Windsor Star.* For permission to use excerpts from a letter to *The Windsor Star* we thank Professor Lawrence LaFave. We acknowledge permission to print excerpts from the following books: an excerpt from *Ludwig Wittgenstein: A Memoir* by Norman Malcolm, reprinted with permission of Oxford University Press, Oxford; an excerpt from *The October Crisis* by Gerard Pelletier, reprinted by permission of The Canadian Publisher, McClelland & Stewart Limited, Toronto; an excerpt from *Consumer, Beware!* by Ellen Roseman, used by permission of New Press, Don Mills, Ontario; an excerpt from *I Can Sell You Anything* by Carl P. Wrighter, copyright by Ballantine Books, a Division of Random House, Inc., New York; an excerpt from *Confessions of an Advertising Man* by David Ogilvy, reprinted with permission of Atheneum Publishers, New York.


Care has been taken to trace ownership of copyright material contained in this text. The publishers will gladly take any information that will enable them to rectify any reference or credit in subsequent editions.

# Contents

... what is the use of studying philosophy if all that it does for you is to enable you to talk with some plausibility about some abstruse questions of logic, etc., and it does not improve your thinking about the important questions of everyday life ...

—Ludwig Wittgenstein (from Norman Malcolm), *Ludwig Wittgenstein, A Memoir* (Oxford University Press, 1958; Oxford Paperbacks, 1962), p. 39.

# Acknowledgements

The list of people to whom the authors are indebted is very long. Our sources for this book include Howard Kahane's *Logic and Contemporary Rhetoric* and Michael Scrivens's *Reasoning*.

We would like to especially acknowledge the help of two colleagues in the Philosophy Department at Windsor: Harry A. Nielsen and Robert C. Pinto, both of whom read extensive portions of the manuscript and made many valuable comments. As the occasion arose we also received helpful advice from other colleagues at Windsor: Profs. Peter Burrell, Harold Clarke, Lawrence Leduc, William Arison, Ray Brown, Lloyd Brown-John, George Stewart. The Reference Department of the University of Windsor Library was unfailingly courteous and helpful in supplying information. Several students and former students made contributions that deserve acknowledgement: John Westwood, John McIlvride, Eric Fournie, Dennis and Mary Hudecki, Kim Christy, Ken Saunders; Larry Flohr and Rick Morrow did research that provided us with many of our examples of fallacies from newspapers across the country. Don McNeill of CBC television news, Don West of CBET news (Windsor), and Robert Pearson, editor of the Windsor *Star*, answered many questions about the media. Budd Johnson helped us with the chapter on advertising. Our Department Head, Peter F. Wilkinson, and Dean, Rev. Eugene Malley, gave us considerable assistance and encouragement. For the patience, endurance, and perfectionism of Cheryl Pollard-Pollock, Violet Smith, and Joan Reid, who typed various drafts of the manuscript, we are extremely grateful.

Our students over the past five years not only served as guinea pigs through various editions, but also exposed numerous mistakes, confusions, and infelicities. We are also enormously indebted to the two McGraw-Hill Ryerson readers who supplied lengthy, sympathetic, and constructive criticisms of an earlier draft, and to our editors, Jane Abramowitz and David Marshall.

Most of all we thank our wives and children, who have sacrificed evenings, weekends, and summers to this text for too long a time.

Ralph H. Johnson
J. Anthony Blair

University of Windsor
September, 1976

# Introduction

Much has been written about the consumer in our society, but little has been done to extend that viewpoint to the area of social, political and economic persuasion. As citizens we are constantly being offered persuasive rhetoric from a multitude of directions. Pick up any newspaper or magazine, turn on the radio or TV, or check the mail that comes to your door. The teachers' union, the school board, the city fathers, irate taxpayers are all trying to gain your support for higher teacher salaries, or lower teacher salaries; to back a strike, or to pressure for provincial intervention; to sympathize with teacher demands, or to reject them. Miles for Millions wants you to walk, a bikeathon wants you to ride, a telethon wants you to call; a political party wants you to canvass, a candidate wants you to listen to a party's program, your MLA wants you to return a questionnaire with your opinions on the latest issues. An editorial thunders that pornography is corrupting the moral fibre of the nation; your buddies want you to go along to a soft-core flick. Mothers write letters to the editor against abortion; mothers write letters to the editor for abortion; you wonder what you'd do if you became pregnant. You're asked to sign a petition supporting Mackenzie Valley Dene land claims; you're told by commercials that petroleum prices must go up in order to finance exploration in the North; you read that the corporations are welfare bums and rip-off artists. You are urged to go out and jog; you're terrorized to quit smoking. Should downtown be saved? Is a home of your own an obsolete dream? Are greedy unions the cause of inflation?

Not only is this bombardment a competition for your attention, but it is also a fantastic competition for your beliefs and support. Groups and individuals constantly vie for your adherence to their way of seeing things, for your acceptance of their picture of what is true, important, and worth doing.

You may think you can simply tune it all out, but, if so, you are deluding yourself. Practically speaking, you have only two choices: you can pretend to ignore these pressures and, as a result, have your beliefs shaped and your conduct directed by uncritical absorption of their appeals; or you can try to arm yourself with the knowledge and skill of the craft that will enable you to defend yourself intelligently against them, rejecting groundless arguments and accepting sound ones.

We have written this book for those who prefer the second

option. We believe that logic can be a useful skill to help you cope better with the world. We have written this text with an awareness of the growing barrage of persuasive appeals pounding daily on your consciousness. We have written it with the conviction that to be an intelligent and responsible person, you must learn logical skills to defend yourself against this onslaught.

Logic is a practical skill, and this book is a means of encouraging and helping you to develop it. The skill we speak of can be readily linked to the contemporary trend toward being a defensive consumer. Among the things you are called on to buy are beliefs, positions, and arguments. These products are intangible, yet the harm that may occur from accepting bad ones can be every bit as real and tangible as that from getting a car or an appliance which turns out to be a lemon.

Some arguments are damaged goods. You can learn how to spot them, what their traits and habitats are, and how to handle them. Our purpose here is to show them to you. It takes time, patience, and practice most of all. We have included exercises, but the best way to learn this skill is to begin to watch for bad arguments.

We would like to have written a definitive text. But, once into the project, we began to realize how vast the area is, how intriguing, and how little practically oriented work has been done. We attribute this deficiency chiefly to the mesmerizing grip which formal deductive logic has had both on logic and on philosophy in the 20th century. One consequence has been to relegate informal (or applied) logic—the study of fallacies—to a position of minor importance. In practice, it has meant one chapter out of ten in a book otherwise devoted to validity, truth tables, etc. It has also meant that those who wish to improve their capacity to appraise everyday rhetoric have been frustrated by texts and courses that teach them about propositional logic and deductive systems, knowledge which does not particularly enhance their ability to deal with the editorial in tonight's newspaper.

We have tried to make the study of *ordinary arguments* interesting and lively. Our main focus is the idea of *fallacy*, and we have tried to put some order and regularity into this concept. Our inventory of fallacies is by some standards incomplete, but we have included the ones which seem most common and most interesting.

Our treatment of fallacies differs from that found in other texts in several noteworthy ways. *First*, our objective is to use the concept of fallacy as a device for learning the skill of analyzing and appraising real-life arguments. All other features of our approach devolve from this premise. *Second*, we emphasize not just tagging fallacies, but also, and more important, understanding what is wrong with each fallacious move and seeing how to argue soundly that it is mistaken. *Third*, virtually all of the examples we use come from actual arguments in newspapers, magazines, and books, and are quoted as they originally appeared. *Fourth*, we downplay disputes about labels. Other texts use different names for many of the same fallacies, contain fallacy categories that overlap with some of ours, and subdivide fallacies that we assemble under a single rubric. Since the labels and categories are merely tools, once you learn to pick your way through arguments and detect the flaws, it's scarcely necessary to use the labels. The purpose of logical self-defense is to expose flaws clearly and offer sound criticism. *Fifth*, our list may appear to some to be incomplete; our organization, untraditional. We aimed to employ the organization and thought that will be most helpful to the learner who wants practical skills rather than theoretical elegance. *Sixth*, we have tried to make our treatment of each fallacy as precise and rigorous as possible by giving a list of the conditions specifying its occurrence. This process should help to screen out cases of apparent fallacy, but its full use guides the construction of arguments showing that the given fallacy has been committed. *Seventh*, throughout the fallacy phase of the text we introduce a series of techniques that apply in the critical evaluation of arguments and promote the underlying skill we are trying to impart.

The real star of the text, we think, is the roster of real-life Canadian examples, both in the body of the text and in the exercises at the end of each chapter. Unless you hone your skill on these or similar specimens, you are unlikely to find any improvement in your practical ability to handle arguments. You may want to compile your own catalogue of examples and keep it up to date, because ours will quickly become dated. We have given our analysis of each example, but you may disagree with or improve on ours: so much the better.

A host of topics has not been covered in this text. We have not, for instance, gone into the distinction between inductive and deductive logic; we have not even mentioned validity, soundness, or inference patterns. All of these topics are more than adequately dealt with in the burgeoning number of formal logic texts, and we could see no point in duplicating their treatments. If such material is important to you, it can be introduced at many junctures in the text. We have said nothing about definition, again a topic well rehearsed in the existing shelf of texts; our experience suggests that very few everyday arguments feature the phrasing of definitions in a central role.

For showing us how interesting this small and overlooked corner of the world of logic can be, we want to acknowledge Howard Kahane's *Logic and Contemporary Rhetoric* (Wadsworth, 1971). The text is lively and, when it was published, contemporary and it includes a healthy sample of the sorts of argument that fill the pages of the newspapers. Our debt to Kahane is great. In some instances, we have simply adapted his general approach to the Canadian scene. In others, we have modified or departed from it, mainly in trying to give a more systematic analysis and explanation of each fallacy. Most recently, we have come into contact with Michael Scriven's *Reasoning* (Edgepress, 1976), a text which has also impressed us. His approach is very different from ours, but our goals are the same.

This, then, is a working text. There will likely be things you find wrong or unsuitable. We would appreciate hearing from you about those, so that improvements can be made in any future edition, and for our own enlightenment. Our address is: Philosophy Department, University of Windsor, Windsor, Ontario, N9B 3P4.

The text has three sections or phases. Phase I quickly introduces the basic concepts: argument and fallacy. Since argument is at the core of most persuasive appeals, since fallacies are violations of the standards of good argument, and since our approach is to provide the tools of logical self-defense for consumers of everyday persuasion, Phase II presents an inventory of the main and representative kinds of fallacy.

In Phase III we turn away from the snippets which were the teaching examples of Phase II and focus on the longer pieces of ill-organized, rambling, many-sided reasoning typical of everyday argumentation. We offer some devices and guidelines for coming to terms with these kinds of argumentation, for sorting the verbiage from the argument and organizing its complex parts in a fashion that allows for the clearest appraisal possible. In the two concluding chapters, we offer brief guidelines for self-defense against those two mammoths of persuasion: advertising and the news media.

*To Maggie and June
and to Jay and Mary and Sean*

# I Fundamentals

# 1 The Basics

## Introduction

**1.1** For starters, we ask you to do a brief quiz, the purpose of which is twofold. First, it will give you a chance to test your logical powers in a kind of warm-up exercise. Second, it will give you a practical introduction to the basic concepts (*argument, premise, conclusion, fallacy*), skills (apprehending the argument, appraising its logic), and material (arguments taken from everyday life) that are the subject of this text.

For each of the four examples, do three things. (1) Determine precisely what is being said; that is, what is the basic point and how is it supported? (2) Make a judgement about the argument's value: is it a convincing argument or not? (3) State the basis for your appraisal.

*Example 1:*

1   Dear Ann Landers:
My 16-year-old cousin sent for your booklet called "Teenage Sex and Ten Ways to Cool it." She sent her 50 cents and the self-addressed envelope like it said at the foot of your column. When the booklet arrived, she read it right away and phoned me to say that it was very good and gave her a lot to think about. Well, Ann Landers, three months later she was pregnant and got married very fast. Her mother almost had a heart attack. What I want to know is why do you recommend booklets if they don't do any good?
HIGHLY DISAPPOINTED

*Example 2:* This is an excerpt from a speech given by Syd Brown to the Police Association of Ontario when he was its president:

2       Surely life in prison was never intended to provide a better way of life than every law-abiding citizen, employed, unemployed, or pensioned has a right to expect. If we maintain the present reckless course of stupidity and senselessness, soon the courts will be issuing rain checks to those sentenced, in case they don't like the surroundings and conditions of the institution they are sent to.

*Example 3:* In 1973, the Canadian Jewish Congress asked the government of Ontario to discontinue religious instructions in public elementary schools. This except from a Toronto *Globe and Mail* editorial (August 1973) seconded that request:

3       The purpose of the public schools is to teach the acquisition of secular skills and wisdom, not to promote denominational beliefs. In a pluralistic society, there is a generally accepted principle that public money should not be used to promote one denomination at the expense of another. Premier Davis, both as Education Minister and Premier, has shown himself determined not to extend the influence of one religion in Ontario's public school system. When will he follow through on his principles and root out all denominational religious teaching from the public schools?

*Example 4:* This comes from a letter, to the Windsor *Star* (December 1973), on capital punishment:

4       It was repeatedly stated in the newspaper that capital punishment is no deterrent. But as we all know, with statistics you can prove anything you want. Yet our common sense tells us that the death penalty is a deterrent. And if that is not enough, read the words of a criminal named Woltowicz: "The Supreme Court will let me get away with this. There is no death penalty. It's ridiculous. You have to have a death penalty. Otherwise this can happen everyday."

**1.2** Before we take up these arguments and give you our own assessments, let us clarify what is meant in logic by the term **argument**. All four examples have one thing in common: they attempt to persuade us of something by citing reasons intended to support that claim and prove its truth. In *Example 1*, the claim made by Highly Disappointed is that Ann Landers' booklet is not effective. The support is that the booklet did not keep Highly's cousin from becoming pregnant. In the terminology of logic, the support provided is called a **premise**; the claim it supports is called a **conclusion**. Simply stated, an argument consists of a set of premises and a conclusion.

We said "simply stated," because one or the other component of the argument may not be explicitly formulated. *Example 2* illustrates this point, for the conclusion of the argument was not actually formulated. However, the context of the argument makes it evident that Brown was arguing against the present trend toward liberalizing prison conditions. By **context** here, we mean the circumstances in which the argument takes place. Whom is the argument directed to? What has occasioned it? What's the immediate background? Answers to these questions will usually be furnished by the context, so you will often have to look to it in order to understand exactly what the argument is.

In *Example 3*, we meet another wrinkle: the conclusion of that argument is stated as a rhetorical question, and we are left with the job of formulating it in literal terms. Why? Because arguments are intended to show that something is true, and that something must therefore take the appropriate form of a statement, or claim, or assertion. Restating that rhetorical question as an assertion, we would have as the conclusion: "Davis should follow through on his principles and root out all denominational religious teaching from the public schools."

The tasks of spotting missing premises and conclusions, and of reformulating and restating pieces of the argument, are aspects of logical evaluation taken up in Phase II. For the present, it is sufficient to understand the logical conception of argument as a set of statements with a premise-conclusion structure. Understanding what an argument is and identifying an argument's components are preliminaries to appraising it, for the practical interest of logic revolves around distinguishing good arguments from bad ones. The first question you need to learn to ask, in logical self-defense, is: *Do the premises of the argument furnish adequate support for the conclusion?* Learning how to ask and answer this question is the skill we are concerned with in this text.

**1.3** Before reading further, complete your appraisal of the four arguments presented in 1.1. Then read our assessments, which follow here:

*Example 1: not* a good argument. The reason: *not enough support* to warrant the conclusion. Highly Disappointed has cited one instance (his/her cousin's case) in which the booklet failed to avert teenage sex. But surely a thorough evaluation of that booklet's effectiveness would have to consider carefully the details in that one instance and the experience of the many other teenagers who have read the booklet. Highly's cousin *said* that the booklet gave her a lot to think about, but did she actually do the thinking? Did she take the advice contained in the booklet, or ignore it? Perhaps the booklet is not effective, but Highly has reached that conclusion on inadequate evidence.

*Example 2:* again, *not* a good argument. The reason: Brown's premises really take the form of sarcasm and ridicule directed against a vaguely specified policy. His first sentence makes it sound as though people in prison were purposely being placed in better living conditions than the rest of us. Clearly, this was neither the intent nor—in most cases—the effect of penal reform. From his distortion of the policy, Brown goes on in the second part of his argument to anticipate an even more patently ridiculous situation in the future—prisoners being issued rainchecks! But that projection is beside the point, because of the original distortion it is based on.

*Example 3:* nothing obviously wrong with this argument. To see this, let's first set it forth in an orderly fashion:

5
**P1:** The purpose of the public schools is to teach the acquisition of secular skills and wisdom, not to promote denominational beliefs.

**P2:** In a pluralistic society like ours, there is a generally accepted principle that public money should not be used to promote one denomination at the expense of another.

**P3:** Premier Davis, both as Education Minister and as Premier, has shown himself determined not to extend the influence of one religion in Ontario's public school system.

**C:** Premier Davis should follow through on his principles and root out all denominational teaching from the public schools.

**P1** states a truth about public schools. **P2** states a generally accepted principle which also applies to public schools. **P3** states a matter of fact about the position Davis has taken in the past. Together, these premises provide good support for the conclusion.

---

**STANDARDIZING** *In extricating the argument from Example 3, stating the propositions in our own words, and restructuring the whole, separating the premises from each other and the conclusion* and listing the premises one by one above the conclusion, we introduce a convention which we shall call **standardizing the argument**. *The premises are marked "P" and numbered for convenience of reference; the conclusion is marked "C." The more complicated the argument, the more necessary is some such procedure in order to get a clear sense of its logical flow. Even with fairly simple arguments, standardizing is a good exercise for learning to identify arguments. As it becomes necessary to handle more and more complicated arguments, we shall add refinements to our standardizing convention.*

---

*Example 4:* again, not a good argument. We are being asked to accept the claim that the death penalty is a deterrent. Because this is an extremely controversial position, powerful evidence is necessary to persuade. How strong is the support? The first piece of support is that common sense tells us that the death penalty is a deterrent. Presumably, that means if you stop and think about it, you'll see that, faced with a choice between murdering someone (thereby risking execution) and not murdering someone, obviously most people will opt for the latter. That argument does seem to be common sense. But how many potential murderers start out that way, coolly considering their options? How many potential murderers are that rational? Our common sense does not answer this question. We need more information, and it is not easy to come by. (How do you poll potential murderers who decided against it because they feared the death penalty?) Taken by itself, this appeal to common sense cannot be accepted as a strong reason for thinking that the death penalty is a significant deterrent. The second premise appeals to the authority of a criminal named "Woltowicz." We're given no reason to think that his opinion carries any special weight: hence, it does not provide much support for the conclusion. So we're not persuaded by that argument.

So *Examples* 1, 2, and 4 are bad arguments, while *Example 3* is a good one. That's about the proportion you can expect to find in your daily reading; it is also the kind of mixture you'll find in the balance of this text. We'll be spending much more time on bad arguments (and *why* they are bad) than on good ones, because the ones you need to learn how to defend yourself against are the bad ones. But in the exercises with each chapter, we reserve the right to sprinkle good arguments in among the bad to keep you on your toes. The craft of evaluating arguments is not enhanced if you know in advance that something is wrong with an argument. For, in real life, arguments do not come with the labels "good" and "bad" on them.

They all claim to be good. They do not announce their logical weaknesses.

**1.4** The flaws and weaknesses we'll be showing you are called *fallacies*. By **fallacy** we mean a violation of one of the criteria which govern good arguments. Our evaluation of each of the flawed examples in the quiz referred implicitly to those criteria, which we now make explicit. Recall that *Example 1* was faulty because its premises did not provide enough support for the conclusion; in other words, the premises gave insufficient evidence for it. *Example 2* illustrated a different flaw: one of the premises was not relevant (because it was a distortion) to the conclusion. Finally, *Example 4* failed because its premises were unacceptable. The criteria implicit in our appraisal of these arguments follow.

First, the premises must be *relevant* to the conclusion. Second, taken together, the premises must provide *sufficient* support for the conclusion. Third, the premises must be *acceptable*. We shall be studying these criteria by looking at arguments which contain typical violations of them—that is, which contain fallacies. It may be helpful at the outset to expand on each one.

**A. Relevance.** Since the purpose of argument is to bring about rational consent to the conclusion on the strength of the premises, those premises must be relevant to the conclusion. Suppose, for example, that someone were to argue because Canadian winters are cold and snowy, *therefore* Canada should merge with the United States. A fanciful example to be sure, yet one that illustrates *irrelevance* of the rankest sort. The word "therefore" is completely out of place here, and one's instinctive response to such an argument is, "What have Canadian winters and climate got to do with whether or not Canada should join forces politically with the U.S.?" The two things are completely unrelated.

When someone puts forth a statement as support for another, that person clearly believes that the two claims are related. But such beliefs can be and often are mistaken. In the next chapter, we take a closer look at the notion of relevance.

**B. Sufficiency.** Taken together, the premises as a *group* must pass a second test: they must provide sufficient evidence for the conclusion. The evidence Highly Disappointed mentioned was clearly relevant; it was just not enough. You ought to get into the habit of asking, then, "Is there enough evidence, enough support, for the conclusion?"

**C. Acceptability.** The aim of any argument is to lay down a path leading from the reasons (the premises) to the goal (the conclusion). So the arguer, to convince us to accept the conclusion, has to pro-

vide us with acceptable premises. The highest standard of acceptability is *truth*. If the arguer can provide premises known to be true,
then (provided they are also relevant, and together sufficient) we are
obliged to accept the conclusion: it also must be true.

Frequently, truth is too hard a mark to attain, and too onerous a
requirement to demand. The arguer cannot claim truth for the
premises presented, yet may still put them forward as **reasonable**.
If the arguer has sifted the available evidence bearing on the truth
of the premises and presents—or is prepared to present—the
reasons why they're believable, then the arguer has met a minimum
standard of acceptability. By "available evidence" we imply more
than the support for the claims that might be conjured up off the
top of the arguer's head. The arguer has a responsibility to judge
carefully what evidence is relevant and to seek it out. At the same
time, this responsibility has limits. The arguer cannot be expected,
for example, to initiate sophisticated research projects. Yet, to the
extent that the evidence falls short of what's needed to conclude the
argument decisively, the arguer ought to qualify the assertions. The
requirement of acceptability implies that premises in arguments
should be reasonable beliefs in this sense.

An example of an unreasonable belief may help to clarify the
notion. In the late 1960s, just after the release of the Beatles' album
*Abbey Road*, many people believed that Paul McCartney was dead.
The evidence they offered consisted of so-called clues on the album
covers of Beatles' records: that Paul was the only Beatle barefoot
on the cover of *Abbey Road*; that he was wearing a black flower in
his lapel in the insert of *Magical Mystery Tour*; that his back was
turned to the camera on the back cover of *Sgt. Pepper*. At the same
time, however, considerable evidence, widely available, suggested
the opposite: there were no reports of the dead body of Paul
McCartney; there had been no funeral; there were steadfast denials
in the press from those close to McCartney. Even when McCartney
himself finally materialized, many were slow to give up their belief
that he was dead. But that belief was based on sheer fanciful speculation and maintained only by a dogged refusal to consider relevant
and accessible evidence. It was a clear instance of an *unreasonable*
belief.

We have just said that in public discourse everyone has a
responsibility to put forward reasonable beliefs as premises in
arguments. The obligation has a corollary: the more controversial
the issue or questionable the claim, then the more important it is
to accompany the premises of arguments with your evidence for
accepting them.

The requirements of *relevance*, *sufficiency*, and *acceptability*, discussed in more detail in Chapter 2, define the ideal persuasive argument.

**1.5** Before studying individual fallacies, a few points require emphasis. *First*, the fallacies discussed in the following chapters are flaws that *typically* beset arguments. They all have labels which serve only one purpose: to make you look for certain kinds of mistakes in arguments; they serve to put you on guard. But detecting the fallacy and labelling it is just the first step. You must also be able to explain why the argument fails to compel assent. Simply tossing out the name of a fallacy is not likely to impress your opponent, nor does it serve the cause of responsible logical criticism.

*Second*, each discussion of a fallacy is accompanied by several examples and an economical statement of the **conditions** for the occurrence of that fallacy. In order to convict an argument of a particular fallacy, you must yourself construct an argument showing that the conditions for the fallacy are satisfied. Thus, learning logic by studying fallacies simultaneously teaches you both offense and defense. You learn defense because being able to spot fallacies is one excellent way to defend yourself against a bad argument. But you learn offense too, for to justify the charge of fallacy you have to go on the attack and construct an argument.

*Third*, although an argument can go wrong by containing a fallacy, the conclusion may very well be true. The point is that it's possible to argue poorly on behalf of a true statement, just as it is to argue well on behalf of a false one. So, when you reject an argument because it contains a fallacy, remember that you've shown only that the route traced by the argument from the premises to the conclusion is no good. You have not claimed no other route is possible (through different premises) to that conclusion.

---

## Exercises for Chapter 1

*Directions:* These exercises are designed to test your understanding of what an argument is and give you an opportunity to practice setting arguments up in premise-conclusion form. Decide, with respect to each of the following passages, whether it is an argument or not. If it is, then standardize it, as we did in Example 5.

1. While we watch it [the unfolding of the Watergate scandals in the United States] with a mixture of fascination and disgust, there is no way that Canadians can feel the total

impact of Watergate. It's not only that Watergate is unlike any political scandal in Canadian history (and we've had our share), what's most important is that the American response to the transgressions of a political leader is completely alien to us. (Peter C. Newman, "The Dark Side of Temptation and What Watergate Means to Us," *Maclean's*, July 1973.)

2. The welfare department has become, in effect, a source of farm labour. The primary motivation behind this development seems to be the need of farmers. The need to employ welfare recipients who are able to work has become a secondary matter, a by-product. (Editorial in the Windsor *Star*, September 1974)

3. Advertising is something we should have in Canada, since it stimulates the economy by inducing people to buy what they do not essentially need; it also creates mass production, employment, and greater physical well-being by informing people of the availability of new and improved products.

4. A letter from B.F. mentions civil liberties and rights of workers in a long argument defending strikes but not the use of force. I could not find any reference to the rights of an employer to decline to give in to the demands of employees. It would seem that B.F.'s liberties would be on one side only. (Letter to the Toronto *Globe and Mail*, May 1974)

5. Freud was a confessed atheist and did not believe in the Bible, so we can see that his view that Moses was an Egyptian is false; the same holds true of his assertion that religion is just a matter of wish-fulfillment. (Adapted from an example found in *Fundamentals of Logic*, James D. Carney and Richard K. Scheer [New York: MacMillan Publishing Co., Inc., 1974], 2nd ed., p. 12.)

6. Thanks a lot to all nurses who are causing such inconvenience to the public. Most likely, a good majority of these nurses are married with husbands bringing in a good salary. And most likely some nurses have two cars and a couple of snowmobiles sitting in their yard, and a couple of TVs sitting in their home. Also, they have conveniently forgotten their Florence Nightingale pledge. (Letter to St. John *Telegraph-Journal*, February 1975)

7. I wish the news media would attack other forms of waste with the same vigor and persistence that it does the loss of 28 million eggs. This astronomical sounding number repre-

sents about one day's egg production. I would be surprised if the wastage in many other commodities would not exceed 1/365 of their total production. What about oil or lumber? And what about time? (Letter to the Ottawa *Journal*, November 1974)

8. Long, long ago words sounded like they were spelled and spelled like they sounded. Then Mr. Dictionary said, "Everyone must write words the same way regardless of how they sound." Over the years people changed the way they sounded words but Mr. Dictionary did not change his spelling along with the new pronunciation. Nowadays only a few who have very good eyes and memory can learn to spell perfectly. Therefore, many people in Canada want spelling and pronunciation to match more closely. (Letter to the Windsor *Star*, May 1975)

9. Over five hundred copies of *Mass Line* were sold in one area of Toronto alone in two days which goes to show that broad masses of people are not anti-communists and, in fact, are eager to read communist literature and apply it in practice. (*Mass Line*, June 1970)

# 2 Three Basic Fallacies

## Introduction

**2.1** The point of this chapter is to discuss in detail three basic fallacies. Almost all the fallacies treated in the groupings of subsequent chapters are variations of these three. We have already met specimens of each in Chapter 1; our purpose here is to fill in the details of that sketchy discussion.

## 1 Irrelevant Reason

**2.2** The first fallacy in our catalogue is known as **irrelevant reason**, though it is still often referred to under its Latin name, *"non sequitur"* ("it does not follow"). *Example 2* provides us with one instance of the fallacy. Mr. Brown's attack on prison reforms was *irrelevant*, because the policies he appeared to be attacking were not really the policies in effect, only distortions of them. Here is a second specimen of this fallacy.

In 1973, Grace MacInnis (then-MP for Vancouver-Kingsway) charged in the House of Commons that the Department of Health had been cooperating with the Kellogg Company in selling a cereal (Kellogg's Corn Flakes) with "little or no nutritional value." That was her charge. In attempting to rebut that charge, Health Minister Marc Lalonde stated:

6    As for the nutritional value of corn flakes, the milk you have
     with your corn flakes has great nutritional value.

Since Lalonde was attempting to rebut MacInnis' charge, we may formulate his unstated conclusion as follows: Kellogg's Corn Flakes have *more than a little* nutritional value.

But how do we know that this is the conclusion Lalonde wished to argue for? From the context, we know that he disagreed with MacInnis, and the conclusion we have attributed to him is the weakest statement which brings him into conflict with her. The reason that we take the weakest is that we are obliged, in filling in parts of any argument which have been omitted, not to overcommit the arguer. We could, for example, have saddled Lalonde with the view that Kellogg's Corn Flakes have *lots* of nutritional value. That would be a much stronger disagreement with MacInnis's claim, but we can't be sure that Lalonde would want to go that far. We do know that he meant to disagree with her, however, so we attribute to him the weakest position in conformity with the context of this argument and the assumptions that go with it.

Reconstructed, then, here is Lalonde's argument:

7    **P:** The milk that one has with Kellogg's Corn Flakes has great nutritional value.

    **C:** Kellogg's Corn Flakes have more than a little nutritional value.

How good is Lalonde's argument? What does his premise afford, by way of support, for his conclusion? None whatsoever! Eating corn flakes may be an occasion for consuming milk, but that fact doesn't make those corn flakes nutritious in and of themselves. Using Lalonde's reasoning, we ought to conclude that salt possesses great nutritional value, because the steak that you sprinkle it on has great nutritional value. In sum, Lalonde's premise is *irrelevant* to his conclusion, and the argument commits the fallacy of *irrelevant reason*.

In 1972, a doll sold in Ontario stores was found to have the unsavory feature of allowing a spike to protrude from the neck area when the head of the doll was removed—a feat many infants and toddlers can manage. When some parents discovered this danger, they complained to the Department of Consumer and Corporate Affairs. An official of the department investigated the doll, but decided that it did not qualify as hazardous under the provisions of the Hazardous Product Act because the spike was not sharp enough nor its diameter small enough. When informed of the complaints, a spokesman for the company that manufactured the doll responded:

8    All of the legislation in Canada isn't going to protect a child from the normal hazards of life.

A firm point on his side, but exactly what is its force? In context, the spokesman seems to have been using this point to further the position that nothing was particularly wrong with the doll and that legislation against it would not be appropriate. But his statement is relevant only if we assume that the doll in question can rightly be classed as one of "the normal hazards of life." Can it be? That category is vague and broad, but one thinks of things like busy urban streets, rusty nails, or icy sidewalks. Is a doll such a "normal hazard"? Hardly. A doll is a toy, a plaything, and by its very nature is not supposed to be dangerous. So, although his claim was true enough—legislation can't protect against normal hazards—it was simply irrelevant here.

**2.3** We have seen enough instances of this fallacy to be able to pinpoint its conditions:

---

### IRRELEVANT REASON

1. M has put forth R as a reason (premise) for Q.
2. R is *irrelevant* to Q.

---

**VARIABLES AND ABBREVIATIONS** *Here and throughout, in stating the conditions, we use the letters of the alphabet in the following ways: M, N, O for names of persons; Q, R, S for statements or claims; X, Y, Z for events, actions, or situations.* **P** *will be saved for the abbreviation of "Premise" and* **C** *for the abbreviation of "Conclusion."*

---

It is one thing to suspect, or to charge an argument with *irrelevant reason*, and another thing altogether to justify your suspicion or charge. To do that, you must show that the conditions are satisfied in the argument you are analyzing. The first step, clearly, is to identify precisely who M is as well as what R and S are in the particular case at hand. The second and more difficult step is to show that Condition 2 is satisfied. This step requires you to *argue* that R is irrelevant to Q. If you simply *assert* that R is irrelevant, you are merely announcing your disagreement with M who obviously believes that R is relevant. But which of you is right? To tip the logical scales in your favour, you have to *show why you are right* in claiming that R is irrelevant to Q. To show irrelevance, you must know what is meant by "relevance."

**2.4** The concept of *relevance* is tricky to explain since it is so basic. Synonyms of "relevant," such as "germane to," "has a bearing on," cannot take us very far towards an understanding, for they need to be explained in turn. You can't depend on your "intuition" of what is relevant, because intuitions about relevance vary. Let us try using a hypothetical example. Suppose that Grant is being tried for the murder of Richard. And suppose it has been established that the murderer was left-handed. Clearly, *Grant is left-handed* is relevant to *Grant is the murderer*. For, if it is true that Grant is left-handed, then, although this fact doesn't prove that he was the murderer, it does marginally increase its likelihood. On the other hand, if *Grant is left-handed* is false, that does increase the likelihood that the proposition *Grant is the murderer* is false. If R is relevant to Q, we might say, then R's being true would increase the likelihood that Q is true, while R's being false would increase the likelihood that Q is false.

With this case in mind, reconsider the corn flakes example. In this case, R is *The milk you have with your corn flakes has great nutritional value* and Q is *Corn flakes have more than a little nutritional value*. Suppose R is true: does that increase the likelihood of Q's being true? No, for the reasons we have already given. Corn flakes and milk are two different and distinct food substances, each with its own nutrient properties. Suppose R were false: would that increase the likelihood of Q's being false? No, even if milk turned out not to have any nutrient properties, it could still be the case that corn flakes did. So R and Q here fail the relevance test proposed above, for the truth or falsity of R seems to have no effect at all on the truth or falsity of Q.

By contrast, instead of R, consider S: *Corn flakes have 1 gram of protein per 30 grams*. Let Q be as before. If S is true, then the likelihood of Q's being true would increase at least slightly: that is, corn flakes have more than a little nutritional value. Suppose S is false. This possibility presents two alternatives: (i) S is false because corn flakes have more than 1 g of protein per 30 g; (ii) S is false because corn flakes have less than 1 g of protein per 30 g. Case (i) is already covered, since, if corn flakes have more than 1 g protein per 30 g, they have at least that much and hence more than a little nutritional value. Case (ii) tests out, for, the less protein, the less likely that they have more than a little nutritional value.

To see if Condition 2 is satisfied, we suggest you try the relevance test: consider how the truth of R would affect the truth of Q and how the falsity of R affects the falsity of Q. If there is no effect one way or the other, then you have ample grounds for your claim that R is irrelevant to Q.

**2.5** We conclude with one final example, followed by an observation about this fallacy. An article in *Time* (October 1971) reported the findings of an American sociologist who "discovered" a new form of discrimination: heightism! This discrimination against short people is "well illustrated by language," says the article:

9   Instead of the neutral "What is your height?" the question is always the invidious "How tall are you?" Dishonest cashiers shortchange customers, and people who lack foresight are shortsighted.

We want to focus on the claim that language illustrates the existence of this form of discrimination against short people. The evidence presented is that the terms "shortsighted" and "shortchange" have a negative connotation and they use the word "short," presumably indicating that the word "short" functions in these expressions to cast aspersions on people of below-average height. These two terms do have negative connotations and the word "short" does occur in each. But the presence of "short" here is evidence of heightism only if it makes some reference to height— only if it is used in the sense in which its opposite is "tall." If, on the other hand, "short" in these terms makes no reference to height, then it has no bearing at all on whether there is heightism in our society. And in fact that's the case here. The "short" of "shortchange" has to do with quantity—as in "I'm short three dollars"— not height. The "short" of "shortsighted" refers to the distance one can see into the future, not to anyone's tallness. This linguistic evidence is simply irrelevant to the claim that short people are discriminated against.

That the question "How tall are you?" is in common use is perhaps offset because most questionnaires ask for the person's height. In any event, we don't deny the existence of this new form of discrimination; we do deny the relevance of the linguistic evidence cited.

We end with the observation that one of the factors causing people to commit this fallacy and to be taken in by it is that the irrelevant premise is very often true. It's true that the milk one has with corn flakes has great nutritional value; it's true that all the legislation in the world won't protect a child from the normal hazards of life; and it's true that "shortchange" and "shortsighted" have negative connotations. The problem is that truth is not enough; the premise must be relevant to the conclusion.

# 2 Hasty Conclusion

**2.6** Even when the premises of an argument pass the relevance test, they may fail to provide sufficient support for the conclusion. This fallacy is known as **hasty conclusion**. We have already seen one instance, Highly Disappointed's letter to Ann Landers. Here is another example.

In early 1975, Dr. Bette Stephenson, then president of the Canadian Medical Association, called for Justice Minister Otto Lang to resign on the ground that his position on the abortion issue was dictated by bias. (Lang was opposed to liberalizing abortion laws and is a Roman Catholic.) Writing to the Halifax *Chronicle-Herald* (February 1975), S.H. claimed that Canadians as a whole did not share Stephenson's views:

**10** It seems apparent that the Canadian public does not share the view of the CMA as expressed by its president. In the last election, after Mr. Lang had expressed on several occasions his opposition to abortion on demand, he was re-elected by his constituents by a large majority. David Lewis, leader of the NDP, whose platform included abortion on demand, was defeated by newcomer, Mrs. Ursula Appolloni, who said publicly during her campaign that she would uphold in Parliament the right to life of babies in the womb.

In context, S.H. seems to be arguing not simply that the Canadian public doesn't agree with Stephenson about Lang, but also that Canadians are generally opposed to abortion on demand. When standardized, S.H.'s argument looks like this:

**11**  **P1:** Justice Minister Lang was opposed to abortion on demand.
**P2:** Justice Minister Lang was re-elected by his constituents with a large majority.
**P3:** David Lewis belongs to the NDP which favoured abortion on demand.
**P4:** Lewis' opponent, Ursula Appolloni, opposed abortion on demand.
**P5:** Lewis was defeated by Appolloni.
**C:** The Canadian public is opposed (apparently) to abortion on demand.

We should note first that the task of interpreting the results of an election is a very difficult one. For S.H.'s interpretation to make sense we must make several assumptions. For instance, we must assume that Lang's stance on the abortion issue was a dominant factor in his being re-elected. This assumption means downplaying that he was both the incumbent and a cabinet minister, two factors which normally give a candidate an edge. We must assume as well that Lewis' defeat had more to do with his stance on abortion than with the fact that, as party leader, he had to spend most of his time campaigning across the country, so he had little left to spend in his own riding. Likewise, we must assume that Mrs. Appolloni's position on abortion played a significant role in her campaign. These assumptions can be challenged, but we'll grant them for the sake of argument, thus granting that S.H.'s premises are both true and relevant.

---

**A NOTE ABOUT ASSUMPTIONS**   *The ability to ferret out the assumptions behind an argument is one of the principal techniques in the logician's repertoire. Most arguments make assumptions— things taken for granted because the context of the argument seems to contain them, or because they are regarded as too obvious to be worth stating. In the present case we have simply stated what we consider to be the operative assumptions in this example, without showing how we arrived at that opinion. If you want to know more about assumptions at this time, look ahead to our treatment of "missing premises," which are one kind of assumption, in Chapter 3, Section 2 (3.7), and to our more general treatment of assumptions in Chapter 6, Section 3 (6.13).*

---

S.H.'s evidence is not sufficient for two reasons. First, S.H. has not incorporated all the evidence that might be culled from an analysis of the election. What about other ridings where the abortion issue was prominent? Did pro-abortionists always lose out to anti-abortionists? The sort of evidence S.H. produced, while clearly relevant, is itself incomplete. Second, other sorts of evidence require consideration here, but are not mentioned. Polls are taken by reputable organizations; questionnaires are sent out by Members of Parliament; the views of interested organizations are publicized. This sort of evidence would also have to be considered before a verdict could be reached. So, on two counts, S.H. was guilty of *hasty conclusion.*

Another example, to bring out another aspect of the fallacy: a letter to the Ottawa *Citizen* from D.I., written in 1972, just after

Jane Fonda—the American movie star who actively opposed the U.S. war effort in Vietnam—returned to the U.S. following a visit to North Vietnam. While there, Fonda had reproached the U.S. for its bombing of the North.

12      Now that Jane Fonda is home again after speaking so strongly against her own country, it should be realized that she has demonstrated to all the people of North Vietnam that freedom of speech is indeed a living thing in the United States.

Surely every person in every Communist country now knows that this is not U.S. propaganda, but a precious freedom, envied by millions. Can anyone imagine a citizen of Communist North Vietnam being allowed to do the same thing?

To D.I., this *one incident* proved that freedom of speech is a reality in the U.S. But should D.I. have been persuaded so easily? Should *we* be? It's our view that the Fonda incident is clearly relevant to the question of freedom of speech in the U.S. But so are a great many other incidents not incorporated into D.I.'s brief argument. Indeed, Fonda was harrassed after her return and threatened with being tried for treason. Recent revelations indicate that many Americans who expressed unpopular views were bugged, wiretapped, and otherwise harrassed by government agencies. All of these incidents would need to be assessed and weighed in coming to any reflective verdict about the myths and realities of freedom of speech in the U.S.

The moral of the last example is: Beware of *anecdotal evidence*— the use of one or two incidents or stories which bear upon a point. Here's another example:

13      University profs really have it pretty easy. Why, my folks have a cottage next door to a prof from a university, and he's there from late April right through September, fishing and relaxing.

One story, one account. Of course, it must be put onto the scales, but so must a great many others. However, people tend to be quite impressed by such isolated stories, especially if they have enough drama and reinforce a perhaps prejudiced opinion already formed.

**2.7** These are the conditions of the fallacy:

---

**HASTY CONCLUSION**

1. M adduces Q, R, S, . . . as sufficient support for T;
2. Q, R, S, . . . , taken together, are not sufficient support for T.

---

As in the case of *irrelevant reason*, you have two tasks in making and adequately defending a charge of *hasty conclusion*. First, you must identify the pieces of evidence given and the conclusion they supposedly prove. That's Condition 1. Then you must not only assert but also defend or argue for your assertion, that the evidence is not sufficient. Generally, this obligation means being able to specify precisely what the evidence presented does show and that the evidence shows less than the arguer concludes. Or you must be ready to specify what sort of additional evidence would be necessary. That may be either more of the same kind of evidence, or evidence of a different sort. Whatever the case, it is never enough just to state that more evidence is needed. If you do no more than that, your argument looks like this:

**14**      **P:** M has not produced enough evidence for S.
           **C:** M is guilty of *hasty conclusion.*

Precisely why this sort of argument is inadequate is the subject of the next section. Certainly the premise is relevant; and if it's true, the conclusion follows. Yet you can glimpse what's wrong if you stop to consider that originally, in giving the argument, M presumably believed that he or she *had* produced enough evidence for S. If all you do is *say* that M has not, why should M change his or her mind? M believes **P** is false; you assert it to be true. The two of you are at a standoff. And that means you haven't tipped the scales in your direction.

**2.8** Let's be realistic on the question of evidence. In the informality that characterizes most ordinary discourse and argument, people don't usually bring out all the evidence at their disposal. They go with the evidence they regard as the most striking or most likely to convince. There's nothing wrong with this situation, as long as the arguer somehow indicates that he or she is aware of the limitations or insufficiency of the evidence introduced. People should learn to qualify their arguments in appropriate ways, by saying things like, "Space and time do not permit me to list all the reasons or evidence" or "These reasons, though not conclusive, are highly persuasive." Such qualifiers, when appropriate, go a long way to improving the profile of an argument. When no such qualifiers are presented, then it is reasonable to assume that the arguer regards the evidence that has been produced as sufficient and hence is open to attack along the lines of *hasty conclusion*.

It may also be observed that an argument which suffers from *hasty conclusion* is really in better shape than one which suffers from *irrelevant reason*. For the former can be strengthened and revised by including the additional evidence, whereas the latter (if the charge is merited) has to start over from scratch.

**2.9** We end this section with a teaser, which may not be an argument at all and, if it is, looks at one moment like *hasty conclusion*, at another like *irrelevant reason*. Thor Heyerdahl is a world-famous adventurer who some years ago crossed the Pacific Ocean on a balsa raft in the Kon-Tiki expedition. Recently, he took to the high seas once again, this time crossing the Atlantic in a papyrus raft modelled after carvings found in ancient Egyptian tombs. When he landed on the island of Barbados, he was greeted by its Prime Minister, Errol Barrow, who declared:

**15**     This has established that Barbados was the first landing place for man in the Western hemisphere.

Perhaps Barrow here is simply parodying the nationalist claims that officials often make. (Think about the furor surrounding where Alexander Graham Bell was when he invented the telephone!) The trouble is that, while Barrow may himself have been purposely mocking such nationalist prejudices, others might have taken him seriously. Such a person might have been persuaded by this "argument" culled from Barrow's jest:

**16**     **P1:** Heyerdahl crossed the Atlantic in a raft designed after carvings on ancient Egyptian tombs.
        **P2:** Heyerdahl landed at the island of Barbados.
        **C:** Barbados was the first landing place for man in the Western world.

One's initial inclination is that the premises, though relevant, are not sufficient. The additional evidence would be supplied by answers to such questions as: What does history show about the settling of the Western hemisphere? What are the earliest pieces of evidence? In the absence of such considerations, the conclusion appears premature.

On further reflection, however, one discovers that so many assumptions are necessary for the premises even to be relevant that one begins to have doubts. We must assume that the Egyptians were the first people to cross the Atlantic and settle in North America. If it were some other people, then the whole experiment is beside the point. We must also assume that the ocean currents and prevailing winds were exactly the same when Heyerdahl sailed as they were when the original sailors crossed. In sum, if one was persuaded by Barrow's remark, that person was not thinking clearly or logically.

# 3 Problematic Premise

**2.10** Suppose you are confronted with an argument which does not obviously violate the requirements of relevancy or sufficiency. Are you logically obligated to accept the conclusion? Consider the following example:

17     **P1:** Liberal policies have been responsible for an increase in the erosion of Canadian culture and the foreign domination of the economy.

          **P2:** Liberal policies have been responsible for the recent recession, for inflation, and for the high unemployment.

          **P3:** Liberal policies have crippled Canada's position in the international community.

          **C:** The Liberals should be defeated next election.

**P1**, **P2**, and **P3** seem clearly relevant to the conclusion and together would be sufficient to persuade most clear-headed people. There is just one problem: as they stand, these premises are mere assertions, unattended and unadorned by any evidence. Quite rightly, a great many people (and not only Liberals) would find them *unacceptable* and would therefore not be persuaded of the conclusion. So relevancy and sufficiency are not enough; if the argument is to work, the premises must also be *acceptable*.

The notion of acceptability is broad and vague, although we intend to give it approximate boundaries. Before we turn to that, however, we want to head off a common misunderstanding. Often people who are first beginning to appreciate logical rigour insist on proof for everything. They want every single premise defended: they pounce on undefended premises as logically suspect. However, it's impossible to require, as a condition of a premise's acceptability, that it be defended. *Some* premises *must* appear without support.

We can show why this is true. Consider **P1** as a premise offered in support of **C**. The requirement we're considering means that **P1** is not acceptable unless it has been defended. So let **P1A** be a premise offered in support of **P1**. **P1** has now been defended, but what about **P1A**? By the requirement, it too must be defended. Suppose that **P1Ai** is offered in support of it. Now **P1A** is acceptable, but what about **P1Ai**? You can see that following the demand that every premise be defended would yield an unending spiral of premises. Either no argument could ever be completed or else every argument would have at least one unacceptable premise. Thus, there are either no complete arguments or no good arguments. Both alternatives seem patently false. Since our supposition (the requirement that every premise be defended before it proves acceptable) has led us to either of two patently false conclusions, that supposition must itself be false. (The sort of argument we have used here is known as a *reductio ad absurdum*. The essence of this strategy is that if a proposition leads to a patently false conclusion, that proposition must be rejected and its opposite accepted. Cf. Chapter 8 [8.3].)

The question that arises, then, is this: Under what conditions must the premise of an argument itself be defended? Since the person who proposes the argument in the first place has taken the initiative, the burden of proof falls on his or her shoulders. That is the idea encapsulated in the following basic principle:

**Principle I:** Each premise of an argument should be defended, unless exempted by the context of argumentation.[1]

The "unless" clause plays a dual role here. As we've seen, it's impossible that every premise be defended. More than that, there are clear cases when the arguer is exempt from the normal requirement to defend. We intend to survey some of these shortly. However, our principle means that if a premise is not defended and if there is no exemption to cover it, then the premise is unacceptable and it doesn't provide support for the conclusion. To say that the premise is unacceptable is simply a way of pointing to a flaw in the argument as it stands. It does *not* mean that the premise is false. And clearly such criticism is not a fatal blow to an argument, for the arguer may well be ready and able to provide the defense needed.

---

[1] This principle is similar to one proposed by our colleague, Prof. Robert Pinto, and the authors have benefited a great deal from their discussions with him. Any defects in our principle here are, of course, solely our own responsibility.

We propose to label the employment of undefended premises *not* exempt from defense by the context of argumentation the fallacy of **problematic premise**. Although it's easy to locate undefended premises, it is not always simple to decide whether they ought to have received support. You need to use restraint in charging *problematic premise*, and to develop an intelligent sense for the viability of premises.

**2.11** What conditions would exempt someone from the necessity of defending a premise? We cannot provide an exhaustive account. Instead we shall consider those situations in which an exemption seems clearly permissible.

1. *The premise is self-evidently true.* If a premise is self-evident, then proof or defense is otiose. But what is "self-evident"? An example: "Either we want to limit foreign investment in Canada or we don't." This statement is self-evident; anyone who understands the meaning of the words is able to see that it is true. A second example is furnished by an editorial in the Windsor *Star* (June 1975), at a time when hearings were under way in Toronto about our immigration policy. A group called The Western Guard was prevented from expressing its views to the parliamentary committee. The *Star* commented:

**18**  But cast the Western Guard in the role of martyr—by attempting to muzzle it, as leftists did in Toronto Wednesday —and its ideas will cease to be exposed for the nonsense that they are. *Any attempt to limit freedom of opinion, even of patently foolish opinions—is an attack on freedom . . .* (Emphasis ours.)

The italicized proposition is, we would claim, self-evidently true and therefore not in need of defense. Anyone who understands the notion of a limit to freedom of opinion can understand that it would constitute an attack on freedom.

2. *The premise asserts a proposition that is a matter of common knowledge in the audience to which it is addressed.* That Canada was once a British colony is certainly a matter of common knowledge in Canada (though perhaps not in Argentina). A Canadian writing for a Canadian audience could justifiably use such a proposition without having to defend it.

The next example illustrates how the two exemptions discussed already apply, and leads in turn to two more. This letter appeared in the Edmonton *Journal* (December 1974):

**19**     During the past few months there has been quite a bit of controversy in the number of articles that appeared in the *Journal* concerning the wearing of seat belts. Because of this I would submit this article, "A Logical Answer," that recently appeared in the *Canadian Public Safety* magazine:

*Logic*

(a)  The average driver is not an expert.

(b)  Racing drivers are experts.

(c)  Racing drivers wear safety-belts.

(d)  Racing drivers agree that public highways are more dangerous than race tracks.

(e)  You drive on public highways, therefore, why don't you wear safety belts?

This logic will answer a lot of questions in the minds of Albertans.

The question we must ask is, Should it? The conclusion, stated in the form of a rhetorical question in (e), is: People should wear safety-belts when they drive on the highway. There seem to be no obvious violations of the relevance or sufficiency requirements, but none of the premises has been defended. Are they acceptable? That is, are they exempted from the necessity of being defended? Take them one at a time.

"(a) The average driver is not an expert." This statement is self-evident to anyone who considers our present methods of training drivers in Canada. An expert driver would be one who practised the driving skills and who possessed the skill of driving a car to an unusual degree. (The premise does not assert that the average driver is not *competent*—a vastly different claim which would certainly require backing of some sort.)

"(b) Racing drivers are experts." This proposition is vague. If taken to mean that racing drivers possess a measure of driving skill, then it is certainly a self-evident truth. If they did not, they could not continue to be racing drivers.

"(c) Racing drivers wear safety belts." Again the premise is imprecise. If it means that they wear safety belts while driving in a race, then it is common knowledge, at least among those who follow sports-car racing.

"(d) Racing drivers agree that public highways are more dangerous than race tracks." Neither of the exemptions mentioned thus far seems applicable to (d). Is it then a *problematic premise*, or is there another exemption which would cover (d)?

There is an exemption which may well apply here:

3. *The arguer has some special warrant, status, or qualification for making the particular claim.*

If, for example, the person who makes the claim is an authority on the subject under debate, then in putting forth the claim the arguer is appealing to his or her own authority. This appeal can be perfectly legitimate. In the case of (d) above, this argument was originally presented in the *Canadian Public Safety* magazine. The editors may have some special authority that allows them to assert (d) without defense, in which case the premise would not be problematic.

Or perhaps the editors of the magazine assert (d) based on previous studies they've either conducted or are aware of. If so, then the premise becomes acceptable and illustrates another excusing condition:

4. *The premise has already been defended elsewhere and that defense is referred to.* If a premise has already been argued for, whether earlier in the argument or in a previous one, then that defense need not be repeated. It should, however, be referred to so that anyone who is doubtful can go to the source and appraise the argument. If the editors of *Canadian Public Safety* were aware of such previous argumentation for (d), they fell down at least in not referring their readers to the relevant source.

Here is an argument in which an undefended premise qualifies for Exemption 4, from a letter to the editor in the Montreal *Star* (February 1974):

**20**     Driving at reduced speeds will not create large-scale fuel savings. Unfortunately the necessary data has not been published for Canada. However, in the European situation (i.e., Germany), . . . of the total amount of crude oil used, about 15% is converted into gasoline for internal combustion engines and approximately 8% into fuel for diesel engines. The remaining 77% is used in home heating and industry. It follows that all traffic economy measures can lead to a minor saving of crude oil. Indeed even a Sunday driving ban intended to save 5% of gasoline reserves gives only a 1.8% overall saving in crude usage (see, *Christophorous* magazine, No. 109, February, 1974).

Here the arguer gave a reference for at least one (and perhaps all) of the premises. Anyone in doubt can refer to the publication cited.

5. *The arguer recognizes the lack of defense and indicates a willingness to provide that defense at some other time.* Sometimes in constructing an argument, an arguer will leave a premise undefended

because he or she does not wish to take the time to defend it at that moment. As long as it is done forthrightly and with evident awareness of the lack of defense, *problematic premise* cannot be charged. It follows, of course, that the argument cannot be fully satisfying until that defense has been provided.

Closely related to 5 is the sixth and final exemption:

6. *The premise if offered as true without defense, for the purposes of argumentation in order to show what follows from it.* "Let's grant, for the sake of argument, that **P** is true; then what follows?" As when Exemption 5 applies, such an argument, though not guilty of having a *problematic premise*, is not going to be fully persuasive until defense for that hypothetical premise is provided.

We believe our list covers the main cases where it is logically permissible to use a premise without defense. At least these six exemptions illustrate the sorts of reason for not defending a premise that the social, public, and interactive context of argumentation would sanction. Since it is difficult and maybe impossible to be sure that all possible contexts have been included, this list should not be treated as definitive.

**2.12** Principle I puts the onus on the person offering an argument to back up his or her premises. At the same time, the critic using that principle needs a degree of restraint. The absence of ideally needed defense will be more devastating to some arguments than to others. Consequently, a second principle may usefully be added to the first:

**Principle II:** The less crucial and less controversial a premise is, the less serious the failure to defend it.

By requiring the person evaluating an argument to think about the relative importance of the undefended premise, Principle II should inhibit a tendency to abuse or overwork the charge of *problematic premise*. The charge is most gainfully employed when the premise in question lacks a defense, qualifies for no exemption, is crucial to the argument, and is not otherwise fallacious.

We believe that presenting Principle I, its list of obvious exemptions, and Principle II, is the most perspicuous way to convey when and why premises should be supported. We must grant, however, that this presentation omits a short and handy list of conditions stipulating when *problematic premise* has been committed. Our discussion indicates the main occasions when a premise may go undefended. However, you cannot use our set of exemptions as a checklist for charging *problematic premise* (i.e., if none of the exemptions applies, and the premise is not defended, then the fallacy). That could be done only if our list included *all possible* exemptions.

Since we cannot provide that assurance, we advise a two-stage approach. First, use Principles I and II, together with the exemptions to Principle I, to check undefended premises and to thereby acquire a sense for when a premise is acceptable without defense and when it is not. Second, move beyond any mechanical application of the principles and exemptions to judge from your own assessment of the context of argumentation when an undefended premise is acceptable. At that point, when you charge *problematic premise*, you will be in a position to cite grounds in each context for why the premise requires support.

**2.13** We conclude with an example of the unguarded assertion of a premise that its author should have realized needs defense. This is a small excerpt from a long letter to the editor (St. John's *Evening Telegram*) arguing for a tougher penal system:

21      Many young people who today hold responsible jobs were once the recipient of the lash, and if there are any bleeding hearts who think this is callous and inhuman, let them read Proverbs . . .

The premise here is that *the Bible says* physical punishment is a good thing ("The rod and reproof give wisdom," *Proverbs*, 29:15). The conclusion is that *therefore it's true* that physical punishment is a good thing. There was a time when virtually all Canadians accepted biblical authority and so when an appeal to the Bible would have required no additional defense in order to be persuasive. But that day has passed. Canada is now a pluralistic society. Not all Canadians are Christians or even subscribe to any form of organized religion. In such a society, where basic religious beliefs are not universally subscribed to, an appeal to the Bible carries no persuasive force. The failure to recognize the pluralistic situation in Canada seems to have led to this *problematic premise*.

## Note

**2.14** We've covered three very basic fallacies in this chapter, and we're about to begin an inventory of more. A general point worth making is that the charge of fallacy against an argument varies in strength. *Irrelevant reason* is a strong charge, because if successfully prosecuted the argument cannot be repaired but must be started over. The charge of *hasty conclusion* is somewhat weaker, for in effect you're saying that what's already in the argument is fine, just that more is necessary. The charge of *problematic premise* is the weakest of the three, for all it means is that the arguer is still faced with the task of supplying a defense for the premise in question.

---

## Exercises for Chapter 2

*Directions:* Determine which of the three fallacies discussed in this chapter—*hasty conclusion, irrelevant reason,* or *problematic premise*—occurs in each of the passages that follow. Be sure to *argue* that all of the conditions for the fallacy are fulfilled.

1. *Background:* There was a dispute in the pages of the Halifax *Chronicle-Herald* recently about the newspaper's policy of publishing photographs of accidents. One reader wrote to support the policy:

> I notice that some of your correspondents speak of lack of "good taste." Do these exponents of imaginary "good taste" realize that these horrors, of which they are presented with images only, have to be actually seen by doctors, nurses, police, ambulance staff, relatives, friends, and others?

2. *Background:* Just prior to her marriage to Capt. Mark Phillips, Princess Anne was the subject of a newspaper report, "Women's lib dealt royal blow by princess," which stated:

> Princess Anne, already on record as having no sympathy for Women's lib, has dealt the cause another blow. When she and Capt. Mark Phillips take their marriage vows on Nov. 14 the princess will promise to "obey" her husband... In recent years, the word "obey" has often been replaced by the word "cherish," usually at the request of the bride.

3. *Background:* The following letter appeared in the Ottawa *Journal:*

> In your editorial on Canada's birthday . . . you referred to July 1 as Canada Day. We are all aware that there has never been an act of Parliament to change the name of Canada's birthday from Dominion Day and I am quite sure you are not ignorant of that fact. When you include in your paper, on the editorial page, such a gross inaccuracy, it is difficult

for your readers to put much faith in any editorial appearing in your paper.

4. *Background:* A letter to the Toronto *Star* complained about an editorial (August 1974) on drinking in public parks:

> Your editorial "Iniquitous picnics" advocates the legalization of liquor consumption in our public parks.
>
> Wherever alcoholic beverages are consumed in public there have always been brawls, fights and disorders, and it is not good enough for the *Star* to say that the drunks should be arrested and the laws enforced.
>
> The facts are that the laws and the police have not prevented drunkenness and tragedies where alcohol is permitted, and it is only common sense to prevent the trouble occurring by not allowing drinking in our parks.

5. *Background:* Here is a letter to the *Canadian Forum,* written during the U.S. Watergate crisis, on the virtues of the monarchy:

> The virtues of the monarchy as an institution need not be rehearsed here. The stability, freedom, non-partisanship, and continuity symbolized by the Crown are obvious and commendable attributes. An elected or appointed head of state lacks some or all of these. Surely the present collapse of the American political structure or the recurrent threat of chaos in republican France is graphic proof of this.

6. *Background:* The pages of the Edmonton *Journal* witnessed an ongoing dispute about immigration policy in late 1974 and early 1975. Here is one sample:

> As the *Journal* said on October 30, the new immigration law will be racist and discriminatory. One wonders, on what basis this discrimination in a country which actually does not belong to white people unless you call grabbing as right of ownership? Has the color of skin any effect on culture and morals? Maybe it has. Otherwise why is it the criminals, rapists, drug addicts, etc., in this country are mostly white?

7. *Background:* In late 1974, the former premier of Newfoundland, Joey Smallwood, let it be known that he was considering a comeback. The St. John's *Evening Telegram* did not respond warmly to the prospect, as this excerpt from an editorial, entitled "J.R.S.—a no-no," in September 1974 makes clear:

> The Liberal party, which was almost wrecked by his going, may well be destroyed by his attempt to regain control of

its machinery. It is an affront to a whole new generation of Newfoundlanders that they should be thought ready to embrace a septuagenarian who was holding the reins of office before they were born.

8. *Background:* This letter to the Vancouver *Sun* (August 1974) came in response to a front-page story about an American who deserted the army:

> As a deserter, Mr. A. should be a man without a country. He had no desire to serve his country when his services were required. Why should he then be allowed refuge in our country when he refused to serve his own?
> I'm sure if Canada was ever in a state of national emergency, these cowards would be of no service to us. Yet they feel no guilt in drawing Canadian UIC and welfare benefits. It's a pity our immigration laws allow the dregs of other countries into ours.

9. *Background:* This excerpt from Richard J. Needham's column, "A Writer's Notebook," concerns unemployment and appeared in the Toronto *Globe and Mail* the fall of 1972:

> In times of large-scale unemployment, two things are supposed to happen—(1) wages go down and (2) the Help Wanted signs and advertisements dry up. Neither of these is happening today. Wages keep going up, and newspapers are running yards of Help Wanted ads. I've decided the reason for this is that everybody who wants to work is already working, and must be coaxed away from his or her present job by better money (hence the wage increases) or by learning about opportunities elsewhere (hence all the Help Wanted columns). So far as I can see, and going also from what businessmen tell me, the people who aren't working don't want to work; at any rate, they don't want to work at what's available, which means that they themselves aren't available.

10. *Background:* The following letter to the Vancouver *Sun* (September 1974) was part of an exchange about the humaneness of trapping furbearing animals:

> This is a trapper's rebuttal to the humane groups.
> Leghold traps—the very name is misleading. I prefer to call them toehold traps, which they are if the right size is used for the animal that is trapped. I have caught many a lynx in a 1½ Victor by one or two toes, and I am convinced

that the animals have not suffered. I use the Conibear for wolverines and fisher because I believe that they are more humane for these animals . . .

11. *Background:* While we aren't in the habit of using advertisements as examples, occasionally one comes along that is too good to resist. This one had the headline "Is this a 'potato chip' or a chemistry set?" The copy read in part:

> The ingredient list on the package of a new so-called "potato chip" reads as follows: Dehydrated potatoes; vegetable shortening, salt; mono- and diglycerides; dextrose; ascorbic acid, sodium phosphates, sodium bisulfite, BHA added to preserve freshness.
>
> Now a chemist probably understands this concoction, but where does that leave the rest of us? Are we supposed to eat what we can't even pronounce, much less understand?[2]

12. *Background:* According to a story in the *Canadian Tribune* (November 1974), the Ontario government was guilty of keeping secret a report which charged that fish from the Wabigoon River system near Kenora, Ontario, contained at most more than one and a half times the methyl mercury which has killed or crippled hundreds of Japanese. The government, according to the story, sent around letters to everyone in the area saying not to eat the fish. The report continued:

> Nobody said anything about stopping the lumber operations that pour mercury into the waters. Nobody ordered the companies to install equipment to stop pollution. Nobody suggested that perhaps other sources of food could be supplied in the interim to the Native people who inhabit that area, or job opportunities created so that they could afford other foods. No, the buck was passed from provincial department to provincial department, each one falling over the other's feet to disclaim any or all responsibility. Just "don't eat the fish." That's government racism. It's directed against Native people, because no action by the Ontario government means that many of them will die.

[2] Thanks to Virginia Kepran for this example.

# II A Roster of Fallacies

# 3 Fallacies of Diversion

## Introduction

**3.1** The four fallacies in this chapter work by diverting attention from the proposition at issue; each accomplishes this diversion in a different way. What is crucial is the *effect*, the tendency to distract or shift the focus of the argument.

Worth noting is the locale of these four fallacies. They typically reside in **adversary** contexts; that is, one person is *attacking* someone else's position, or is *defending* his or her position from someone else's attack. Examples of such contexts are political campaigns, management-labour disputes, public controversy about issues of extreme importance such as capital punishment. In such cases, the arguer runs the risk of wanting too much to defeat the opponent, a desire that can work at cross-purposes to the goal of arriving at the most reasonable position available. This fallacy can happen when the arguer diverts attention from the topic under dispute to territory the arguer thinks provides better ground for victory. So watch for these fallacies, particularly in the adversary context.

## 1 Straw Man

**3.2** You're having an argument with someone. The topic is one you're pretty emotional about. You are aware of several positions that you consider dead wrong. Now your antagonist makes a claim that sounds awfully close to one of those dreadfully mistaken views. In that kind of situation, in the heat of controversy, it is tempting to jump on your opponent for holding that view you're familiar with and (you think) know to be false. You have little patience to be attentive to what may be a fine distinction between what your opponent actually said and the position you are eager to demolish. Or if you think your opponent's stand sounds downright dangerous, or morally loathesome, your emotional antagonism can completely blind you to significant differences between what was said and what it reminds you of. You can find yourself launching into a defense of democracy, free enterprise, or the institution of marriage when your opponent didn't really mean to put any of those in question. Or, finally, if you're devious, you can deliberately misrepresent the views of your opponent, and proceed to make your opponent look silly for saying something you're quite aware he or she didn't say at all.

In any case, when you misrepresent your opponent's position, attribute to that person a point of view with a set-up implausibility that you can easily demolish, then proceed to argue against the set-up version as though it were your opponent's, you commit **straw man.**[1]

**3.3** Here is the sort of thing we're talking about. The following letter to the Windsor *Star* was a response to an article quoting the opinions of several men about women's voting habits. Both the article and the response appeared in the paper just after the 1974 federal election.

22          . . . Under the title, "Victory was no big surprise . . . but the size of it was!" you printed several quotes which read as follows, "There are a great many women who simply don't know who to vote for. They just ask their husbands and vote the way they are told," also, "Seventy per cent of the women vote for the person their husband tells them to." Of course these misguided gentlemen are entitled to their own opinions, but the fact that the *Star* would print such ridiculous statements is unbelievable. Surely your writers could have replaced this drivel with something more intelligent.

To set the record straight, women need rely on no one in making their decision as to which way to vote. Contrary to the beliefs of many, women have the power to think, and reason out problems without having to rely on the so-called

---

[1] The term probably originated from the practice of making a straw effigy of someone under severe criticism, then burning it. Cf. Alfred H. Holt, *Phrases and Word Origins* (New York: Dover Publications, 1961), p. 172.

"stronger sex" for answers. In the future, I suggest that your newspaper staff think more carefully before printing statements such as these.

The writer is taking issue with the statements quoted in the article. He contends that they are so obviously false ("ridiculous") that the *Star* shouldn't have bothered to print them. The writer proceeds to argue against those statements in order to "set the record straight." But does he?

Look more closely if you think so. What the quotes included in his letter assert are claims about how many or most women *actually do decide* whom to vote for. However, his argument instead refers to claims about whom women *need to rely on* and about their *capacity* for independent deliberation, in deciding how to vote. These points are different. How people actually *do* behave can differ from how they *need* to and from what they are *capable* of doing. Another way to see the difference is to notice that evidence which would show how women *actually do decide* how to vote (e.g., questionnaire responses in which a representative sample of women confirmed or denied that they followed their husbands' advice) would *not* show whether they were *capable of deciding* for themselves. (Evidence for the latter would include such things as tests of women's ability to understand political issues and to deliberate on them.)

---

**DISTINGUISHING PROPOSITIONS**   *Spotting straw man requires a skill in distinguishing different but look-alike assertions. Above, we showed two techniques for telling such assertions apart:*

*1. Compare subjects, verbs, and predicates for operational differences. In this case, one claim was made in terms of what women do, the other in terms of what they can do or need to do. Look, too, for conflations of what people do (how they conduct themselves) and what they should do (how they ought to conduct themselves).*

*2. Consider the evidence that would be relevant in verifying each claim. If there is a difference, the claims are different.*

*We cannot overstress the importance of developing extremely fine tuning in your ability to discriminate between different propositions.*

---

So our writer's argument is addressed to the position that women are incapable of deciding for themselves how to vote. He points out—what is obvious and hence easily defended—that women are perfectly capable of deciding for themselves how to vote. But the position he *sets out* to criticize, the position he labels "drivel," is different. It is the claim that, whatever they may be capable of doing, many women in actual fact do simply follow their husbands' leads in voting decisions. Our writer misrepresents the position he's attacking, and criticizes the misstated version as if it were the original. He thereby commits *straw man*.

**3.4** A lovely run of straw man fallacies appeared in an exchange over capital punishment in the Windsor *Star* a few years ago. First, here is part of the letter to the editor from Prof. Lawrence LaFave against capital punishment that started the debate off. *Please read this excerpt carefully:*

23    The vast majority of Canadian policemen appear to favor capital punishment, especially when one of their colleagues is murdered in the line of duty. These policemen are entitled to their opinion. However, the public should not take their views on this subject seriously and the mass communications media (with special reference to the Windsor *Star*) should not continue to give so much space to their views.

---

**READING COMPREHENSION TEST** *Without glancing back at Example 23, answer the following questions about it:*
*(a) Prof. LaFave opposes letting police express their opinions. True__ False__*
*(b) Prof. LaFave thinks the public should disregard the views of police on capital punishment. True__ False__*
*(c) Prof. LaFave thinks the media should not report the views of police on capital punishment. True__ False__*
*(d) Prof. LaFave thinks the pro–capital punishment view of police should be suppressed, censored, or ignored. True__ False__*
    *The correct answer is, in each case, False.*
    *(a) The only thing LaFave says that might relate to whether policemen should be allowed to express their anti-capital punishment views is his statement that they are "entitled to their opinion." That might be understood to imply he thinks they should be allowed to express it; he certainly nowhere says they shouldn't be allowed to.*
    *The second statement, (b), is tricky. LaFave does say the public shouldn't take police views on capital punishment seriously, but that's not the same thing as disregarding their views. For instance,*

you may not take the views of terrorist revolutionaries seriously, yet still think it important not to completely disregard those views. You don't ponder their ideology trying to decide whether to adopt it yourself, but you do make a point of noting it, particularly since it represents a threat to international security.

Third, (c), LaFave didn't encourage the media not to report police views; he merely urged them to reduce the amount of space devoted to reporting the police viewpoint. Finally, (d), he said absolutely nothing at all about suppressing or censoring police opinions, nor did anything he said lead to such a suggestion. What we've said about "disregarding" goes for "ignoring" those opinions, too.

If you answered "True" to any of the questions, you did not read carefully enough. It is an imperative starting point we cannot stress too much that you read or listen to the statement of a position with great care. Unless you do, you won't be evaluating the actual assertions you're looking at. You'll be reviewing some different position— if you criticize it, you'll be committing straw man yourself.

---

The point of this little exercise was not just to emphasize the importance of careful reading. It was also to prepare you for the Windsor *Star*'s editorial response to Prof. LaFave's letter. The *Star* began by quoting the segment of the letter we've been looking at, and then went on to say:

**24**      Wrong, Dr. LaFave. The policemen are entitled to their opinion, as your letter says. But policemen—and any other group—are also entitled to express their opinions and have them reported. The media would be failing in their responsibility if they did not give space to the opinions of such groups. And on the subject of capital punishment, a good case can be made for greater attention to the view of police groups, which are close to the situation. Nor should such views be disregarded by the public.

The *Star* agrees with Dr. LaFave in his opposition to capital punishment, and disagrees with the anti-abolition stand which he feels is the majority view of Canadian police officers. But the *Star* does not agree that the view should be suppressed, censored, or ignored. Democracy is a process of making choices after the facts are known and the alternatives discussed and the opinions weighed.

We want to charge the *Star* with four counts of *straw man* in this rejoinder. The fallacy can be characterized in general in terms of the following conditions, so we'll need to show that the *Star's* response to LaFave qualifies on each point:

---

**STRAW MAN**

1. *M* attributes to *N* the view or position, *Q*.
2. *N's* position is not *Q*, but a different one, *R*.
3. *M* criticizes *Q* as though it were the view or position actually held by *N*.

---

We've already covered the first two. By basing our four questions on quotes from the editorial (see Reading Comprehension Test, above), we've shown that the *Star* misrepresented the writer's position. And the *Star* went on to criticize the views it falsely attributed to LaFave. It wrote, "Wrong, Dr. LaFave," referring to the first three claims, and in the second paragraph proceeded to disagree with the fourth. If you'll reread the *Star's* rejoinder, you'll see that it is engaged in *supporting* claims it takes to be *opposed* to Dr. LaFave's position. That's one standard way of criticizing a position: show its opposite to be true. Of course, this procedure also reinforces the erroneous impression that LaFave actually did hold the opposite view.

The parade of *straw men* in this exchange did not end there. Prof. LaFave wrote a rejoinder to the *Star* exposing the *straw men* we have noted, adding:

**25**     The *Star* suggests I am anti-democratic. By its view of democracy, if an inmate of a feeble-minded institute, innocent of physics, argued he had refuted Einstein's theory of relativity, his statement ought to be granted as much press coverage as the same claim by an eminent physicist. If 10 out of 10 physicians believe a man has measles, while 11 out of 11 street cleaners deduce he does not, then by *Star* logic he (by a vote of 11 to 10) does *not* have measles.

The writer's point here is that the *Star* is committed to a view of democracy that would give the incompetent as much voice as the expert and permit majority to rule to decide in matters best left to specialists.

---

**INTERPRETATION AND EXTRAPOLATION**  *We shall turn the tables on LaFave and accuse him of committing* straw man *in the* above passage. But before we do, we must take time out for two ancillary observations.

1. Look at our sentence following this last quotation from the writer. In that one sentence we have compressed his views, and given an interpretation of what he's saying or actually committed to. We've tried to cut through his vivid metaphors and express the point that it seems he meant to make. Slipping your fingers through the murk of rhetoric and withdrawing the kernel of assertion is a skill you'll need to become proficient at to evaluate arguments in ordinary situations. That is, a requisite skill of applied logic is identifying and stating the proposition that's actually being conveyed in a text of heavily rhetorical speech or writing.

2. Notice, too, that LaFave was extrapolating the view of democracy he attributed to the Star. He drew an inference from what was said. The position he attributed to the Star was one he took to be logically implied by what it stated. Specifically, he took three points: (i) the Star's insistence that it should give space to police opinions about capital punishment, (ii) the Star's disregarding his own claim (argued elsewhere in his letter) that the police have no special competence to judge the merits of capital punishment, and (iii) the Star's lecture on democracy. From them he drew the inference that the Star endorsed a view of democracy that would extend majority rule to decide matters of specialized knowledge and give equal media coverage to the views of both laypersons and authorities on subjects calling for expertise.

This move, extrapolation from a stated position, is frequently a means of exploring the merits of the position. To avoid straw man, it is essential to stick to inferences logically warranted by the original position.

---

Now to Professor LaFave: he committed *straw man* himself in this part of his rejoinder because he attacked (by ridicule) an extrapolation not entailed by the *Star's* stated views about democracy. We say it's not entailed because we don't think enough is said in the brief response to be able to pin this theory onto it. The *Star* may hold this view, but neither LaFave nor we can know that from the scant bit that's been said. In ridiculing a theory of democracy that he had no adequate grounds for attributing to the *Star*, LaFave committed the very fallacy which he had rightly accused the newspaper of.

**3.5** A final example. R.R. wrote the following letter to the Vancouver *Sun* (November 1974):

**26**  I was shocked to read about the Canadian Bar Association's proposal to make heroin legally available for addicts to prevent them from being the "criminal menace" they are now.

Such an absurd proposal coming from a prestigious body as the CBA must be a sure sign that they feel no other workable solution exists for the handling of the heroin addiction problem. It is frightening to realize that the bar association is willing to condemn a man to a life of addiction on a deadly drug just to keep him from stealing and to keep him out of their legal hair . . .

Ignore the *hasty conclusion* in the second sentence and look at the last sentence. R.R. asserted there an extrapolation from the CBA's proposal. He was assuming that making heroin legally available to addicts would condemn them to lifelong addiction. For that reason he denounced the proposal as "absurd."

R.R.'s objection would be fair enough if indeed a probable consequence of the CBA's suggestion would be guaranteed addiction for present addicts. But why expect that outcome? If heroin became legally available to addicts, most of these addicts would be more easily identified as needing treatment. There would be no reason to expect that rehabilitative programs would cease to function with the legalization of heroin. On the contrary, they might be more successful, since they would not have the added obstacle of dealing with the criminal subculture. For these reasons, we believe that R.R.'s extrapolation is iffy; consequently, his slam against the CBA's proposal is based on a distortion. The conditions for *straw man* are satisfied.

**3.6** To detect *straw man*, you have to keep abreast of the positions taken by others on matters you're interested in. If you don't know who holds what position, then your defenses are down and you'll find yourself persuaded by implausible criticism. All argumentation in the adversary context must abide by this principle: The position under attack must actually be the position held, not a counterfeit. If we add the realization that even the best intentioned critic may alter the position he or she is attacking, we come up with another basic principle of logical self-defense: When N and M are on opposite sides of the issue, you should be very hesitant to accept M's characterization of N's views. Be cautious of arguments with this move: "Now my opponent believes that . . . but I believe that . . ." Find out for yourself what N's position is; don't take the opponent's word for it! Use these principles and you'll avoid being diverted by *straw man*.

# 2 Ad Hominem

**3.7** When you disagree with something, the logically appropriate response is to aim your critical arrows at that position itself. We have just seen how one diversion from the issue consists instead of attacking a straw man. Another common tactic in adversary contexts is to ignore the issue altogether and go for the person who asserted it. An irrelevant attack on the person, instead of the position, is the fallacy called **ad hominem.**

In April 1976, Paul Desrochers launched a scathing attack on the media in a speech before the Montreal Chamber of Commerce. (Desrochers was an advisor to Quebec Premier Robert Bourassa from 1969 to 1974.) In that speech (according to an editorial in the Windsor *Star*, April 1976), Desrochers urged businesses to withdraw advertising from the news media that do not admit errors and falsehoods; claimed that the press was conducting "a systematic campaign . . . aimed at weakening our institutions and the men who run them so as to bring them down more easily"; stated further that the media "are conducting hate campaigns against businessmen and their 'natural allies' politicians, reminiscent of the inquisition of the Middle Ages"; and charged that the press is destroying careers and reputations without reason. As the *Star* itself commented, "Pretty heavy stuff, that."

The *Star* could have attacked Desrochers' *position* by, for example, claiming that his allegations were vastly overstated or by challenging Desrochers to back them up with specifics. Instead, it chose to attack Desrochers *personally* and thereby attempted to discredit his position without actually confronting it:

27   We shall temporarily overlook the fact that the 1975 Cliche Commission Inquiry into Labor Violence: said that he was "imprudent" for having held shares through his family in a Montreal building where the provincial government rented space while he was a Bourassa adviser;

revealed that patronage appointments to senior James Bay hydro project jobs had been done through his office, completely bypassing the Quebec Public Service Board;

discovered that Desrochers attempted to negotiate a 10-year no-strike deal, illegal at that time, with construction union leaders at James Bay, and approached the same leaders at election time . . .

And perhaps it is pure coincidence that he resigned his governmental post just after a story broke about his part in awarding a $25 million television contract to the Olympics, suggesting a substantial bribe, and just prior to the Cliche Commission report.

Note what the *Star* has done. It has attempted to discredit Desrochers' character by suggesting, with its reference to the findings of the Cliche Commission, that he is a shady operator. But the *Star* managed to say nothing about the charges made by Desrochers. It attacked his person rather than his position. But *even if* Desrochers were guilty of the misdeeds the *Star* imputes to him, what would that tell us about the truth of his position? Would it follow that his charges were untrue? It would only if we were to add a **missing premise** like this: "A man who has been guilty of shady practices cannot hold true views about the media." Such a missing premise would, if added to the *Star*'s response, connect its attack on his character to an assessment of his position. But should we accept that missing premise?

---

**MISSING PREMISES**   *By a missing premise, we mean a proposition which, though unstated in the argument, nevertheless is needed to link a stated premise with a conclusion. In the case just considered, the obvious conclusion seems to be:*

   **C:** *Desrochers' views about the press and the media are not valid.*

*The stated premise is:*

   **P:** *Desrochers is a person of bad character.*

*In looking for the missing premise, we are seeking what must be taken for granted in order to connect the stated premise with the conclusion. In this case, the Star is taking for granted some sort of connection between Desrochers' allegedly unsavory character and the untenability of his criticisms of the media. In formulating this intermediary premise—as is always the case when making explicit something implicit in an argument—we are obliged to pick the weakest possible candidate that will do the job.[2] Otherwise we risk attributing to the Star a position it does not have to accept, and thereby setting up a straw man. Here are two of the possibilities, either of which will connect P to C:*

   **MP₁:** *A person of bad character cannot hold any true views.*
   **MP₂:** *A person of bad character cannot hold any valid views about the newspapers.*

---

[2] Recall the care we had to take in attributing an implicit conclusion to Marc Lalonde's argument about milk adding to the nutritional value of corn flakes in **2.1**.

*Clearly* **MP**$_2$ *is weaker than* **MP**$_1$ *in the sense that it states less and would be easier to prove than* **MP**$_1$. *Thus, when standardized and supplemented with the missing premise, the argument is:*

**28**
**MP**   **P1:** A person of bad character cannot hold true views about the media.
        **P2:** Desrochers is a person of bad character.
        **C:** Desrochers' views about the media are not valid.

*Detecting and formulating missing premises is one of the essential skills in logic. Many fallacies which would otherwise seem persuasive lose their seductiveness when these culprits are detected. The Star's argument is a case in point. Even if Desrochers were an unsavory character, his character obviously wouldn't prevent his accusations against the media from being true.*

---

June Callwood's article about Margaret Trudeau's campaigning for her husband in the 1974 federal election appeared in *Maclean's* of August 1974. It evoked this response from a couple in Sardis, B.C.:

**29**   Re: Article on Margaret Trudeau, all we need is another millionaire's child telling us how to live on $9,500 a year. She can afford to be a "beautiful" person.

Without knowing what Mrs. Trudeau said or what Ms. Callwood reported about her views, you can appreciate the message conveyed in this short response. We want to focus once again on the implicit premise at work here. The writers appear to think that because Mrs. Trudeau is wealthy, whatever she had to say about how to live can be ignored or rejected. They draw attention to her millionaire father —a fact about her background—as though this information had something to do with the merits or validity of her views. They respond by attacking her person (background) rather than her views, and hence commit *ad hominem*.

A House of Commons debate several years ago concerned whether a parliamentary committee holding hearings across the country on the Income Tax Act was really open to the views of the general public. David Orlikow (Winnipeg North, NDP) contended that the committee was mostly hearing from the corporate sector and the wealthy—those who had the ability, knowledge, and money to hire experts to represent their interests. "The vast bulk of people," he said, "the ordinary wage and salary earners who pay every penny of income tax which the law requires them to pay . . . were not able to make representations." Orlikow was interrupted by the Liberal MP from Winnipeg South Centre, E. B. Osler, who claimed that ordinary citizens had made their views known to the committee at a meeting in Winnipeg just the previous week. To this Orlikow replied:

**30**     It is an interesting development we see in regard to the hon. member for Winnipeg South Centre. When he was running as a candidate he was careful to try to create the impression that he was just an ordinary citizen like everybody else. But since he has come down here, increasingly we find in his interjections and his speeches . . . that the real person comes out. He is from one of the few top families in Winnipeg. They've got it made, and he is going to keep on seeing that they are protected.

Here's a classic example of an adversary context—a debate in the House of Commons. Did Orlikow respond to Osler's challenge? No, he attacked his background ("He is from one of the few top families in Winnipeg.") and interests (". . . he is going to keep on seeing that they are protected."). Another case of *ad hominem*.

Both the B.C. couple and Orlikow seem to believe that if someone is rich, that makes their views untrue or unacceptable. Since it has never been demonstrated that belonging to a particular socio-economic or ethnic group causes a person to have false views, no attempt to rebut someone's claim by identifying him or her as a member of such a class is ever defensible.

**3.8** "Ad hominem"—from the Latin phrase *argumentum ad hominem* meaning "argument against the person"—is characterized by the following conditions:

---

**AD HOMINEM**

1. M responds to a position N has taken by attacking N rather than N's position.
2. N's position can be judged without any reference to N's person.

---

The attack on the person can come in a variety of forms: a criticism of his or her personality or character, a derogatory crack about the ethnic or racial background, a condemnation of behaviour ("People in glass houses shouldn't throw stones" is an example of that one), or speculation about motives or special interests. In fact, *any* response qualifies as "attacking *N*" for purposes of *ad hominem*, if the response steers attention away from the substance of what is under debate and toward the person who proposed it by seeking to discredit that person.

However—and we want to put this "however" in flashing lights —finding a controversy in which someone has been personally criticized is *not enough* to charge *ad hominem*. In certain situations it *is* relevant to attack a person as a means of discrediting that person's views. That's why we require Condition 2: to say, in effect, that *ad hominem* cannot be charged when reference to the person can be relevant to an assessment of his or her position.

**3.9** It's difficult to come up with a rule of thumb for distinguishing legitimate from illegitimate criticisms of the person when the dispute is over a position. You will have to judge each case on its merits.

Try on this next example. First the background: in July 1972, novelist Joan Didion wrote an essay-review of the literature on "The Women's Movement" for the *New York Times Book Review*. In reviewing a sample of 15 books, Ms. Didion argued that the literature was "mired in trivia" and didacticism; that "half truths, repeated, authenticated themselves"; that many women supporting the movement were "converts who want not a revolution but romance." In sum, she concluded, "the Women's Movement is no longer a cause but a symptom." Her article brought in a flood of replies. Here's one:

**31**    So Joan Didion can afford the luxury of intellectualizing the Women's Movement . . . *I* can't. My reaction to her article is pure, gusty anger. "Litany of trivia," she writes. "Not revolution but romance!" Miss Didion, may your next review for the *Times* be written while one diaper needs changing, one grilled cheese needs tending, and a lasagna needs to be made for company dinner. Baby, that's how I'm writing this letter . . .

Once again, we need to sift through the rhetoric, and identify the point being made. The writer thought Didion was mistaken in her assessment of the Women's Movement, but instead of arguing her point, she challenged Didion's credentials as a critic of the Movement. Her point seems to have been: Unless you've tried to do something outside the role of homemaker, while at the same time having to look after babies, make meals, and so on, you can't know what it's like, so you're in no position to criticize the Movement. The writer attacked Didion, but did not try to show that her criticisms were wrong. The first condition of *ad hominem* is met, but is the second? *Can* a person sufficiently understand the Women's Movement and its literature to assess it intelligently without having experienced the confinement and frustrations of the roles of homemaker and mother? Was this slam at Didion's qualifications in fact irrelevant? (Consider analogous questions: Can one understand what it is like to live in poverty without having been poor? Is the experience of poverty necessary for a fair assessment of discussions of poverty?) Since we see arguments in both directions, we reserve judgement about whether Didion's critic committed *ad hominem* until we can follow them up.

Consider a different example. M.M. of Edmonton wrote to *Maclean's* criticizing a profile of Tommy Douglas and the "Education" column, both written by Heather Robertson:

**32**    Two articles by Heather Robertson in the January [1975] issue of *Maclean's* deserve careful consideration. The first of these about Tommy Douglas in its introductory page is nothing less than disgusting. Here we have Heather, *a relatively unknown person*, writing in a most patronizing manner about one of Canada's most distinguished citizens . . . It reminds me of the thistle trying to patronize the rose.

   In her article on schools, *Heather's attitude seems to have been based on the fact that one teacher once had the temerity to scold her!* Apparently she has hated all schools and all teachers ever after this terrible insult . . . (Emphasis ours.)

In the first paragraph, M.M. attacked Robertson's article *indirectly* by referring to her as "a relatively unknown person." The intended persuasive force of this passing remark was, we guess, that because Robertson was unknown, we do not need to take the substance of her article seriously. The second paragraph introduces a variation in M.M.'s attack on Robertson. This time, it was not her lack of fame but *her motives* that were advanced as relevant to a judgement about her article. M.M. seemed to be saying that, since Robertson had an unjustified bias against schools and teachers, her criticisms of education may be dismissed. We strongly suspect that Robertson did not commit the *hasty conclusion* that M.M. attributed to her here. But suppose she had. Suppose, that is, Robertson had a blind bias against schools and teachers. Would that fact about her be relevant when evaluating an article in which she was critical of education? It depends on the kind of charges she made. If she were presenting evidence for a certain claim (e.g., that teachers are lazy, or repressive; that schools are inefficient, or counterproductive), knowledge of her bias would lead us to wonder whether she had looked hard enough for evidence pointing the other way. But if she were making a criticism backed by reasoned arguments, her contentions could and should be assessed on their own merits, without reference to her personal motives for advancing them.

**3.10** Instead of a rule of thumb or a general principle indicating when it is relevant to attack the person, and hence when such a criticism cannot be called *ad hominem*, we can give a partial list of sorts of circumstances.

**A. Appeals to authority, or to expert opinion.** If I ask you to believe something I say using the argument that an authority or expert on the subject says it's true, you may legitimately question the background or motives of that authority. If I'm asking you to accept the point just because she or he says so, then it's fair to challenge credentials and to be critical of the authority's interests. Suppose I tell you that a certain make of ski is good and cite Kathy Kreiner's endorsement of it as my authority. If you point out that Kreiner is employed by that manufacturer and makes a percentage on gross sales of those skis each year, you don't commit *ad hominem* —even though you are attacking her motives in endorsing the product instead of evaluating the skis on their own merits. For, in the case we're imagining, Kreiner's endorsement of the skis may be judged—indeed, *should* be judged—in the light of her tie with the manufacturer. She would have an interest in people's buying those skis whether they were good ones or not. On the other hand, she might have chosen to endorse one manufacturer's skis over the other brands because of their superior merits—and this fact should be noted in the argument too.

**B. Candidates for positions of public trust.** No matter what arguments a candidate puts forward for being qualified for the office sought, it is always legitimate to consider his or her character and background. Not every facet would be fair game for critical appraisal. It wouldn't particularly matter if the leader of a party turned out to have a preference for the Rolling Stones rather than Ravel. If, on the other hand, he or she had a history of coronary attacks, or were suffering from an incurable and interminable disease, these factors would probably outweigh even the best arguments and someone who made them known would not be guilty of *ad hominem*. The reason is clear: in electing an official, we elect the human being, not just the mind that shapes the policies.

**C. Cases of credibility.** Courtroom proceedings furnish the clearest examples here. Suppose someone has testified in court. If that person is found to be a habitual liar, then this fact damages his or her credibility. The lawyer who points out this personality trait is attacking the person as a means of discrediting the testimony, not as an alternative to confronting it.

**3.11** It should be clear why *ad hominem* is a fallacy. An argument is an attempt to elicit our consent to the truth of a proposition by appealing to other propositions we accept—not by appealing to force, flattery, or personality. If you disagree with a claim, logic demands that you inspect the reasons put forward to support it. You normally need know nothing about the person who happens to put forward the claim, whether he or she is rich or poor, Indian or WASP or *québécois*, votes Liberal, Conservative, or NDP.

*Ad hominem* is obviously fallacious. Why do people continue to commit it and be persuaded by it? Maybe because there's something satisfying, emotionally, about putting down someone you disagree with. It's irritating to admit that someone you dislike has made a valid point. Also, when you identify with a view, an attack on it seems like an attack on you, so it's natural to counter with a personal challenge of your own. Logical self-defense requires some detachment from your beliefs—the Socratic ideal of pursuing the truth, wherever the path to it may lead.

# 3 Guilt by Association

**3.12** Suppose one of your friends works for a day-care centre and another for a family-planning bureau; because of these friends, your parents conclude that you're "one of those Women's Libbers" and a pro-abortionist. Suppose you express agreement with environmentalists' concerns about pollution from petroleum exploration in the Arctic, so your parents accuse you of being "a damned socialist." What has gone wrong? Certainly people who associate with one another have some common interest, but that doesn't mean *all* their beliefs are identical. And people and groups can have some beliefs in common without accepting everything the others believe.

These obvious rules can be ignored in the heat of debate. Especially in adversary contexts, you can be tempted to transfer some perceived discredit to an opponent, based on some association that person has with a supposedly discreditable individual or group. The attack is usually (though not always) *ad hominem* in form, since its objective is to refute or discount the opponent's position by focusing on his or her person. But it is an *indirect* strike against the person, made by transferring alleged "guilt" that has accrued to someone else, or to some other group or doctrine, from them to the opponent, using the connection between them as a bridge. The move is the fallacy called **guilt by association**, when the mere association is *not* reason enough to attribute any opprobrium to the opponent.

Some examples should elucidate the fallacy. In 1975 (before their anti-inflation program), the federal Liberals proposed a pay raise for MPs. The New Democrats opposed it and soon the debate hit the newspapers. At one point, an NDP worker wrote to several papers outlining his party's position. That letter was soon followed by a reply from a Liberal party official, from which we take this excerpt:

**33**    Every NDP member accepted the parliamentary increase in 1970, even when they spoke against it; and Ed Broadbent, the NDP parliamentary leader, has already admitted that he will accept any new increase. It seems to me that the NDP is engaged in a large scale exercise in hypocrisy. This impression is strengthened by the knowledge that the NDP government in British Columbia doubled members' salaries there shortly after taking office.

Are the *federal* NDP members of parliament hypocrites because the B.C. *provincial* party increased MLAs' salaries in the Victoria legislature? The "guilt" alleged here is inconsistency—a respectable line of political criticism if it can be backed up. But the federal NDP cannot be held responsible for the policies of a provincial New Democrat government. The two are independent authorities, dealing with different social, economic, and political exigencies. The Liberal official who wrote the above letter tried to get us to accept that the association in name and general political outlook would carry over to particular political policy. Since it does not, he committed *guilt by association*. (We must be careful not to charge the federal Liberal Party with the fallacy. If we did so, we'd be guilty of it ourselves—tarring the whole party with the brush that can in fairness only be used against one of its over-zealous officials.)

When Dr. Bette Stephenson was president of the Canadian Medical Association in 1974-75, she pressed for liberalized abortion laws. Her stance provoked this letter from L.M. to the Edmonton *Journal* (January 1975):

**34**    Perhaps it is not Canadian law which ought to be called into question but the arrogant attitude of the president of the Canadian Medical Association. Laws should be designed to afford reasonable protection for all human life. Statutes made and enforced by sensible, civilized societies should not provide for the thoughtless, wholesale slaughter of those considered to be less than human by some. Remember Dachau and Auschwitz.

L.M. associates Dr. Stephenson's position with the Nazi concentration camps where millions of Jews and other "undesirables" were murdered under Hitler's horrifying program of genocide—and invites enormous antagonism to her views. To suggest that association, L.M. had first to create a straw man, by describing Dr. Stephenson's proposals for more liberal abortion laws as entailing "the thoughtless and wholesale slaughter of those considered to be less than human by some." With the distortion in hand, L.M. had only a slight jump to make to forge a link with the Nazi extermination camps. But the link is complete fabrication. The CMA president wasn't calling for thoughtless and wholesale slaughter. Furthermore, favouring liberalized abortion laws does not require believing that the foetus is less than human. Finally, even if Dr. Stephenson did believe that a foetus is "less than human," that's a far cry from considering it subhuman in the way Hitler and the Nazis viewed so-called non-Aryans. L.M. committed *guilt by association* by alleging a non-existent association. That's a slightly different blunder from the one in the Liberal official's attack on the NDP, where an association did exist, but wasn't strong enough to support the connection based on it.

**3.13** The following conditions cover the central cases of this type of fallacy:

---

### GUILT BY ASSOCIATION

1. M attacks N (or N's position), on the basis of some alleged association between N (or N's position) and some other person, group, or belief(s).
2. Either (a) the alleged association does not exist at all, or else (b) it does not provide adequate support for M's criticism of N (or N's position).

---

*Guilt by association* crops up in a variety of forms. It took a curious turn in the reaction of a political official to a rowdy reception given Queen Elizabeth in Stirling, Scotland, by anti-royalist students (AP, October 1972):

**35**     Four hundred students chanted obscene songs and hurled insults at the Queen, jostling the royal entourage during a ceremony at the university . . .

The scenes involving the Queen, the worst in Britain of her 20-year reign, were criticized by leading Scots. The Conservative party chairman in Scotland, Sir William McEwan Younger, said: *"The damage done to all Scotland's image across the world is incalculable."* (Emphasis ours.)

Sir William's fear would have foundation only if we assume that people the world over would commit *guilt by association*. For there is no reason to condemn "all Scotland" just because of the behaviour of a few hundred Scottish students. Did Sir William commit the fallacy, or did he merely assume that *we* would?

**3.14** Identifying *guilt by association* becomes dicey when it is not clear whether the association does justify the criticism based on it. This problem is well illustrated by a passage in Gérard Pelletier's *The October Crisis.*

The crisis began on October 5, 1970, when a cell of the *Front du Libération de Québec* kidnapped James Cross, then British Trade Commissioner in Montreal. For his release they demanded the release from jail of people they claimed were political prisoners, and the dissemination through the media of a "manifesto." The manifesto was read and its description of economic conditions in the province aroused the sympathy of many beyond the terrorist fringe. But the prisoners were not released and on October 11 a second *FLQ* cell kidnapped Quebec Minister of Labour, Pierre Laporte. Five days later the federal government invoked the War Measures Act, claiming that a state of "apprehended insurrection" existed in Quebec. The army was called in to protect MPs in Ottawa and to police Montreal, civil liberties were suspended, it was declared illegal to have belonged to the *FLQ*, and over four hundred people were arrested without warrants. On October 17, the body of Laporte, assassinated, was found in the trunk of an abandoned car. Several weeks later the police located the *FLQ* hideout where Cross was being held. The government negotiated his release in return for allowing the kidnappers and their families to leave Canada for Cuba.

The following passage comes from the section of Pelletier's book entitled, "The confusion between the *FLQ* and the *Parti Québécois*." The latter is a provincial political party devoted to bringing about the separation of Quebec from Canada by legal political means; the *FLQ* was an underground urban guerilla group committed to the goal of independence by any means, legal or illegal. Pelletier was generally careful to distinguish the two, but he argued that the *Parti Québécois* should "purge itself of its undesirable elements," and went on to berate Pierre Bourgault, a leading member of the party:

36    When Mr. Bourgault declares: "We are five million political prisoners," he is clearly saying: "The *FLQ* is leading the action and it is they who represent us. The political prisoners are being punished for our sake because they tried to free us from slavery." These words are proof of an unconscious indulgence on Mr. Bourgault's part towards the strategy of the *FLQ*. When Mr. Lévesque says that people are doing their utmost to confuse the *PQ* with the *FLQ*, he should begin by cleaning his own house.[3]

In extrapolating the way he did from Bourgault's statement, Pelletier left himself open to a charge of *straw man*. Still, he may have just overstated an otherwise valid case. Did the similarity of Bourgault's rhetoric to that of the *FLQ*, pronounced in the midst of the crisis, warrant the conclusion of "an unconscious indulgence" towards the *FLQ* strategy? We can imagine arguments on both sides in answer to that question. However, Pelletier goes further and uses his association of Bourgault with the *FLQ* to criticize in turn the *Parti Québécois*. Can the entire party be discredited because of the views of one of its members? The answer is not so clear, since Bourgault was a leading figure in the party. In this sort of case, the decision to charge a fallacy must finally be based on a judgement about political responsibility.

# 4 Red Herring

**3.15** Victory is the obsession of most adversary-context arguments. Often the goal is not the triumph of truth, but the triumph of your views; not the elimination of error, but the elimination of your opponent. We have seen how this pressure to win produces distortions of opposing positions (*straw man*), and even irrelevant attacks on the person opposing, both direct (*ad hominem*) and indirect (*guilt by association*). **Red herring** is another fallacy in this genre. It's the ploy of introducing an irrelevant issue into adversary debate, thus inviting a digression away from the original topic.

    The origin of the term "red herring" makes it a good descriptive label for this fallacy. It comes from the sport of foxhunting, in which the hunters on horseback follow a pack of hounds tracking a fox's scent. To divert the hounds from the hunt—either to save a good fox for another day's chase, or to call off young hounds being trained —a red herring (one that's been dried, smoked, and salted) was

[3] McClelland and Stewart Limited, Toronto/Montreal, 1971, paperback edition, p. 179.

drawn across the fox's track ahead of the pack. The dogs would be diverted by the fresher, stronger scent. The term's application to this fallacy is evident.

**3.16** A typical *red herring* was committed by then-Senator Paul Martin, well-known for extolling the virtues of his hometown of Windsor, Ontario. On this occasion, Senator Martin rose to defend Windsor against a slur contained in Arthur Hailey's novel about the U.S. auto industry, *Wheels*. Hailey wrote of "grimy Windsor" across the border from Detroit, "matching in ugliness the worst of its U.S. senior partner." According to press reports, Martin responded:

**37**     When I read this I was incensed . . . Those of us who live there know that [Windsor] is not a grimy city. It is a city that has one of the best flower parks in Canada. It is a city of fine schools, hard-working and tolerant people.

Martin's first point does tell against Hailey's appraisal, for a city with an attractive flower park cannot be completely ugly. But the Senator didn't continue building his case for Windsor's beauty (as he might have) by extolling its splendid rose gardens and miles of riverfront parkland. Instead he *changed the subject*. Fine schools and hard-working, tolerant people are no doubt an asset, but they have nothing to do with whether a city is fair or ugly.

The Senator's shift here is a common type of *red herring* move. Martin began his defense of Windsor on topic, then shifted to an associated point, not strictly relevant to the attack. Perhaps Martin interpreted Hailey's criticism of Windsor's physical appearance as part of a general critique of the city. That would explain his more general defense. It wouldn't alter the fact, however, that Hailey's comment was restricted to Windsor's appearance. Nor would it make the Senator's second point any less a distraction, inviting a step away from Hailey's claim. The effect, whether intentional or not, was to move the argument onto different ground to terrain much more favourable to Martin. (It's harder to document the allegation that the quality of life in a city is lamentable than it is to show that the city is physically grimy and ugly.)

A typical case of *red herring* as counterattack in an adversary context occurred in the following exchange. Recall that Prime Minister Trudeau and the Liberals were swept into power in 1968 promising to build a "Just Society." During the 1972 federal election, on an open-line radio program in Regina, a caller asked Mr. Trudeau what had happened to the "Just Society" he'd promised. The Prime Minister replied by suggesting that his questioner ask Jesus Christ what happened to the just society that Christ had promised 2000 years ago.

Trudeau was probably trying to suggest that if it was impossible for Christ to keep His promise, the Liberals can be forgiven for failing to keep theirs. But his reply invites a shift of focus to the tenuous analogy. There is an enormous leap from the reasons a Canadian political party didn't keep a campaign promise in the mid-twentieth century to the reasons that the two-millenia-old Christian hope of peace on earth and goodwill towards men (and women and children) hasn't come about. Left behind was the caller's question about the social justice the Liberals had promised four years earlier.

**3.17** *Red herring* might be defined in terms of the *intention* of the person who introduces the red herring to divert his or her opponent from the opponent's original line of attack. Because it is difficult to be sure about people's intentions, this definition would restrict our employment of the *red herring* tag. It would be an undue restriction, because we often want to mark a distractingly irrelevant response whether or not the person was *trying* to change the subject. However, to define the fallacy in terms of the *effect* a response has in diverting the opponent's attention to a different topic would mean that we could charge *red herring* only when the opponent was duped by the irrelevant rejoinder. Hence, the presence of the fallacy would depend on the cleverness of the opponent—an odd situation, since we'd want to say that the clever opponent exposed the fallacy or avoided it; we would not want to say, paradoxically, that the fallacy didn't exist because the opponent spotted it! Certainly a paradigm of *red herring* would be an exchange in which someone deliberately introduces a red herring to try to divert the opponent's attention from the point under controversy, *and* as a result the opponent is distracted by the red herring and follows it up, leaving behind the original issue. We find it more useful, however, to use the label for responses to attacks in adversary contexts that, because they are close but not strictly relevant to the topic, invite the opponent to digress, whether or not the distraction is intended or successful. More formally:

---

### RED HERRING

1. N has made a claim, or posed a question, that is implicitly or explicitly critical of a position M holds or identifies with.
2. M's response to N introduces an issue that is not strictly relevant, and thereby instigates a shift of focus in the exchange.

---

**3.18** Beginning students of logic often have the mistaken idea that the defining conditions of each fallacy will always clearly and sharply delineate each occurrence of that logical flaw and, what's more, will do this automatically, like a compass needle picking out North. They also have a misplaced expectation that each fallacy can be neatly distinguished from the others. Such hopes stem from a misunderstanding of how the defining conditions are determined and how they relate to actual arguments.

The defining conditions in fact have either of two origins. In some instances they are generalizations derived from a variety of similar but not identical logical errors. Such conditions have to be stated in general terms to fit these variations in actual arguments. Other defining conditions describe an "ideal type" which is only approximated in practice, though it serves as a useful exemplar for fallacy detection. The indeterminacy and variety of actual argumentation responsible for this imprecision cannot be avoided. In either case you can see that you are required to use your own judgement to decide which label fits most closely the actual fallacy you have found. Proper use of the defining conditions also calls for your judgement when different fallacy conditions overlap or when an actual logical mistake has some features of each of two different sets of fallacy conditions.

The whole point of introducing the concept of fallacy is as a learning device, something like training wheels for a bicycle. The goal is not to be able to stand up at a meeting and cry, "*Ad hominem!*" or to mutter "*Straw man!*" under your breath while you read the paper. The goal is to be able to see what's going on in an argument, to appreciate the strengths and weaknesses of persuasive appeals. Learning to identify fallacies sharpens your analytical skills and your capacity for logical evaluation. These are your best defense against bad reasoning. Once these skills are refined, the exercise of attaching the proper label to the fallacy becomes superfluous.

The fallacy under discussion here, *red herring*, provides ample illustration of these points. 1. Many arguments that are clearly flawed logically, and approximate *red herring*, also blend into *irrelevant reason* or *ad hominem*. 2. Many arguments, that may look like cases of *red herring*, on closer examination seem not to be fallacies at all. Some examples will bring these points home.

1. In November 1975, a government official responsible for investigating and prosecuting misleading advertisements gave a talk on the subject to a group of Windsor businesspersons. He pointed out that, since 1969, 28 000 new files had been opened on misleading advertising, and he cited a wide variety of cases. His speech left the impression that much advertising is unreliable. One of his listeners responded during the question-and-answer period:

**38**     It would be far better if you didn't go around making speeches and discouraging people from entering this business.

The point of the talk was the reliability of advertising and whether business people were upholding their responsibility to provide reliable information in their advertising. But the critic's objection had nothing to do with reliable advertising. Why not, then, call this a case of *irrelevant reason*? We prefer *red herring* for two reasons. First, this is an adversary context, and irrelevant replies in the context of attack and defense have a strong tendency to change the subject. Calling this irrelevant reply *red herring* acknowledges that fact. Second, the critic did not proceed to draw any explicit conclusion from his remark. Had he done so (assuming his suggestion quoted above to be irrelevant to that conclusion), then, even though it's an adversary context, we'd have preferred the label *irrelevant reason*. For in that case it would have been clear that he had *intended* it to be relevant, so he could not have been trying to introduce a digression. In this case, however, the critic's comment clearly invited a change of topic from the reliability of advertising to the advisability of criticizing unreliable advertising. Using the label *red herring* underscores this feature of the irrelevant objection.

The next example emphasizes the blurry boundary between *red herring* and *ad hominem*. Its setting was a meeting of a group of touring Ontario (Conservative) cabinet ministers and local citizens at Sault Ste. Marie. An NDP supporter charged that the "Government was too slow to act on mercury poisoning in the Kenora area and lung cancer dangers facing uranium miners in Elliott Lake until the NDP 'screamed for action'" (Toronto *Globe and Mail*, September 1975). According to the newspaper report, Ontario Health Minister Frank Miller responded that he was

**39**     tired of people complaining about health hazards facing Indians in Northwestern Ontario while the complainers go on killing themselves with what he called diseases of choice by exercising too little and smoking too much.

"I get a bit cynical about reactions of society that totally ignores my warnings about smoking and wearing seat belts, killing more people every day than mercury ever will," he said.

*Was* Ontario slow to act on the dangers of Minamata disease from mercury poisoning and of cancer from uranium radiation? Mr. Miller's reply was clearly irrelevant to the accusation. It invited a digression onto the topic of the consistency of the government's critics or even to the extent to which people were heeding warnings about smoking and seat belts. Thus, it seems to qualify as a case of *red herring*. Yet Mr. Miller was also launching a personal attack against the critics of the Government (charging inconsistency) instead of responding to the merits of their case. Thus, the fallacy meets the conditions of *ad hominem*.

If our goal were simply to teach you to identify fallacies, we'd be in a quandary. Which one is it? Or is it both? Our answer: if you can see how it could be either, or both, you have appreciated the three dimensions of Mr. Miller's answer—its irrelevance, its direction against the person instead of the issue, and its invitation to change the subject. Which fallacy? It doesn't matter. Our definitions allow for an overlap here. They show that with one response in argument, a person can be doing more than one thing.

2. Finally, consider an example where the choice is not between two fallacy labels, but between *red herring* and no fallacy at all.

D.C. of St. Lambert, Quebec, wrote a long letter to the Montreal *Gazette* (February 1975) in which he made a case against some suggestions for gun control laws. He began:

**40**    Reading your editorial "Drop those guns," made me 'do a slow boil.' It is quite evident you know very little about game laws, and even less about sport shooters, i.e., target shooters.

There is far more ammunition used each year on targets, either paper or clay, than on living things. You say nothing in your editorial on this point.

[D. C. next argued against a proposal to have licensed rifles kept at target shooting ranges. He proceeded:]

I believe John Diefenbaker had the best idea, when he said that people who commit crimes with guns, should get an automatic five years prison term, with no parole, in addition to any other sentence received for the crime.

Please start blaming the people, not the guns.

*Also, why is so much time and effort spent on this subject recently? How about the people killed on snowmobiles each year? How do their numbers rank with killing by guns? Much higher. And how about traffic deaths? Drunken drivers? Why not do something about them?* (Emphasis ours.)

The last paragraph looks like a *red herring*. What has the number of people killed in snowmobile and traffic accidents got to do with whether guns should be controlled? D.C. seems clearly to be changing the subject. On the other hand, it cannot be denied that most of the letter responded to various arguments for gun control. Why not give the letter this interpretation: first, it dealt with the arguments favouring gun controls; then it suggested that there are other, more pressing, problems for public attention. Once again we reply: It doesn't matter which interpretation you settle on, provided you recognize the considerations weighing in favour of each one.

**3.19** With *red herring*, we complete our list and discussion of fallacies of diversion. When evaluating an argument in adversary contexts, you ought to be on the lookout for them. We have followed a sort of logical declension in presenting them. First case: when faced with an argument or criticism, the respondent attacks an argument; but instead of attacking the real McCoy, he or she attacks a distorted version (*straw man*). Second case: when confronted with an argument or criticism, the respondent attacks the person instead of the argument (*ad hominem*). Third case: when confronted with an argument, the respondent attacks the person or position, but does so indirectly by some imagined or real association between some other individual or group and the person who proposed the argument (*guilt by association*). Fourth case: when confronted with an argument, the respondent changes the subject (*red herring*). You can see how in each case the argument gets further and further away from the response logically appropriate in adversary contexts: *an attack on the precise argument or position asserted by the opponent.*

---

# Exercises for Chapter 3

*Directions:* Determine which of the four fallacies discussed in this chapter occurs in each of the passages that follow. Be sure to *argue* that all of the conditions for the fallacy are fulfilled. Some of the passages contain more than one of the fallacies; some may contain more than one instance of a given fallacy. In several cases it will be controversial which of the labels to assign to a particular fallacy.

1. *Background:* A television station in Toronto used to show adult ("blue") movies late Friday night. This programming occasioned a spate of letters to the Toronto *Globe and Mail* about current mores. One of them was from W.J.T. of Aurora (November 1973):

> There appears to be a popular belief that persons who do not subscribe to lewd conduct and loose behavior, either in

fact or fiction . . . are suffering from some sort of hangup from which they need to be liberated. One wonders whether the individuals harboring this belief are suffering from a a rather pathetic hangup of their own?

2. *Background:* Just after *Saturday Night* magazine announced in October 1974 that it was being forced to fold because of lack of capital, N.H. wrote to the Edmonton *Journal:* "As far as I'm concerned, *Saturday Night* could have quit many years ago. I think *Reader's Digest* is an excellent magazine and the only one in Canada now or ever that will give such a variety of material so well written and authoritative." N.M. of Crestwood responded:

> The intemperate remarks of N.H. . . . on the subject of all things Canadian, especially our magazines, need not be taken too seriously, since her taste runs to the predigested pap of *Reader's Digest.*

3. *Background:* In a letter devoted to an attack on abortion, R.K. wrote to the Detroit *Free Press* (September 1972) as follows:

> The anti-abortion story has not been presented in detail. How many readers have seen pictures depicting babies aborted by various methods at various stages of conception? The pictures are shocking for sure, and may be considered by some as in bad taste but abortion is by no means good. If the woman having an abortion performed were to witness the results, do you think there would be as many abortions as there are in the world today? . . .

4. *Background:* In 1973, a group with the acronym PUSH (People Under Social Hardship) made a presentation to the city council of Sarnia, Ontario. Sarnia Alderwoman Marie Coulter greeted the brief with the statement, "There is no disadvantage to being poor." In an editorial (July 1973), the Windsor *Star* commented:

> Surely such a gem of political philosophy deserves to be enshrined along with such other Canadian political milestone slogans as the one attributed to C. D. Howe: "What's a million?"
>
> Putting it more in perspective, perhaps the statement should be enshrined alongside *The Wit and Wisdom of Archie Bunker . . .*
>
> Such foolish comments, Ms. Coulter, only serve to reinforce the feelings of male chauvinists who feel that a

woman's place is in the home and not in public where she may make ridiculous and embarrassing statements.

5. *Background:* Back in the summer of 1974, registered nurses (RNs) in Ottawa were arguing for higher salaries. One issue was that registered nursing assistants (RNAs), with lower educational and training standards and less responsibility than RNs, got paid almost as much. The RNs thought they should get an increase that would put them further ahead of RNAs. Another issue was the nature of the work: the responsibility for 25 patients each, double shifts (16 hours straight), insufficient time to complete assigned duties. They pointed out the work is physically exhausting and emotionally draining. One RN said, "You are always aware you are working with sick people, and it effects you emotionally and physically." The RNs' case was described in an article in the Ottawa *Journal* (July 1974). In response to that article, an irate RNA, F.F., wrote to the *Journal* (July 1974):

> Another point that roused me was the "emotionally draining and physically exhausting" bit. It would appear that since we are but RNAs, the work does not affect us emotionally and physically, or that ill patients never take out their frustrations on us.

6. *Background:* In January 1975, the St. John *Telegraph-Journal* ran an editorial against the decision of New Brunswick teachers to "work to rule"—to cease donating their free time to supervise extracurricular activities. R.D. responded, praising the unselfishness of teachers and citing examples. He continued:

> I think the public should ask themselves if there is any other group in the community which gives so freely of its spare time. Do you see dentists, electricians, lawyers, etc. giving up comparable amounts of their free time to benefit the community? By what right does the community demand that teachers give up their spare time so that you can get something for nothing? I wonder how much time the editor of the *Telegraph-Journal* donated to the community last year. Do we have the right to suggest that it is immoral if he gave less than X hours?

7. *Background:* In 1973, the city of Windsor, Ontario, was considering the expansion of its airport. In August 1973, S.L., the president of a Windsor firm, wrote to the *Star*: "As a citizen of this community, speaking no doubt for the silent majority of Windsor and Essex county residents, I wish to express my full

support for . . . plans to expand the present Windsor airport facilities." F.W. responded:

> In his letter, Mr. S.L. lavishes praise on the . . . expansion plans for the airport of Windsor, while purporting to be "a citizen of this community, speaking no doubt for the silent majority of Windsor and Essex county."
>
> Mr. L. certainly displays no careless habits of accuracy. He is not a citizen of the community of Windsor, but resides according to all records in the bucolic splendor of Colchester [a town near Lake Erie, about 25 miles from Windsor]. If he has no doubts at such a distance, I have them at close proximity. I doubt, for instance, that Mr. L. has a mandate from any majority, and I also doubt that any majority would remain a silent one once Mr. L. joined it.

8. *Background:* In the fall of 1974 the government was considering regulating Canadian content in print media. One of the guidelines called for any new *Time* Canada company to be 75% controlled in Canada. It must also be substantially different from the foreign-owned original. In a telephone interview (as reported by James Farrabee, Southam News Services, in the Windsor *Star*, November 1974), Stephen Larue, president of *Time* Canada, said that his company was rethinking what it might do to exist in Canada, but the question of government control of content was a major stumbling block:

> No editor is willing to turn his product over to a government or anyone else to decide what's in it.

9. *Background:* Bob Talbert writes a daily column for the Detroit *Free Press*. He covers a variety of local activities and issues. Like most columnists who receive letters from their readers, Talbert devotes an occasional column to the response. Here is one letter he received (August 1972) from someone who used the pseudonym "Sam Detroit," along with Talbert's reply:

> S.D.: The danger of writing a witty(?) column such as yours is that eventually, being in the public eye, hob-nobbing with celebrities, you begin to acquire a false sense of importance, which some psychiatrists call delusions of grandeur. Come down off your white charger and try writing an amusing article for a change.
>
> B.T.: Wonder what psychiatrists would call hiding behind a pseudonym?

10. *Background:* With reference again to Arthur Hailey's

charge that Windsor is ugly, here is the response of another Windsor politician, then–Minister of National Revenue and MP for Windsor West, Herb Gray:

> I don't think Hailey's impressions are correct. The fact that thousands of people choose to live in Windsor even though they work in Detroit, and that even larger numbers of Detroiters come to Windsor for shopping and entertainment, shows that the negative aspects of life in Detroit, fortunately, are not found in Windsor.

11. *Background:* In the 1972 Olympics, the black nations of Africa stated they would boycott the games if Rhodesian athletes were allowed to compete. The International Olympic Committee subsequently voted Rhodesia out of the games. In an editorial entitled, "Racism in Black Africa, too," (August 1972), the Detroit *News* stated:

> The black nations of Africa, citing racism by the white supremacist Rhodesian regime, almost wrecked the Olympic Games opening this weekend by using their political muscle to force Rhodesia out of the games. It was coincidental that the day they won their point, Uganda, one of the leaders of the movement, confirmed its own brand of racism by spelling out the details of its arbitrary ouster of Indians and Pakistanis who have for generations lived in Uganda.
>   Racism is clearly a two-way street.

12. *Background:* Times change. In November 1973, when M.C.K. wrote the following letter to the Toronto *Globe and Mail*, Mitchell Sharp was Canadian Minister for External Affairs, Greece was under a military dictatorship, Salazar still ruled in Portugal, and South Vietnam had not been taken by the NLF:

> I note with dismay that A.A.'s letter (Political Prisoners— November 26) is critical of the alleged failure of Mitchell Sharp to intervene on behalf of political prisoners in Spain, Chile, Greece, Brazil, South Africa, South Vietnam and Portugal which have been acknowledged as repressive rightist regimes but made no mention of political prisoners in Cuba, Poland, North Vietnam, Czechoslovakia and Hungary which are ruled by equally repressive Communist regimes debasing and dehumanizing their citizens who, in any way, manifest opposition to political policies.
>   Has she forgotten the ravage inflicted upon Hungary,

Czechoslovakia and Poland by the Soviet Army when peoples of those countries dared to express their desire for human liberty and freedom . . . ?

# 4 Fallacies of Impersonation

## Introduction

**4.1** It has been held that all fallacies impersonate good arguments. No doubt a significant feature of most fallacies is that they counterfeit sound patterns of argument.[1] As such a widely shared characteristic, this masquerading role played by most of them wouldn't normally be expected to set apart one particular subgroup of fallacies. However, the three we discuss in this chapter exhibit this feature more than any other. Three of the most common and useful kinds of argument in public discourse are: (1) arguments from analogy, (2) appeals to fairness and precedent, and (3) arguments about causal claims. *Faulty analogy*, *two wrongs* (and its variants, *common practice* and *past practice*), and *questionable cause*, respectively, impersonate these three types of argument.

## 1 Faulty Analogy

**4.2** An analogy is a comparison between two things, or situations. It may serve a variety of functions. Thus, an analogy may be used to describe: "He looked like death warmed over." Or to explain:

---

[1] Cf. the title of W. Ward Fearnside's and William B. Holther's book: *Fallacy, The Counterfeit of Argument* (Englewood Cliffs, N.J.: Spectrum Books, Prentice-Hall, Inc., 1959).

"To show that a fallacy has been committed is like producing enough evidence to convict the accused in a court of law." Or to state a point in provocative language, as James Eayrs did when he wrote (in a column about the demise of the Allende regime in Chile in September 1973):

**41**   Like a group of bystanders unconcernedly gazing at a mugging, the world's democracies stood to one side last week as one of their number was brutally beaten to death . . .

Samuel Johnson used an analogy for humorous effect when, on being asked for his response to the idea of a woman preaching a sermon, he replied: "Sir, a woman preaching is like a dog's walking on hind legs. It is not done well; but you are surprised to find it done at all." An analogy can also be used in order to persuade, and it is strictly such uses—*arguments* employing analogies—that we are concerned with here.

**4.3** Here's an example from a letter by E.P. to the Winnipeg *Free Press* (August 1974):

**42**   . . . I believe the citizens of this province, whether they be drinkers or dry, might consider it only fair that liquor sales revenue be further increased to cover the costs to society of the extra costs that seem to fall in the wake of imbibing. In other words why cannot the full costs of the effects of drinking be met by the sales tax on alcoholic beverages *just as the cost of highway maintenance costs are met by the sales tax on gasoline*? What would we expect this additional revenue from liquor to cover? For openers, about $10 million is the annual provincial loss through absenteeism from drinking workers. (Emphasis ours.)

Notice what E.P. has done here. He or she has taken an accepted belief—that the cost of highway maintenance should be met by a sales tax on gasoline—and used it to pave the way for the proposal for an increased tax on liquor. The argument says: The two situations are comparable (i.e. analogous), so if you accept the principle in the case of gasoline taxes, you should also accept it in the case of liquor taxes. One's acceptance of the conclusion based on this argument depends entirely on the adequacy of the analogy.

Does the analogy support the conclusion? We don't think so. It is true that the revenue from taxes on gasoline is used in part for the maintenance of roads and highways. That's fair enough, since virtually everyone who buys gasoline contributes to the wear and tear on thoroughfares, and roughly in proportion to the amount of gas purchased. It is quite true, as E.P. pointed out, that drinking, like driving, can cost society money. But the analogy supports E.P.'s conclusion only if drinkers are responsible for the social costs of drinking in proportion to their purchases of alcohol—the way drivers are responsible for the costs of road repair in proportion to their purchases of gasoline. However, not everyone who uses liquor contributes to the social costs due to the consumption of alcohol; only those who *drink too much* are responsible for those costs. The respect in which the two situations (gasoline and liquor consumption and attendant costs) must be analogous to support E.P.'s conclusion is this:

$$\frac{\text{amount of gas consumption}}{\substack{\text{responsibility for roadway} \\ \text{wear and tear}}} = \frac{\text{amount of liquor consumption}}{\substack{\text{responsibility for social costs} \\ \text{of alcohol abuse}}}$$

The two situations are not similar in this respect, so the analogy does not support the conclusion. E.P. has committed **faulty analogy.**

Another example. In August 1975, Thomas Middleton wrote an article for *Saturday Review* calling for stricter gun control legislation. A reader responded:

**43**    I wish to protest the article written by Mr. Middleton. Can Mr. Middleton be so naive as to really believe that banning ownership of firearms would significantly reduce murders and robberies? Did banning booze significantly reduce drinking?[2]

Standardizing this argument helps make the role of the analogy explicit:

**44**    **P1:** Prohibition did not significantly reduce drinking.
**MP**    **P2:** Banning ownership of firearms is analogous to banning booze in precisely the respect which led to the failure of prohibition.
         **C:** Banning ownership of firearms won't work either.

The analogy is contained in the missing premise. Does it support the conclusion? The answer requires a brief look at why prohibition failed. There was a host of reasons: it didn't have the support of most people; liquor, beer, and wine are relatively easy to make in one's own home; it was difficult to enforce. The question is, would banning private ownership of firearms be subject to the same limita-

---

[2] Thanks to Brian Savard for bringing this example to our attention.

tions? Hardly. While gun proponents are vocal, they are relatively few in number; it would be very difficult to manufacture guns in one's home or secretly; given the need for factories for gun manufacture, firearm distribution should be much less difficult to police than booze distribution was. So, although it is undeniable that prohibition was a failure, the reasons it failed do not apply in the case of gun control. The analogy does not support the conclusion.

**4.4** The conditions for the fallacy are these:

---

### FAULTY ANALOGY

1. An analogy is offered in support of the conclusion of an argument.
2. The two things* being compared are not similar *in the respect required to support the conclusion.*

---

* By "thing" we mean to allow for the inclusion of events, situations, etc.

The analogy may be explicit (as in Example 42), or implicit (as in Example 43). Usually, the exact way the two analogues must be similar, if the analogy is to support the conclusion, is not made explicit. The first steps in arguing that *faulty analogy* has been committed are, correspondingly: (a) identify the two things being compared and (b) figure out the *precise* respect in which they must be similar if the analogy is to support the conclusion. The last step is to argue that the two things are *not* similar in that particular respect.

In typical cases, the *faulty analogy* gets its plausibility because the two things compared are indeed similar in some respects. So you needn't try to argue that they are in no way alike. And obviously, since they are *two* things being compared, they will be dissimilar in many respects. Hence, it won't be enough to argue that they are not alike in some respects. What you must do is *zero in on the particular feature that the two things must share for the analogy to lend support to the conclusion.*

To illustrate this one last time, we will take an argument from analogy and present two attempts—one bad and one good—to charge the argument with *faulty analogy*. The example comes from a letter from J.S. in New York City in *Time* magazine (October 1971) that appeared when the United States was still actively engaged in the Vietnam war:

**45**     Contrary to your article, the events that are taking place in South Vietnam's presidential election offer the best opportunity for the U.S. to make a "decent" exit from Southeast Asia. Under the existing circumstances, the U.S. should declare that South Vietnam is unable to sustain a political democracy, that there is no reason for us to remain there, and that we should withdraw our remaining forces. By doing this, we would leave the image of a patient who died despite the extraordinary efforts of a good doctor.

First, we standardize:

**46**  **P1:** By withdrawing from South Vietnam with the declaration that South Vietnam can now be seen to be unable to sustain political democracy, the U.S. would be acting like a good doctor who, despite extraordinary efforts, lost the patient.
 **P2:** No one would blame a doctor whose patient dies despite the doctor's extraordinary effort.
 **C:** No one could blame the U.S. for withdrawing from South Vietnam under the circumstances.

First look at an *unsatisfactory* attempt to show that J.S. committed *faulty analogy*:

**47**  The U.S. and South Vietnam cannot be compared to a doctor and his patient because a doctor receives pay for his services and the U.S. did not receive any pay from South Vietnam.

Although it's true that the U.S. did not receive any pay, this attempt to defeat the analogy seizes upon a minor feature of the analogy and overlooks the important ones. Even if the U.S. had been paid by South Vietnam, the analogy would fail, for, and here we begin what we regard as a satisfactory defense of the charge,

**48**  in order for the analogy to be applicable, the analogue of the patient's life would have to be a democratic South Vietnam, and the analogue of the doctor's extraordinary fight to save that life would have to be the U.S.'s extraordinary efforts to create (or sustain) a democratic South Vietnam. The record is clear, however, that the U.S. was willing to tolerate clearly undemocratic regimes in South Vietnam so long as they were fairly stable. Both the Diem and the Thieu regimes, though patently undemocratic, were sustained and supported by the U.S. with little effort to make them more democratic. The analogy fails, then, in the respect relevant to support the conclusion: the doctor did not make an extraordinary effort to save the patient's life.

It also fails because the doctor-patient metaphor has certain built-in assumptions not warranted here. It assumes South Vietnam was a single patient, but that assumption is questionable. The war there can be interpreted as a civil war, with the United States in the role of a doctor treating Siamese twins, one of whom does not want the doctor. Finally, whether the U.S. can reasonably be termed "a good doctor" in terms of this analogy is open to question. A "good doctor" here would be one who sought to make democracy a workable form of government. In fact, U.S. foreign policy throughout the 1950s and 1960s can be interpreted as more anti-Communist than pro-democratic— witness the U.S. support of the undemocratic regime of Batista in Cuba, of the military dictatorship in Greece, and so on.

**4.5** We said at the outset of this section that *faulty analogy* labels, exclusively, bad *arguments* from analogy. We also noted that analogies function outside arguments—to describe, for instance, or to explain. A particular analogy may be a poor one for any of those other purposes, too; that cannot make it a logical fallacy, however, since in those cases there is no argument present.

The distinction between an argument and an explanation, particularly, can be blurry in practice. It's worth a digression at this point to set out their differentiating characteristics. Our discussion will in turn lead into a review of the contextual indicators marking arguments which have been tacitly employed for some time now.

---

**ARGUMENTS VS. EXPLANATIONS**   *Perhaps the best approach to distinguishing these two modes of discourse is to think about their respective functions. When and why do we explain something? When and why do we attempt to argue for something? Generally, an explanation is an attempt to indicate how or why an event occurred. Where explanation is appropriate, there is usually no question whether or not the event did occur. That much is either known to be true or accepted as true. The explanation is an attempt to make the event more intelligible or understandable. An argument, on the other hand, is an attempt to show that something is true. We employ arguments precisely when doubt exists about a statement's truth.*

*For example, to argue that Igor is healthier than Ivan, you would have to show that Igor has fewer colds, is less susceptible to disease, is in better physical condition than Ivan is. On the other* hand, suppose it is known that Igor is healthier than Ivan, so that it doesn't need to be proven. To explain why Igor is healthier, you might point out that he exercises regularly, has sound eating and sleeping habits, and has a check-up once a year, whereas Ivan does none of these and smokes like a fiend, while getting very little rest and being under constant pressure.

The difference between an argument and an explanation is clear enough in the abstract, but it can be very difficult to decide, in concrete instances, whether a passage is an argument or an explanation. It's possible, we should note, to have a passage in which there is both an argument and an explanation. It is not possible, however, for one and the same set of propositions to function simultaneously as an argument and as an explanation.

---

**4.6** Up to this point we have introduced our examples as arguments, and the exercises at the end of Chapters 1, 2, and 3 have consisted primarily of arguments. To be more exact, we have introduced passages which *contain* arguments. In some cases we have extricated the arguments from those passages, setting them out by means of our standardizing convention. In others and in the exercises, we have left it to you to identify the argument in the passage.

When you identified the arguments in those passages or when in your reading in general you spotted arguments, you were implicitly making use of a variety of clues that signal the presence and the contents of arguments. It is now time to mention those clues explicitly, for in everyday discourse people do not necessarily announce their intention to offer an argument; you will need to be able to recognize the signs of argumentation for yourself.

1. *Verbal indicators of arguments.* Certain words and phrases usually signal the presence of an argument and simultaneously distinguish premises and conclusion. These markers can be divided into two lists. The terms in the first set immediately *precede the conclusion* of an argument, and *follow the premises.* That is, they point backward towards the premises and immediately forward to the conclusion:

> (Premises) **therefore**, (conclusion).
> (Premises) **hence**, (conclusion).
> (Premises) **so**, (conclusion).
> (Premises) **accordingly**, (conclusion).
> (Premises) **it follows that**, (conclusion).
> (Premises) **thus**, (conclusion).
> (Premises) **consequently**, (conclusion).

These words may or may not begin a sentence, but the conclusion —or at least part of it—is always contained in the clause which they introduce.

The terms in the second set immediately *precede a premise*. In most cases, they don't also point towards the conclusion, which may equally well follow or precede the proposition they introduce:

> **Since** (premise) . . .
> **Because** (premise) . . .
> **Granted that** (premise) . . .
> **Assuming that** (premise) . . .
> **Given that** (premise) . . .
> **For** (premise) . . .

A note of caution must accompany these lists. First, they are not complete: other words and phrases occasionally mark premises and conclusions. Second, they aren't infallible guides, just rules of thumb. Words such as "because" and "since" frequently mark a premise, but they can and do serve other functions as well. For example:

**49**     Leon went to the store *because* he wanted a pack of cigarettes and couldn't get anyone else to go for him.

Here "because" introduces an explanation rather than a premise: it doesn't precede a premise which proves that Leon went to the store; it precedes a proposition which explains why he went. If you can differentiate between an argument and an explanation (see 4.5, above), then the word "because" should give you no trouble.

One pair of words which frequently appears in arguments but is absent from both our lists is the "if . . . then" of conditional or hypothetical statements. A conditional statement is a qualified assertion, but it is one single assertion just the same. For example, "She would love you if your teeth were sparkly white" does not assert two things: that she does or would love you and that your teeth are sparkly white. It says one thing: namely, she would love you on the condition that your teeth were sparkly white. So "if" doesn't mark a premise, nor does "then" mark a conclusion. (Frequently "then" is omitted from a conditional statement.) This is not to deny that a conditional statement can be a premise in an argument. The point is merely that the "if" does not mark it as a premise. Actually, conditional statements can be either premises or conclusions of arguments. So if you see an "if . . . then . . ." statement, you cannot assume that it is a premise. You have to see how it functions.

2. *Contextual indicators of arguments.* Some contexts are much more likely to contain an argument than others. Here are a few of them:

editorials (newspaper, radio, TV)
opinion columns (newspapers, magazines)
political speeches (during campaigns, in Parliament)
scholarly works (books, journal articles).

Again, this list is neither complete nor infallible. In these contexts it is almost always the intention of the speaker or writer to persuade the audience to accept some claim or point of view. In the end, this must be your touchstone: each time you're confronted with a doubtful case, you must determine whether the evidence indicates *the intention to persuade.*

These contextual indicators mark customary habitats of arguments; they don't help, the way the premise markers and conclusion markers do, to isolate the individual components of arguments. Don't look for any surefire aids to do the job for you here anyway. Instead, work at developing your sense for the flow of reasoning.

# 2 Two Wrongs

**4.7** The fallacy we're calling **two wrongs** is a *logical* fallacy employed primarily in *ethical* arguments, and appealing to very strong *emotional* and *psychological* factors. This deceptively simple manoeuver is one most children are capable of mastering and using. Remember when your father or mother *criticized* you for hitting your little brother or sister and you *defended* yourself by saying, "But she (or he) hit me first!" The idea is simple and attractive, isn't it? You were wronged (your brother or sister slugged you— something they shouldn't have done) and that act justified you in returning that wrong (hitting back). The fallacy of *two wrongs* seeks in effect to elevate the instinct to retaliate into an argument. Let's look at a few examples.

Our first needs a bit of background. In July 1974, a group of militant Indians took possession of a small park on the outskirts of Kenora, Ontario. They claimed that they had exclusive rights to its use. The occupation made national headlines because the Indians were armed, so there was the possibility of violent confrontation. An agreement was eventually reached and the occupation ended peacefully. It stirred a great deal of comment in the press, and the following passage is from a letter by J.G. to the Winnipeg *Free Press* (August 1974), defending the actions of the Indians against the criticisms which had been aired:

**50**   The occupation of a 14-acre park by the native people in the Kenora area is completely justified. After all, what's a mere 14 acres when they have been robbed of 14 million square miles—the entire North and South American continents.

Notice the pattern here; it is a recurrent one. It begins with the criticism of the action. There follows a defense which takes the form of citing some other wrongdoing, the implication being (in this case it is explicitly stated) that the act which comes under criticism is justified. If we standardize this compact argument, we get:

**51**   **P1A:** The Indians were robbed of North and South America.

**P1:** The Indians were wronged long ago.

**C:** The Indians were justified in occupying the 14-acre park in Kenora.

---

**STANDARDIZING**   *Note the refinement to our standardizing convention introduced here. A statement that functions as support for one of the main premises of the argument is placed above the premise it supports and numbered in two ways: "P1" to indicate that it supports P1, to which is added "A" to give it a marker of its own. Had there been another premise supporting P1 in the above argument, it would have been labelled "P1B", and so on. Notice that in effect P1 is at once the conclusion of one argument and a premise in another.*

*Such an argument (i.e. an argument in which one of the premises is itself the conclusion of yet another argument) we call a* **compound argument**. *We shall refer to the overall conclusion of a compound argument as the* **main conclusion**, *and to the premises supporting it directly as the* **main premises**. *The main premises and main conclusion together make up the* **main argument**. *Any argument that supports one of the main premises, or indeed any other premise, we shall call an* **internal argument**.

Clearly, an implicit premise or assumption operates behind the scenes here, but what is it? J.G.'s reference to "a mere 14 acres" suggests that he or she is thinking of some version of the principle that persons who suffer wrongdoing are entitled to compensation. The idea would be that 14 acres is little enough compensation, given the magnitude of the original wrong done to the Indians. In claiming that the Indians were justified, J.G. would no doubt concede that the seizure of the park by just any group would, in normal circumstances, be wrong. Thus, the complete idea behind the argument is this: an act which would otherwise be wrong (occupying the park) is justified because of a previous wrong. The second "wrong" corrects the first one: two wrongs make a right.

Such arguments seem plausible because they appeal to our sense of justice and fair play; they model legitimate arguments. They go wrong, however, because they involve either a misapplication of the principles of justice, or because they involve unwarranted assumptions, or both.

J.G.'s argument involves a host of assumptions in addition to the one just noted. It assumes that the Indians were in some real sense the owners of North and South America. Second, it assumes that no attempt has been made to compensate them for their losses. Third, it assumes that the Indians themselves are in the best position to decide what sort of compensation is appropriate. When these assumptions are identified and brought to the fore, J. G.'s claim that the Indians were completely justified loses a great deal of its plausibility.

Having mentioned compensation, we should say a word about an ancient principle of justice, the *lex talionis*: "an eye for an eye, a tooth for a tooth." The point of that law (which defined a sort of combination of retribution and compensation) was that *no more than* an eye could be taken for an eye. It placed a *limit* on compensation, or retribution. The law did not stipulate that the person who suffers the wrong be the one to exact retribution from the wrongdoer. That was usually left to the State.

The next example arises from the recent debate about whether or not to restore capital punishment. Taking issue with the abolitionist viewpoint, A. P. wrote to the Edmonton *Journal* (December 1974):

**52**   Mr. E. stated "capital punishment is legal vengeance based on emotion instead of logic." Really! *What kind of "reason and logic" do killers use who snuff out the lives of innocent people?*

   *I don't think any murderer can produce a logical reason for taking a life. So why should society be hesitant to give*

> *him the same treatment he meted out to others? . . .* (Emphasis ours.)

A. P.'s meaning is clear. Murderers act without reason and logic, so we are justified in paying them back in the same coin: we should act without reason and logic by taking their lives from them. Once again, an action which has come under criticism (the State's punishing murderers with death) has been defended by pointing to another wrong (the murder). There may be valid reasons for reinstating the death penalty, but A. P.'s argument, assuming as it does that two wrongs make a right, isn't one of them.

**4.8** The next two examples bring out interesting variations on the pattern we've been looking at. They're close enough in spirit to *two wrongs*, we think, to be considered here.

In early fall of 1974, Minister of Agriculture Eugene Whelan came under a good deal of criticism because the government agency responsible for storing eggs had bungled and over 27 million eggs had been allowed to spoil. In an interview reported in the Windsor *Star* (September 1974), Mr. Whelan, taking issue with his critics, stated:

**53**    I wouldn't call that a surplus. It was only two days consumption for the whole province of Ontario. *They think that's a lot, but how many billions, and I mean billions, of potatoes were dumped in Prince Edward Island years ago. Nothing was said about that.* (Emphasis ours.)

The *two wrongs* motif is evident here. Whelan has been (indirectly) criticized for wasting eggs (a misguided action), and he defends himself by pointing to another bad situation (the potatoes dumped in P.E.I.). His argument differs from the two we've seen already because Whelan does not appear to be arguing that the earlier wrong somehow justifies the present one. Instead, he's saying: Nobody jumped all over the P.E.I. people, so why are you all jumping on us now? Whelan's point is that he and his agency are being subjected to *unfair* criticism. Our sense of justice and fair play is being appealed to: similar cases should be treated similarly.

If the two situations were indeed similar, then Whelan would have a legitimate grievance. But what follows? Not that the egg marketing board was wrongly or even unfairly criticized, for it truly goofed. What follows from Whelan's appeal to fair play is that the P.E.I. people should have been criticized, but weren't. That they weren't does not mean we should repeat the oversight; the way to correct the situation is *not* to compound or double the wrong by withholding criticism here. How strange the principles of justice and consistency would be if they required us to blind our eyes to obvious wrongdoing, simply because similar wrongdoing had once escaped detection and criticism in the past!

**4.9** Our second variant on two wrongs is exemplified in a situation that involved a philosophy professor at an Ivy League college in the United States. To supplement his income, this professor took on a second teaching job at another university, in violation of his contract with the first university; and he did not inform either institution of his dual role. An extremely able and mobile person, he apparently managed to do a competent job at both institutions. Alas, he was discovered and promptly lost both jobs. According to a report in *Time* (March 1972), he admitted a mistake, but not a fault; and in a 15-page letter, reminded the president of the Ivy League institution that:

**54**      *. . . there are faculty members who spend time doing extensive consulting, who write bestsellers, introductory textbooks or columns for popular magazines*—all of which do not contribute to scholarship or teaching, but which earn substantial amounts of money while requiring large amounts of time. (Emphasis ours.)

Professor M.'s argument here is that since other faculty members do outside work which takes time from their teaching and scholarly work without blame or penalty, his taking an outside job should not have been blamed or penalized.

This argument serves as an example of a feature often present in *two wrongs* arguments. Prof. M. is drawing an analogy between his holding two jobs and many other faculty members' consulting and writing novels, textbooks, or opinion columns. He is assuming that all their actions belong to the same general class, which could be described as "doing outside work that takes time from teaching and scholarly work." It's possible, then, to commit *faulty analogy* in the process of committing *two wrongs*, and we would argue that Prof. M. *does* commit *faulty analogy* when he puts writing introductory textbooks on a par with moonlighting. First, his contract explicitly prohibited him from taking another job, whereas the activities he mentions were not then prohibited. Second, introductory texts can be contributions to teaching, and they can also include conceptual innovations that are contributions to scholarship, so that people occupied with them aren't necessarily doing outside work. Writing a newspaper column can hardly be compared, in terms of the time it requires and the sort of effort that goes into it, with holding a second full-time job. So the analogy is faulty.

Quite apart from that, however, Professor M.'s reasoning is fallacious. If faculty members are not doing their work because outside work is interfering, then they should be dealt with in the appropriate way. The existence of such wrongdoing, even when it goes undetected and unpunished, is no reason for letting Professor M. off. These other wrongs can't be used to justify his conduct.

**4.10** Clearly, *two wrongs* is a fallacy to look for in the adversary context, when someone is attempting to defend some action (or course of action) against criticism. The conditions for the fallacy are these:

---

### TWO WRONGS

1. M's action, X, has come under criticism.
2. N (or M) tries to defend either X or M by citing Y, Z, or W—allegedly similar actions (the wrongness of which is granted or at least not challenged).
3. Y, Z or W have no relevance to the defense of X or of M for having done X.

---

*Two wrongs* is a fallacy simply because, at least in the paradigm versions, it is an attempt to do the impossible—to prove that a wrong act is not wrong. A wrong act, multiplied no matter how many times, cannot become right. The variations on the basic pattern of the fallacy don't go quite as far. They are attempts to excuse, or to mitigate blame, or to block criticism. They don't try to justify the wrong. But their appeal to an earlier wrong remains an irrelevant line of defense. A wrong, repeated, becomes no more excusable, blame is no less in order, criticism is just as appropriate.

To show that *two wrongs* has been committed, you need to identify the two actions involved in the defense, and to sort out just what kind of defense is offered. Does the argument attempt to justify the act (as in Examples 50 and 52) or to mitigate the blame or censure (as in Examples 53 and 54)?

We've already indicated why *two wrongs* is an *impersonator*; that is, its plausibility and air of respectability come from its apparent similarity to various principles of justice. The defense of the Kenora occupation imitates the principle of retributive and compensatory justice that when a wrong has been done, the victim deserves compensation. The Whelan example trades on the principle of justice that similar cases be treated similarly. Both of them warp the principles of justice in the naive belief that the interests of justice can somehow be served by either compounding or ignoring wrongdoing.

**4.11** You've surely heard (or used) this defense before: "But Honey (officer, Mom), *everybody's* doing it." Such a move is so common that it deserves its own label, closely related though it is to *two wrongs*. We call it **common practice**. Examples of both fallacies occur in the following brief excerpt from the reminiscences of Vincent Theresa, a former Mafioso:

**55**    There are plenty of good things about [mobsters] . . . most are [patriotic]. We don't think about undermining the government. We corrupt politicians, but that's only so we can do business. *We cheat on taxes, but let's face it, there isn't a damn business executive who doesn't.* If you want to know the truth, I think everyone's entitled to swindle a little bit on taxes because they are too high and politicians spend like drunken sailors on all their pet deals to help out their buddies anyhow. (Emphasis ours.)

According to Theresa, since the government takes money from us (taxes are too high), we are justified in taking money from it (withholding taxes we are legally obligated to pay). Also, politicians use our money in self-serving ways (spending like drunken sailors on deals to help out their buddies), so we are justified in using their money in self-serving ways (keeping for our own use money legally owed to the government). "They did it first to us, so we're justified in doing it to them."

Even if Theresa's *allegations* (and that's all they are—vague, unspecified charges without any evidence) were true, that wouldn't provide justification for not paying taxes. *Two wrongs.* The fallacy of *common practice* occurs when Theresa says: "We cheat on taxes, but let's face it, there isn't a damn business executive that doesn't." It doesn't matter whether Theresa's unsupported statement that *every* business executive cheats on taxes is true. Suppose it were: that doesn't make it right. That all, most, or many people engage in some wrongdoing hasn't the slightest tendency to make it right or to justify it. Like *two wrongs, common practice* is a fallacy that occurs in adversary contexts, when a person finds it necessary to defend his or her action against criticism. It differs from *two wrongs* in that, instead of citing the actions of some one or two other people, it cites what is supposedly a common or widespread practice. Many people engaging in a certain practice does not make it right, any more than many people believing something makes it true. (Compare *common practice* to *popularity*, a fallacy we discuss in Chapter 7.)

**4.12** For some people, when something has always been done in a certain way, it acts as a blinder in face of reasonable challenge. The result is the fallacy we call **past practice**. Here is an example.

In 1974 the city of Regina was debating whether to build a new city hall. The city council favoured the idea, but not all ratepayers shared its opinion, as the following excerpt from a letter V. M. wrote to the Regina *Leader-Post* (September 1974) attests:

**56**      A new city hall will cost many millions of dollars and that cost will increase the mill rate as well as other taxes.

In the opinion of many tax-payers it is undemocratic for the mayor and city council to bypass the public on this important issue. *Past councils would never have gone ahead with the scheme until the people had approved of it.* (Emphasis ours.)

In the last sentence, V.M. is appealing to the way Regina city councils did things in the past. This appeal sidesteps the crucial question: were they right? Did they forsake their leadership duty by giving in to the vocal demands of short-range popular opinion, or did they responsibly consult the wisdom of the people when the public's choice ought to have been sovereign? Just because previous Regina city councils went to the people on such issues does not establish that they did the right thing. And if we do not know whether their past actions were right, we cannot treat an appeal to those actions as a warrant for accepting V.M.'s claim that the present council should seek public approval before going ahead with a new city hall. Instead of appealing to past practice, V. M. would have done better by citing the reasons why the council should seek popular approval in the present case. And that's perhaps the basic problem with the appeal to past practice (tradition, custom), particularly in an adversary situation, where it is used as a means of buttressing a specific practice that has come under criticism. Usually it is the practice or tradition itself that has often come under fire. Consequently, it cannot be used to support itself.

This point can be seen particularly clearly in the following example. D.W., writing in the Edmonton *Journal* (January 1975) against gun-control legislation, used the following argument:

**57**      The people in Canada are accustomed to living in a state of individual liberty. *Part of our heritage is the privately owned firearm* . . . (Emphasis ours.)

This heritage is precisely what the proponents of stricter gun control legislation want to put an end to. D.W.'s appeal to tradition is beside the point. What he needs to do is produce reasons why the tradition should be continued.

**4.13** Here are the conditions for these two variants of *two wrongs*:

---

### COMMON AND PAST PRACTICE

1. M defends an action, X, against criticism by citing that X is widely practiced (everyone does it), or that X has always been the practice (that's the way it's always been done).
2. This is the only defense M offers for X, and M considers it a sufficient defense.

---

As with *two wrongs*, it is important to zero in on the action under attack when trying to see precisely how the fallacy has been committed.

In the final analysis, many of the examples you run into will not fall neatly into any one of the three fallacies we've treated in this section. And there will be examples that seem to fit as easily into *common practice* as *two wrongs*. Deciding what label to apply is much less important than understanding just where and how the argument goes wrong, and being able to defend your judgement clearly and soundly.

Look back at Theresa's remarks in Example 55. It seems to us that Theresa intended to justify the Mafia's cheating on taxes by appealing to the common practice of business executives, and without conceding any wrong there. That, he seemed to be saying, is just how the system works. On the other hand, there is some plausibility in taking Theresa to be defending the mob's tax evasion on a *two wrongs* model. Perhaps he intended to concede that it is wrong to cheat on taxes, but to argue that if business executives don't lose respect or aren't criticized for doing it, then neither should mobsters. The point is not to quibble over the fallacy tag, but to recognize that Theresa's argument, taken either way, is fallacious.

# 3 Questionable Cause

**4.14** Think, for a moment, of some of the hotly contested public issues of the past few years. Should capital punishment have been abolished? Should pornography and marijuana be legalized? How should we fight unemployment? inflation? Should something be done about the violence on TV? To be able to give intelligent answers to these and scores of similar questions, we must make judgements about **causal relationships**. For example: Does capital punishment serve as a deterrent to murder? Does the open availability of pornography decrease the incidence of sexual crimes? Does marijuana have detrimental long-term side effects? Do tax cuts increase spending, hence increase production, hence increase jobs? Does violence on TV lead to violent behaviour in viewers? Obviously a good deal of the discussion about public policy, and the persuasive argumentation directed at the consumer connected with it, must consist of or presuppose arguments about causal claims.

Roughly speaking, a **cause** is an event which produces another event, its **effect**. Causes are, as it were, the moving forces of the world. We refer to them in various ways: we may say that one event leads to another, produces it, brings it about, makes it happen, forces it, stops it, prevents it, stems it, increases it—the list could go on to some length. No one or two or three terms can be depended on to cue causal arguments. You will have to judge from the context whether a causal claim is involved.

A systematic account of causal reasoning is beyond the scope of this section. Indeed, the theory of causal inferences is still much debated in philosophical circles. As it happens, however, detection of the kinds of mistake typically found in causal reasoning does not depend on theoretical subtleties. Moreover, causal fallacies are best understood through the examination of concrete examples. Our approach is to work through a healthy sample of representative errors in arguments employing causal claims, introducing the necessary theoretical background information as we go. These errors, we shall say, constitute cases of the fallacy, **questionable cause**.

A distinction between *arguments to causes* and *arguments from causes* is useful to keep in mind. The former are intended to establish that one thing is the cause of another. The latter take it as a premise that one thing is the cause of another, and go on from there to argue for some further claim, usually a recommendation for action or policy. Of course, the two may be combined, so that someone argues first that X causes Y, and second proceeds to argue that, since X causes Y, something should be done to prevent or bring about X, on the ground that Y is undesirable or desirable. Keeping clear about the distinction between arguments *to* and arguments *from* causes can aid in spotting flaws. For instance, it may be true that X is a cause of Y, but not the only one. Hence, an argument, based on the assumption that X causes Y and concluding that preventing X will therefore prevent Y, is clearly a case of *questionable cause*, for the other causes of Y will still be operative, even if X is stopped.

Although most arguments found in the public domain involving causal claims push recommendations that an action be taken or that a policy be implemented, and thus are arguments *from* causes, their flaws are usually due to some error in reasoning *to* a causal claim. Therefore, in the inventory of examples that follows, we focus primarily on arguments *to* causal claims and the typical ways they can go wrong.

**4.15** Arguments to causes can be subdivided into two groups. Some deal with the causes of particular events—events unique in time. Belonging to this group of *particular causal claims* are arguments about the causes of World War II, the causes of the rise and fall of the Diefenbaker government, the causes of the emergence of rock music in the 1950s, and so on. The other kind of argument to causes covers *general causal claims*, claims about the causes of recurring types of events, such as cancer, revolutions, inflation, rape, and so on.

As a rule, particular causal claims must invoke general ones and consist of showing what general causal laws work in the particular case in question. So, for example, in looking for the cause of someone's lung cancer, the doctor would seek to find what general cancer-causing factors were present in that medical history. This model is less clearly applicable when dealing with social events. In arguing about what brought about Joe Clark's victory at the 1976 Progressive-Conservative leadership convention, one would have to look for the sorts of factor that would influence this kind of party, given the kinds of circumstances it found itself in at the time, to prefer a young, relatively unknown backbencher to the sorts of leader the other available candidates represented. Yet all of these conditions are likely to be unique, and certainly their juxtaposition is. The bearing of general causal claims on Clark's victory is not so obvious.

**4.16** *Particular causal claims.* The following examples will illustrate some of the variants of *questionable cause* possible in arguing to the causes of particular events.

In the spring of 1975, government weather reporting went metric. Among many who complained was a gentleman from Cape Breton Island:

**58**      Ever since we changed over to Celsius, the weather has been unusually irregular.

The implication is that the switch from Fahrenheit to Celsius *caused* the irregular weather. We can smile at this inference, but the *kind* of mistake he made is not always without dangerous possibilities. In the context of defending RCMP surveillance of university campuses in 1963, Commissioner C. W. Harvison alleged that criticism of the RCMP was Communist-inspired. He argued as evidence that prominent Canadian Communist Party leader William Kashtan had spoken at an international Communist conference in Prague the previous summer on how to combat anti-communism and that, "It was only a short time after his return that we began to see increased criticism aimed at the RCMP."[3] Harvison's inference was that because criticism of the RCMP increased following the return to Canada of a Canadian Communist who wanted to combat anti-communism, the former was caused by the latter.

What is wrong in both these arguments is that the mere existence of a before-and-after sequence is never by itself sufficient foundation for any causal claim. For a number of events immediately precede any effect, yet not all can be its cause. The gentleman from Cape Breton's inference was silly, we know, since we are familiar with the kinds of hypotheses meteorologists employ to try to explain weather changes, and the influence of the units of temperature measurement is not among them. Commissioner Harvison's claim was not silly, for the hypothesis that a Communist activist freshly returned from the inspiration of an international meeting could generate a round of criticism of the militantly anti-communist RCMP is very plausible. But the Commissioner's causal argument was still unsound, since it was also possible that given the circumstances at the time other hypotheses were even more plausible, and Mr. Kashtan's return merely coincided with independently inspired sources of RCMP criticism. (As it happened, the clearly non-communist Canadian Association of University Teachers had responded to revelations of RCMP surveillance on university campuses with a resolution urging its members not to cooperate with such investigations.)

Such arguments are said to commit the fallacy of *post hoc ergo*

---

[3] House of Commons *Debates* (May 31, 1963), p. 513. The incident is reported in Lorne and Caroline Brown, *An Unauthorized History of the RCMP* (Toronto: James Lewis & Samuel, 1973), p. 104.

*propter hoc:* "after this, therefore because of this." What gives this reasoning its appeal is that often a cause of an event immediately precedes it. Looking for an event just prior to the one whose cause is being sought is therefore quite appropriate. What is fallacious is moving straight from the fact that X came immediately before Y to the conclusion that X caused Y. It is necessary, further, to have some hypothesis connecting the two events and, finally, to rule out alternative hypotheses as less plausible.

Someone we know received the following chainletter in the mail:

**59**     "Trust in the Lord with all your heart and knowledge and He will light the way." This prayer has been sent to you for good luck. The original copy come from the Netherlands. It was sent around the world 9 times . . . You are to receive good luck within 4 days of receiving this letter. This is not a joke. Don Elliot received $60,000, but lost it because he broke the chain. While in the Phillipines, General Walsh lost his wife 6 days after he received the letter and failed to circulate the prayer. Please send this letter (20 copies) to people you think need good luck and see what happens on the 4th day after . . . Take note of the following: Constantine Diary received the chain in 1933. He asked his secretary to make 20 copies and send them out. A few days later he won the lottery of $4,000,000 in his country. Carlos Broodt, an officer employer, received the chain, forgot it and lost his job. He found the chain and sent out 20 copies. Nine days later he found a better job. Aaron Barachilla received the chain and threw it away; 9 days later he died. For no reason whatever should this chain be broken . . .

No harm done in sending the prayer and letter on, right? After all, why take a chance? Well, this sort of superstition will readily intimidate those who have no defense against the *post hoc* version of *questionable cause.* (Actually, even a prior consideration is the reasonableness of these claims. How could anyone have access to all this information? How could anyone follow the progress of the chain?) Assuming for the sake of argument that the information is correct, what we are given are some cases of "good luck" and some cases of "bad luck" all consisting of before-and-after sequences. The numbers can have no significance unless compared to the total number of people involved in the chain. (And if it's been going since at least 1933, that would include a lot of people.) Also, no connecting hypothesis is offered, unless perhaps it is the implicit suggestion that God will reward those who circulate the prayer and punish those who do not. But no reason is offered, or obvious, why

God might take such an interest in this chain letter. This is a good example of how *post hoc ergo propter hoc* can underlie superstitious beliefs.

What about this example (from the Edmonton *Journal*, December 1974)?

**60**    In Australia, where seat belt use is mandatory, hospital occupancy, one of the highest prices society pays for traffic accidents, has been reduced by 25 per cent.

The implication is that the use of seat belts caused the decrease in hospital occupancy, and the sole basis seems to be a before-and-after sequence. It is clear why wearing seat belts might be expected to cause a decrease in serious injuries, thereby reducing hospital occupancy. This intervening principle might save the *Journal* from the *post hoc* version of *questionable cause*. But what about the reductions in speed limits that occurred widely at about the same time, partly as a result of the world-wide fuel shortage? They too could be responsible for fewer accidents. The *Journal* doesn't mention whether that could have been a factor in Australia.

A more careful statement on the same subject was reported by Canadian Press in July 1976:

**61**    Staff Supt. John Marks of Metropolitan Toronto police said in an interview, "there is absolutely no doubt that the seat-belt law is working." [Use of seat belts became mandatory in Ontario on January 1, 1976.]

"Our sharp drop in death and injury statistics has more to do with seat belts than it does with lower speed limits. Our jurisdiction does not include the major provincial highways, where speed-limit reductions have played a major part in lowering accident statistics."

Here, Staff Supt. Marks acknowledged the alternative hypothesis, and explained why it was unlikely to have been a factor.

**4.17** Another kind of mistake in arguing to causes consists of treating an explanatory hypothesis as an account of *the* cause of an event, without sufficient evidence. Here's an example from a *Time* magazine story some years back. The city of El Paso, Texas, is about one-third the size of Dallas, but the number of El Paso residents found in state mental hospitals was then one-seventh the number of Dallas residents in such institutions. Other things being equal, one would expect roughly similar proportions, so how might the difference have been explained? A University of Texas biochemist offered this explanation:

**62**      . . . El Paso's water is heavily laced with lithium, a tran-
quilizing chemical widely used in the treatment of manic
depression and other psychiatric disorders. Dallas has low
lithium levels because it draws its water from surface
supplies.

An intriguing hypothesis: El Paso citizens were ingesting amounts
of the tranquilizer in their drinking water, which helped to prevent
or to remedy the symptoms of mental disorders for which they
might otherwise have sought treatment in a state mental hospital.
But more investigation was needed. Were there other cities with
high lithium levels in their water supply? If so, how did their mental
hospital admission rates compare to those of El Paso? Also, how
did admissions from Dallas compare with those of other cities
with similar lithium levels? Furthermore, could there be alternative
explanations? Did life in Dallas tend to put great pressures on its
citizens? Did the considerably smaller El Paso have a more serene
pace? Without investigating further the correlation between lithium
intake and mental hospitalization and without checking alternative
explanations, the biochemist would be guilty of *questionable cause*.

As it happened, *Time* had come across a competing hypothesis:

**63**      . . . State mental health officials pointed out that the mental
hospital closest to Dallas is 35 miles from the city, while the
one nearest El Paso is 350 miles away.

We shall not commit *questionable cause* ourselves by asserting that
the health officials' explanation provides us with the cause of the
higher incidence of mental hospital admissions from Dallas. But,
since the biochemist ignored that possibility, he can be charged with
the fallacy.

Here's another example, from a Canadian Press report (August
1973) from London, England:

**64**      A 16-year-old youth dressed in white overalls, a collarless
shirt, high boots and a bowler hat, kicks a younger boy
unconscious, smashing his ribs and disfiguring his face. Why
did he do it?

In the opinion of a British judge, who sentenced the
attacker to a term in reform school, it was simply because
he had watched a "wicked film," Stanley Kubrick's *A Clockwork Orange*.

The judge noted that the young man had launched his
attack while wearing clothes similar to those of the
"violence-crazed" characters in the film.

The judge did not argue in *post hoc* fashion. He reasoned from the fact that the crime resembled acts committed in the film and that the youngster was obviously imitating in his manner of dress the style of characters in the film. Still, the judge made a causal claim of a sort that is difficult to substantiate: a claim about the cause of a person's behaviour. We cannot play this youth's life back over again to see what would have resulted had he not seen Kubrick's film. Moreover, as the liveliness of the current debate attests, there exists no established general causal claim about violence in films or TV causing violent behaviour in their viewers. Finally, the judge's claim, that the youth had committed the crime "simply because" of seeing the film, is unclear. Does he mean that it was *the sole cause*, or that it was one of the contributing causes?

The clothing, style, and manner of the attack do suggest a connection with *A Clockwork Orange*, but we must consider alternative hypotheses. Perhaps the movie started a clothing fad, and it was due to the fad that the youth was dressed in that particular way, and not to his having seen the movie. And perhaps the violence of his attack could be explained as plausibly or more plausibly in terms of factors unique to that youth. Did he have a history of outbursts of uncontrollable temper? Was he acutely sensitive on some point and had the boy teased him about it? Was he acting under peer-group pressure to meet some misconceived standard of manhood? Had the judge offered his opinion merely as a possible and reasonable hypothesis, he would have been on safe ground. Since he asserted it as an unqualified causal claim, without assessing alternative possibilities, he was guilty of *questionable cause*.

What the *Clockwork Orange* and the El Paso lithium examples have in common is the premature elevation of one possible explanation to the status of *the* cause. In both cases, alternative hypotheses were available and should have been investigated. A more thorough check might have revealed one of three possibilities: (a) one or more of the *other* hypotheses correctly described the cause; (b) the factor proposed *together with* one or more of the other hypotheses all operated as independent but mutually reinforcing causes; (c) the hypothesis proposing the causal factor did indeed describe the sole cause. So *questionable cause* may be seen to be a special case of *hasty conclusion*—in the two examples above, the hasty jump to (c) without checking out (a) or (b).

**4.18** We turn now to an example of an argument to a *general* causal claim. The following passage is from an article published a few years ago:

**65**     Psychiatry kills. It kills because of the ruthless, unprovable treatments used on those entrusted to its care . . . These are just a few of the facts. The bodies of no fewer than 21 people have been discovered in shallow graves in California —all killed with machete blows and knife thrusts by one man in a period of less than two months. The murderer, a Mexican-American, had previously been committed to a mental hospital. Sixteen people were shot to death by a student from the top of the Texas University Tower. The student had previously received psychiatric treatment. The Manson family killed seven in brutal murders in California. Manson had previously received psychiatric treatment . . .

The article went on to multiply instances of people who had previously received psychiatric treatment and later engaged in some form of violent, anti-social behaviour.

Note that the article is not *assuming* that what had caused such behaviour in each case was that these people had received psychiatric treatment. On the contrary, it is using these cases to establish a correlation between psychiatric treatment and violent behaviour. This is the correct move to make in trying to establish a general causal claim. If events of type X cause events of type Y, then when instances of X occur, instances of Y will tend to be found. Hence, to establish that Xs cause Ys, the first thing to look for is such a correlation.

Be careful not to make excessive demands of such a correlation. The claim is not necessarily that psychiatric treatment *always* causes people to become violent. More likely, and more typical of general causal claims of this sort, what is being argued is that psychiatry *can* cause violence. Nor was the article claiming that psychiatry is the *only* cause of violence. In fact, it's a claim of the same variety as the assertion that smoking cigarettes in sufficient quantity causes lung cancer. Pointing out such counter-instances as that Somerset Maugham smoked four packs a day for most of his life, yet died a natural death at 91, does not refute the latter claim. Nor would showing cases of people who received psychiatric treatment but did not commit murder refute the former claim. And just as the fact of other causes of cancer besides smoking does not show that smoking isn't also a cause, so the fact of other causes of violent behaviour besides psychiatric treatment would not show that psychiatry is not an additional cause of violence.

Does the article then establish that psychiatry is a cause of violent behaviour? Clearly not. To show precisely why not, however, we must say more about the method of establishing this kind of general causal claim, and it will help to use the example of the established general causal claim that cigarette smoking is a cause of lung cancer.

To establish that claim, researchers first had to demonstrate by carefully systematic studies that the incidence of lung cancer is significantly higher among the smoking population than among non-smokers. By "significantly" is meant, roughly, that the difference is too striking to be explained by chance. It was reasonable, therefore, to hypothesize a causal link between cigarette smoking and lung cancer. To corroborate this hypothesis, however, researchers had to rule out other factors that might have coincidentally been related to smoking, and have been the actual causal agents—e.g., cigarette paper, or the fumes from the match or lighter. Experiments were run in which these factors were present but the tobacco was absent, and the correlation with lung cancer disappeared. The experiments were refined until it was established that the nicotine and tar in cigarettes are the causally operative factors. Researchers have not yet succeeded in discovering the precise mechanism at work (largely because they do not yet know enough about cancers generally), but it's considered a well-established causal claim that smoking is a causal factor in contracting lung cancer.

We can now take stock of the differences between the article's argument that psychiatric treatment is a cause of violent behaviour and the argument establishing smoking as a cause of lung cancer.

1. The psychiatric treatment–murder correlation is inadequately established. The evidence is anecdotal, not systematic. What should have been done (the sort of study done to establish the smoking-cancer correlation) is this: obtain representative samples of those who have and those who have not received psychiatric treatment. Check each group for its incidence of subsequent violent behaviour. Only if there is a statistically significant difference between the two groups, with the treatment sample showing the higher incidence of violent behaviour, has a correlation worth further consideration been established.

2. Additional correlations that might turn out to signify causal connections are not ruled out. (In the cancer example, the tar and nicotine were isolated as the causal factors, and the cigarette paper, match fumes, etc. eliminated.) For instance, what led the people cited in the article's examples to seek or be referred for psychiatric treatment? Chances are good that some underlying disorder first showed symptoms that resulted in their receiving psychiatric treatment and *in spite of* that treatment later resulted in the murderous behaviour. At the least, the article did not produce evidence to rule out such an additional correlate as a causal factor in these murders.

On these two counts, then, we consider the article guilty of *questionable cause* in arguing to the general causal claim that psychiatric treatment can cause violent behaviour.

**4.19** We have been concentrating on these examples as *arguments to causes*. However, in almost every case, the argument was intended as the background for a further inference based on it. The gentleman from Cape Breton was suggesting that perhaps we ought to return to Fahrenheit degrees; the RCMP Commissioner was proposing that criticism of the Mounties be dismissed; the point of the arguments about seat belts was to commend their use; the London judge went on to urge the censorship of movies like *A Clockwork Orange*; and the psychiatry article argued that people ought to avoid psychiatric treatment. (We're not sure whether the Texas chemist was making any recommendations about the introduction of lithium into water supplies.) It's possible, now, to compile a rough catalogue of mistakes found in *arguments from causes*, using these examples as a starting point.

First, arguments from *particular* causal claims:

A. The recommendation is based on a pure *post hoc ergo propter hoc* inference, without even any connecting hypothesis proposed. (Cf. the Cape Breton gentleman's anti-Celsius argument and the chainprayer, Examples 58 and 59.)

B. The recommendation is based on a hypothesis offered to explain a spatio-temporal connection, but alternative, equally plausible hypotheses exist and have not been ruled out. (Cf. the *Clockwork Orange* and the El Paso lithium examples, 62 and 64.)

Second, arguments from *general* causal claims:

C. The recommendation is based on a claim supported only by a spotty correlation, one that hasn't been systematically established.

D. The recommendation is based on a claim supported by a correlation only, without other correlations checked out and found not to account for the cause. (Cf. for C and D the "psychiatry kills" example, 65.)

**4.20** We have not yet fully discussed another fairly common error in arguments from general causes:

E. The recommendation is based on mistakenly taking what is merely *one* cause among others to be *the only* cause or *the main* cause.

There are two quite distinct versions of E. First, what is one among several independently operative causes is taken to be the only or the main cause. Here's an example, from a letter to the St. John's *Evening Telegram*. The writer was concerned about vandalism in the city:

**66**     The real problem was pointed out recently by assistant
          police chief Brown in the talk to the St. John's Kiwanis

Club. He pointed out that the main cause of all this vandalism in the past 20 years is permissiveness in the families and in the schools.

The writer went on to urge an end to the "permissive" treatment of children as the way to end vandalism. But even supposing that permissiveness is *a* cause of vandalism—and that is certainly conceivable—it doesn't follow that ending permissiveness will eliminate vandalism. For it's very likely that the phenomenon has other causes as well—for example, drunkenness, resentment against authority, or youthful bravado. (Vandalism has not been restricted to the "permissive" 1950s and 1960s.)

The other version of the mistake of taking one cause for the only cause consists of the failure to see that factor as merely one component in a set of causal factors, all of which operate together to bring about the effect. Here is an example, from a letter by S.L. to the Detroit *Free Press* (April 1974):

**67**    This is written in reply to the dogma espoused by the *Free Press* and other gun control proponents—the claim that the availability of firearms is the root cause of all the killings in the land. I was born in 1913 and was 15 years old before I was anywhere within 100 miles of anyone who was shot with a pistol and that was a thief who was shot by police. Everyone we knew had guns in their home and knew how to use them . . . If the availability of guns is the cause of the killings, why weren't we all murdered back in those days? Guns were everywhere.

The *Free Press* position was that the availability of guns was one factor that fitted together with others to result in murders, and hence by removing guns from the scene (the aim of gun control legislation), that causal set would be broken up and a major cause of murders removed. S.L., however, took the *Free Press* to be holding that the availability of guns *by itself* led to murders: this was the position he or she was arguing against. It's a case of *straw man* because S.L. confuses necessary with sufficient causal conditions.

---

**NECESSARY AND SUFFICIENT CONDITIONS**   *Philosophers and scientists have developed a convenient terminology for describing S.L.'s error. They distinguish between* **necessary** *causal conditions and* **sufficient** *causal conditions.*

*By a* sufficient *causal condition is meant an event or factor that suffices to bring about another event. "X is a sufficient causal con-*

dition for Y" means "If X occurs, Y occurs." A burnt-out bulb, for example, is a sufficient causal condition for a light not to go on. So is a broken switch, or a burnt-out fuse, or a power failure. The occurrence of any one of these is enough to cause the light's failure.

A necessary causal condition is an event or factor whose absence prevents another from occurring. "X is a necessary causal condition for Y" means "If Y occurs, X must have occurred." So, for example, an unbroken electrical circuit is a necessary condition for a light to go on. If the light does go on, the electricity must be flowing through an unbroken circuit. And if this condition is absent—if the current is broken—then the light is prevented from going on.

Many causes consist of a collection of factors where each one is causally necessary, and all together are jointly causally sufficient, to bring about the effect. To speak of "a cause" in such a situation is to refer to one of the necessary conditions. This was the Free Press's position on the way the availability of firearms was a causal factor in the increased frequency of murders. The availability of guns, it held, was a necessary condition, but not alone a sufficient condition, for the increase in the murder rate. S.L. mistakenly took the Free Press to be arguing that the widespread possession of guns was a sufficient condition for the murder rate increase.

So the second version of treating one cause as the only cause can be described as confusing a necessary causal condition with a sufficient causal condition.

---

**4.21** We hope our discussion of these examples will serve as a useful indication of the complexities to be found in causal arguments, of the varieties of causal claims found in daily discourse, and of the sorts of critical questions to which you should subject them. We can summarize in a general way the conditions of the fallacy we've been discussing as follows:

---

### QUESTIONABLE CAUSE

1. (a) M argues to a *particular* causal claim without providing adequate support; or
   (b) M argues to a *general* causal claim without providing adequate support;
or 2. M argues *from* a causal claim (particular or general) to a recommendation for action or policy, and (a) the causal claim is not warranted, or (b) the causal claim does not adequately support the conclusion.

In detecting instances of *questionable cause,* the first and most important step is to ferret the causal claim (or implication) out into the open. Once that is done, the rest is a matter of looking at the sort of evidence that has been proposed for it. To defend your charge, it is not necessary that you prove that X is *not* the cause of Y. You need only show that the case for the causal connection hasn't been adequately made. An argument that can or might be strengthened by further evidence, so that the causal claim turns out in the end to be true, can still be guilty of *questionable cause.*

---

## Exercises for Chapter 4

*Directions:* Determine which fallacies occur in the following passages. You may decide that some passages contain explanations rather than arguments. You may also decide that some of the fallacies are more perspicuously classified under labels from Chapters 2 or 3 than those from Chapter 4. You may discover fallacies that do not seem to be accurately described by any set of conditions set out up to this point. Finally, you may decide that some passages are innocent of fallacy. Always argue carefully in support of your judgements.

1. *Background:* Here is an excerpt from an open letter from columnist James Eayrs addressed to Premier Alexei Kosygin on the occasion of the latter's visit to Canada in 1971. In that letter, Eayrs listed a number of persecutions being carried on by the Soviet state in Russia. He then said:

> Some Canadians are saying that this is no time for such reminders. That so long as you are in our midst, protest demonstrations are in poor taste and out of place. That you are entitled to the same courtesies a family should extend to a guest within its house.
> I say this is a false analogy. Your presence here has nothing to do with the hospitality of the Canadian people. It is the result of the decisions of our respective governments. Demonstrating for or against visiting statesmen is one of the very few ways our citizens can participate in foreign policy.

The question is: Did Eayrs succeed in pinning "some Canadians" with a charge of *faulty analogy?*

2. *Background:* In 1973, Israel shot down a Libyan airliner

when it strayed over Israeli territory. The act was widely criticized. A.L. wrote to the Detroit *Free Press* (March 1973):

> People of the world condemn Israel for shooting down the Libyan airliner over Israeli territory. If Israel did not have stringent security, there would be no Israel. So she is condemned for her actions. But people easily forget about the attack by Palestinian guerilla-hired Japanese terrorists in an Israeli airport, killing many men, women and children; the Munich murders, where bound and blindfolded men were slaughtered; the many men, women and children who have been murdered by Palestinian Arab guerillas in Israeli border settlements.

3. *Background:* This is an excerpt from a long article by Robert Coates, Progressive-Conservative Member of Parliament for Cumberland-Colchester North (Halifax *Chronicle-Herald*, January 1975), arguing for capital punishment:

> The government has not allowed capital punishment since 1962. Since that time, there has been a heavy toll in deaths of police officers in the performance of their duties. At the same time, there has been a severe breakdown in the operations of our penal institutions.

4. *Background:* Soviet Premier Alexei Kosygin visited Canada in 1971 at a time when Russia was under criticism in the West for alleged discrimination against minorities. A Canadian Press report of a meeting with Members of Parliament at the time (October 1971) stated:

> When MPs asked Mr. Kosygin about problems with Jews and Ukranians, he said such problems exist around the world. He mentioned blacks in the United States and the Irish in the United Kingdom.

5. *Background:* An alderman from the city of Windsor, Ontario, proposed to the council that cats be licensed, just as dogs are. In an editorial, "The Last Free Spirits," the Windsor *Star* argued:

> Cats are free spirits, the last really independent creatures around. You can no more license cats than you can license the wind. Dogs may submit to bureaucracy. Cats won't. The same spirit tends to rub off on cat owners. They have enough trouble being pushed around by their cats without being asked to submit to man-made laws. Besides, there's an economic factor. They've never had to buy licenses, so why start? No . . . it just won't work.

6. *Background:* In an editorial in September 1975, the *Toronto Star* made the claim that abortion is a matter entirely between the woman concerned and her doctor, and that "making this change needn't violate the consciences of those women and medical practitioners who are opposed to abortion." Several weeks later, J.D. of Walkerton argued:

> Your concept of conscience is indeed narrow.
>
> One who is opposed to smoking, for instance, is not content to leave the matter between the child and the tobacconist. Indeed he or she seeks to have glamorous advertising of the product banned and tries to make smoking as difficult as possible (i.e., forbidding it in schools, in food establishments, etc.) to create a deterrent to immature as well as casual smokers . . .
>
> Similarly, one who is opposed to abortion cannot possibly leave this matter between an often immature or panic-stricken woman and a doctor often too busy and too materialistic to oppose her wishes.

7. *Background:* Toronto *Globe and Mail* columnist Scott Young once began a column with the following apology:

> The late Blair Fraser once chided me—or maybe it was more than once, but once that I remember: "All you old sports-writers can't get away from trying to make your points in sports-page lingo," he said. Maybe so, but there are a lot of old sportswriters in the world, including Bruce Hutchison, James Reston and Stuart Keate, who have not been tarred and feathered for it . . .
>
> So okay, I'm sucked into the old sin by the current Toronto mayoralty situation . . .

8. *Background:* Following the 1974 Canada-Russia hockey series, Senator Godfrey, objecting to Rick Ley's role in a fight with Valeri Kharlamov, called Ley a hooligan. K.K. responded in a letter to the Windsor *Star* (October 1974) of which the following is an excerpt:

> I just could not believe my eyes when I read [Senator Godfrey's criticism]. After the effort that our boys put out to come home to a welcome like that from one of our prominent public figures must be pretty disheartening.
>
> Do not get me wrong. I do not condone unreasonable violence in any sport. But "what is good for the goose is good for the gander." Did Godfrey see the Russian's kicking, spearing and slashing the Canadians continually? . . .

9. *Background:* This is a passage from one of the first "exposés" of advertising, *Confessions of an Advertising Man,* by David Ogilvy.[4] He points out that readership of ads drops off quickly up to the first 50 words, but then stays fairly constant from 50 to 500 words. Ogilvy continues:

> In my first Rolls Royce advertisement I used 719 words . . . In the last paragraph I wrote, "People who feel diffident about driving a Rolls-Royce can buy a Bentley." Judging from the number of motorists who picked up . . . "diffident" and bandied it about, I concluded that the advertisement was thoroughly read.

10. *Background:* The following is part of a much longer letter to the Halifax *Chronicle-Herald* in which the writer was defending capitalism:

> It is interesting to note that the "disadvantaged people" are far better off than they would have been had capitalism not existed at all, since they couldn't avoid absorbing some of the benefit of technology. Their lot is now described as inferior but only is it so in comparison with the affluent of today's society. Compared to their pre-capitalism condition, they are well-off indeed, so it is apparent that their "disadvantage" only arose as a result of other people choosing to progress while they did not choose to do so.
>
> This is analogous to the hypothetical situation in which two people of similar capabilities are forced to start from scratch on a desert island. As long as both are industrious or both are lazy, they face their destiny as "equals" and can get along. But if one is lazy and fails to provide himself with the necessities of survival while the other has initiative and succeeds, then the lazy person, through whatever distorted logic, considers himself disadvantaged by the other and demands some sort of "equalization."
>
> The distorted logic of which I speak is provided by altruism . . .

11. *Background:* This letter from E.L. (August 1974) to the editor of the Halifax *Chronicle-Herald* was prompted by Justice Minister Otto Lang's opposition to further liberalization of abortion:

> What about the rights of the ones who are already born?

[4] David Ogilvy, *Confessions of an Advertising Man* (New York: Dell Publishing Company, Inc., 1963), p. 135.

Legislated morality may be fine for P.B. [the writer of an earlier letter]. To a young mother, be she Canadian or South American, who has a dozen children already it does not make sense.

No, abortion is not nice; it is most undesirable. However, I find no dignity in the crying of hundreds of millions of skeletal children around the world who suffer from hunger pangs.

12. *Background:* In early April 1975, the Windsor *Star* carried on its front page a forecast that the next federal budget would reduce or eliminate the 12% sales tax on new cars. In a letter two months later written on behalf of the Essex County Automobile Dealers Association, M.K. had this to say:

The Essex County Automobile Dealer's Association agrees that any form of tax break would be enthusiastically received. Unfortunately the upshot of this premature speculation, three months before the budget becomes public knowledge, is that buyers who were in the market for a vehicle postponed their purchase, and created a lull in sales, adversely affecting dealers, manufacturers and their personnel.

The Essex County dealers, a substantial advertising body in your publication, and members of the communities serviced by the *Star*, request that you recognize the effect of the media on our businesses and be prudent in your articles concerning the auto industry.

# 5 Fallacies of Sleight of Hand

## Introduction

**5.1** Have you ever wanted to have on hand the conceptual tools which would enable you to say what's wrong with calling capital punishment "legalized murder," or dubbing abortion "the murder of innocent lives"? Have you wanted to defend yourself against being labelled a "bleeding heart" or a "do-gooder"? Those are the sorts of move we want to expose in this chapter. The fallacies we introduce here come from a larger class of what are often called "verbal fallacies," because the culprit usually turns out to be a word or a phrase. Since these fallacies are deceits that depend on verbal trickery, they tend to victimize those who are not sensitive to the need for precision and to the dangers of vagueness in language.

*Questionable classification, ambiguity,* and *vagueness* are the principal verbal fallacies we take up. (There are others, but they occur so rarely as to be easily bypassed.) These fallacies are akin to card tricks in their effect: you're sure that something fishy has gone on, but it's hard to see just what. Understanding these three fallacies will provide you with the instruments to expose such rhetorical sleights of hand.

## 1 Questionable Classification

**5.2** Language functions in many ways, and a pre-eminent role it plays is to classify. A thing is classified when it is assigned to a group or set with which it shares some common feature. Let us illustrate how the main parts of speech serve this classifying function. And at the same time we want to show how a classification can sometimes be "questionable."

Take nouns first. To call imprisonment "punishment" is to classify it as inflicting undesirable treatment upon people who are imprisoned. The classification of imprisonment as punishment is, in all but the most unusual cases, accurate and uncontroversial: rarely does anyone desire such a constraint on freedom. Similarly, to call marriage "oppression" is to classify—in this case, to place marriage into that group of social arrangements that wrongly restrict the freedom of at least some of the people enmeshed in them. In some quarters marriage has come under severe criticism; undoubtedly, many marriages lead to the oppression of one spouse or both. But it is incorrect to classify marriage in general as oppression, for that classification says all marriages are oppressive, a dubious contention at best.

Any use of a noun labels or classifies what the noun refers to. Most such classifications will be uncontroversial; a few will be open to dispute or be plain wrong: these classifications are called "questionable," and cause problems.

Consider adjectives next. It's old hat to call our border with the U.S. an "undefended" border. That puts it in the group of borders, such as those in Western Europe, that are not fortified by military installations. It distinguishes the Canada-U.S. border from the one separating West Germany from East Germany, from the Sino-Soviet border, and from the Franco-German border in the pre–World War II days of the Maginot line. This description is surely a correct one, too. Can the same be said of the phrase "our benign neighbour to the south"? We wager that the adjective "benign" would start an argument with the Committee For An Independent Canada. The label "benign" classifies the influence of the U.S. on Canada as harmless or beneficial. In the last few years, the nationalist movement in the country has challenged that belief; consequently, we must tag this classification as questionable. That's not claiming it is mistaken; only that it is open to debate.

You probably get the picture of how language classifies by now. We can cap the point with a brief reference to the role of verbs and adverbs. In 1976 the Montreal Canadiens *won* the Stanley Cup. (To use "won" is to categorize them as victorious, and to set them apart from teams that lose or tie.) But did they *romp* to victory? Well, they beat Philadelphia in four straight games in the final series, but each game was closely fought. If they "romped" to victory, their wins would have had to have been easy ones. So to call their win a "romp," under the circumstances, would be a questionable classification—in this case, an outright mistaken one, we'd argue. But did the Canadiens win *decisively*? This adverb classifies too: it puts the Canadiens' Cup win in the class of those that leave no doubt as to the superior team. Our hockey judgement would accept "decisively" as accurate in 1976. Did Montreal beat the Flyers *easily*? Another classifying adverb, but considering how close and hard-fought the games were, we would be inclined to challenge "easily" as questionable.

**5.3** We must make one more preliminary point before getting down to some examples of the fallacy. That point is simply that the terms you use in an argument usually carry persuasive force, because the classifications entailed by your choice of words tend to strengthen or weaken your conclusion.

The importance of language can be seen using some of the examples we've given above. Since imprisonment may be called *punishment*, that serves as a reason for not imprisoning people innocent of any crime. Were marriage *oppressive*, it would follow that marriage should be avoided. If it is correct to describe the U.S. as a *benign* neighbour, then it would be foolish of Canada to take an aggressive posture in our relations with it. Finally, one might use the statement that Montreal *decisively* defeated the Flyers in the 1976 Stanley Cup playoffs to support the claim that had the Canadiens played the Soviets that spring, instead of the previous January, they would have won.

This fact—the persuasive force of the classifications built into our language—permits questionable classifications to do their mischief in arguments. Once you let a description that should be challenged slip into an argument, you can find yourself in no position to deny a dubious conclusion. The fallacy we call **questionable classification** is quite simply the employment *in an argument* of a term or expression that involves either a false or debatable characterization.

**5.4** Here are some examples. The first is taken from a letter to the London *Free Press* (November 1974):

**68**   The *Free Press* published an article concerning a proposed performing arts school and the involvement of Provincial Treasurer John White and Mayor Jane Bigelow.

When, if ever, will politicians wake up and stop directing funds derived by taxes at these *make-believe* projects? . . .

Government should not invest one dime in . . . art or culture.

This would accomplish two things. Taxes would be diverted to where they are needed, or reduced, and we would return to a society where work is not bad. (Emphasis ours.)

There is no doubt that the writer intends "make-believe" as a pejorative term, though it's not clear just how cultural projects are make-believe. (There seems to be an assumption here that art and culture are somehow not part of reality. In Chapter 7 we introduce the fallacy that occurs with such a move: *dubious assumption*.) But is it accurate to classify the arts as "make-believe" in a bad sense? The world of the imagination seems not only inescapable, but at the very least a valuable adjunct to our daily toil. The writer employs this challengeable classification in an argument designed to convince the government not to invest in cultural projects such as the London performing arts school. So he or she commits *questionable classification*.

(Notice, too, how the writer implies an equivalence between a society that supports the arts and one that considers work to be bad. If you accept that equation, and you value work, you will be propelled towards this conclusion. Yet surely it wants defense. Not only do artists work very hard, but to be able to afford funds for cultural projects, a society must work to produce surplus capital. Here we are inclined to charge *problematic premise*.)

Our second example comes from an advertising supplement circulated in a number of Canadian magazines like *Maclean's* and *Saturday Night* by the Imperial Oil Company. Esso was arguing for more "realistic"—i.e. higher—prices for petroleum products. The pamphlet contained a section called "Prices in perspective," which read, in part:

**69**    Over the past quarter century, because world prices for crude oil have been *depressed*, and because of intense competition, petroleum energy has been available in Canada at *bargain* prices. The price of energy generally in Canada has been so low that, in the words of the Ontario Government Advisory Committee on Energy, it has been taken for granted and regarded almost as a free commodity. (Emphasis ours.)

The thrust of this passage in the overall argument is that since prices in the past have been lower than they could justifiably have been, it is not unwarranted of Esso and the petroleum industry to demand and expect higher prices now. Note how that argument gains support from the classification of world prices for crude oil over the past 25 years as "depressed," and the classification of the prices of petroleum energy in Canada as "bargain." If world prices for crude oil were *depressed*, that implies they are lower than they ought to have been; if we've been getting our petroleum energy at *bargain* prices, that implies we've been getting it more cheaply than we have a right to normally expect. But these classifications are questionable. Economic dogma, at least, has it that fair market prices are established by competition. In arguing that world crude prices have been "depressed" by *competition*, Imperial would appear to be undercutting its own commitment to a free market economy. Further, we note that Esso is arguing that Canadian petroleum prices have been "bargain" just at a time when it wants money for more exploration to come out of higher prices instead of out of retained earnings. Gasoline and heating fuel had hardly been "almost free"—despite what the Ontario Advisory Committee on Energy might have said. Our point is that the case needs a good deal more support; without that further support it's questionable to classify these prices as "bargain." Given that these classifications are used to support the intended conclusion that petroleum prices should be increased, Imperial in this ad is guilty of *questionable classification*.

Clearly the conditions of this fallacy fall into two parts, *each of which* must be satisfied:

---

**QUESTIONABLE CLASSIFICATION**

1. M classifies something, X (a person, act, event, situation, etc.) in a way that is either debatable or else false;
2. M uses that classification of X as support for some conclusion, Q.

---

The *fallacy*, we repeat, occurs only when the questionable classification functions as a premise in an argument. A challengeable classification which occurs outside an argument is not a fallacy, although of course that doesn't mean you should accept it.

**5.5** We must emphasize that *questionable classification* is a special case of *problematic premise*. Essentially what you are doing in locating a term which has questionable application is pointing to a premise which requires defense; that is, the arguer needs to provide some reason for thinking that the term does indeed apply. Therefore, a charge of *questionable classification* must not be pictured as a devastating rebuttal of an argument. It's more appropriately seen as exposing the argument's weak or tender spots. There is no presumption that the arguer cannot produce the needed defense of the classification that is questioned. For instance, Imperial Oil may well be able to demonstrate that, despite the questions we have raised, all the evidence taken together does justify their describing world crude oil prices as "depressed" and Canadian petroleum prices as "bargain."

Here is an example of an argument in which we consider the charge of *questionable classification* justified, but without prejudice to the possibility of an adequate defense. Columnist Dalton Camp was arguing, during the 1972 federal election (Windsor *Star*, September 1972) that Liberal policies since 1968 had given aid and comfort to the NDP:

**70**       . . . cynicism and suspicion of so-called big business and
the free-enterprise ethic have been the certain legacy of the
past four years of harassment of the business community
by the Trudeau administration.
       The seed programs for this fundamental change in public
attitude are best represented by the ill-fated competition
act and the frenetic attempts at tax reform . . .

Mr. Camp's calling the Liberals' treatment of the business community "harassment," and his characterizations of the competition act as "ill-fated" and the attempts at tax reform as "frenetic" are classifications that lend support to his conclusion that the government's measures had left the impression that the business community needed control—a conclusion long argued by the NDP. But to describe the government's actions as "harassment" is to imply that they were illegitimate; to call the competition act "ill-fated" is to suggest it was misconceived to start with; and to construe the tax reform measures as "frenetic" is to imply they were hurried and ill-thought-out. In the adversary context of an election campaign, these are surely charges the Liberals would be at pains to deny. By baldly using these debatable classifications to support his conclusions, Camp committed *questionable classification*.

Mr. Camp did not take the time to defend these classifications in his column. But we aren't saying he could not have done so. Charging the fallacy is in effect returning the ball to his court—and at the same time alerting ourselves to the weakness of the argument as it stands.

**5.6** We cannot leave *questionable classification* without saying something about the members of a notable subgroup, labels that might be called **loaded terms.** These are terms that have acquired by convention either pejorative or commendatory connotations. Employed in argumentative contexts, they slip in undefended value judgements to stack the deck for their advocate's point of view.

These loaded terms are familiar to everyone. When someone alludes to "those Right to Life kooks," referring to people who oppose abortion, his or her use of the word "kooks" suggests the people holding this position on abortion are irrational and fanatics. The implication is that their views are false and that it's unreasonable to hold them. Or, you have heard proposals put down as "airy-fairy" ideas. The implication is that the plans are totally impractical. Again, people speak of "knee-jerk" leftists (or free-enterprisers), thereby suggesting that the leftists (or free-enterprisers) in question respond to situations with uncritical loyalty to their point of view and without sufficient perceptiveness to realize when a dogmatic interpretation distorts the facts.

Of course, if people holding a position *are* "kooks" (i.e. are fanatics who won't listen to reason), if a proposal *is* "airy-fairy" (i.e. lacking in substance), and if a response *is* a "knee-jerk" one (i.e. without thought and critical reflection), then condemnation is appropriate in each case. The trouble is that these epithets should be accepted only when defended, whereas they are usually used without any supporting evidence—and furthermore are themselves deployed to support further conclusions.

Because loaded terms come into and fall out of fashion, there can be no fixed list. Many are slang words—a region of language with a high turnover. Others can trigger diametrically opposed associations in different circles. It's of interest in this connection to note that the word "democracy" had highly negative connotations until about one hundred years ago: democracy was considered a bad thing.[1] Now, of course, to call a procedure or decision or state "democratic" is in this country to accord it the highest praise. Possibly the term "socialism" is now at the point "democracy" occupied in the late 19th century. But "socialism" is also an example of a word that has a different persuasive thrust in different constituencies. For some, a socialist state or proposal is automatically good; for others, it's automatically bad. "Communist" is another example of this phenomenon. What all these words have in common is a built-in evaluation which gives them automatic evaluative force in one direction or another whenever they are used.

Our example of the use of these loaded terms comes from a letter to the Windsor *Star* (February 1976) from R.R. By way of background, Sandra Precop writes a daily column in the *Star*; the capital punishment debate was at one of its heights at the time; and Millhaven is a federal penitentiary near Kingston, Ontario:

[1] Cf. C. B. Macpherson, *The Real World of Democracy*, The Massey Lectures, Fourth Series (Toronto: CBC Publications, 1965), p. 1.

**71**   Well, I see one of your esteemed columnists has added her name to the list of *bleeding hearts* concerning capital punishment.

Ms. Precop, and her band of *pseudo-intellectuals*, and politicians in general take the attitude that the public is, at best, near imbecile, and must therefore be led around by the nose mentally all their lives.

Let's put an end to all this rhetoric once and for all, place the subject on the ballot for a public referendum, and let the *do-gooders* busy themselves sending CARE packages to Millhaven. (Emphasis ours.)

Would we be going out on a limb if we were to guess that R.R. favours capital punishment? His or her position seems to be that the opposition to capital punishment is based on a mistaken perspective. Abolitionists are "bleeding hearts." In other words, they lack the moral fortitude to face up to the need for such a harsh penalty. They are "pseudo-intellectuals." That is to say, presumably, their arguments are pretentious, lacking the tough-minded analysis that would conclude that capital punishment is necessary. They are, finally, "do-gooders." We take this to mean that they are indiscriminately soft-hearted in their concern for those who may suffer, and fail to reserve their benevolence for those who—unlike convicted murderers—genuinely deserve it.

*If* R.R.'s labels were legitimate, then he or she would have gone some way towards making a case against the opponents of capital punishment. The trouble is, to defend the labels adequately, R.R. would have to demonstrate for each one that the claim which would justify its use is sound. "Bleeding heart," "pseudo-intellectual," and "do-gooder" here serve as *substitutes* for argument.

At this point we must acknowledge a fair question: why isn't such *questionable classification* simply a kind of *ad hominem*? It certainly can look like *ad hominem* when the loaded epithet is used to characterize a person. However, there is a difference. Using R.R.'s letter as an example, you can see that he was not actually shifting the argument to an attack on Ms. Precop's person. Rather, he was tagging the position she defended and represented. It *is* relevant to argue that opposition to capital punishment can be explained only as a case of moral cowardice, that the arguments defending that view are intellectually flabby, and that sympathy for convicted murderers betrays a failure to make a needed moral distinction. So R.R.'s logical sin was not responding to Precop's column with an irrelevant attack on her person, but using emotionally loaded terms as substitutes for reasoned argument.

In addition to giving the appearance of argument without the substance, the use of these loaded words frequently violates the very spirit of rational persuasion. Labels like "bleeding heart," "pseudo-intellectual," and "do-gooder" are hardly invitations to the opponent to share in a reasoned pursuit of the truth of the matter. Their appeal is solely to the converted. They serve to ratify and entrench the views on one side of the dispute, while they simply aggravate and antagonize the other side, or those who might be uncommitted. Their only hope of persuasive success is through sleight of hand or mouth, not laudable means to anyone who seeks truth through reason.

**5.7** R.R.'s entreaty, "Let's put an end to all this rhetoric once and for all," is deliciously ironic. This letter is a fine example of sheer rhetoric which required a bit of ingenuity to unpack. As such, it serves as a cue for a discussion of how to extract the bare bones of an argument from its rhetorical dressing.

---

**ELIMINATING RHETORIC**   *Here are some rules of thumb that can help:*

1. *Look for and focus on the argument. Use contextual clues and premise and conclusion indicators as guides to the conclusion and premises.*
2. *Set aside phrases, sentences and even paragraphs that are extraneous to the bare argument—such items as background information, explanations, asides, repetition, elaborations, rhetorical trappings.*
3. *Separate each statement that belongs to the argument as a distinct premise (or conclusion), marked with its own number tag (**P1**, **P2**, **P3**, etc., and **C1**, **C2**, etc. as necessary). This requires breaking up compound sentences so there will be just one single point made in each set-out premise or conclusion.*
4. *Reformulate the premises and conclusion(s) if it is necessary in order to have all the points stated in straightforward and clear language. This especially requires transposing rhetorical questions into assertive sentences.*
5. *Doublecheck to make sure that no changes you make alter the meaning. Your restatement of the argument should not add new ideas, nor take any away, nor give any new twists or shadings to the sense of the argument in the original passage.*

---

To follow these suggestions you will usually need to do some detective work. Using the *context* and what is actually *said* in the passage as your clues, you will have to deduce from them what is actually *meant*.

Our treatments of these examples of fallacies illustrate this extraction of the argument from the rhetoric. However, in most cases we have placed before you only the results of our inferences, not the process whereby we arrived at those interpretations. Below is an excerpt from a long letter about capital punishment, together with our standardization of the argument we think it contains and our explanation of how we arrived at it. J.B. wrote to the Montreal *Gazette* (January 1975):

**72**     We have in recent times witnessed the death of three policemen, a doctor, a family of five and a foreign visitor. The common denominator for all these murders was escape, either by killing to avoid immediate capture or elimination of living witnesses to the crimes committed.

Killing those who could be instrumental in either was included free in the package deal to which our government subscribes for all crimes valued at 20 years in our Criminal Code. The murders were the logical conclusion of the crimes.

This built in incentive to kill must be eliminated . . .

First, you have to read this passage several times before it begins to make any sense. (Believe us, the rest of the letter doesn't help to make this section clearer.) Please reread it now.

Gradually, you begin to see that, in the first paragraph quoted, J.B. told us that, on several recent occasions, after crimes had been committed the criminals killed people to try to keep from being caught. In the second paragraph, J.B. seemed to be making some connection between those murders and "crimes valued at 20 years in our Criminal Code." Here some detective work is needed. Under what interpretation would this reference make sense? We note that the final sentence of the excerpt refers to this paragraph: "*This* built in incentive to kill . . ." Somehow there must be a connection between killing to avoid being caught, crimes with a 20-year sentence attached, and an incentive to kill—*if* J.B.'s contentions tie together coherently. Here is a possible interpretation of what was meant.

By "the package deal to which our government subscribes for all crimes valued at 20 years in our Criminal Code," J.B. may have been referring to the law at the time which carried no capital punishment for murder (except in the case of police officers and prison guards), and instead a 20-year sentence. We could then see how he or she might have thought there was an incentive to kill. Were someone to commit a crime that carried a heavy sentence, and kill in order to try to escape, but be caught anyway and convicted of murder, the worst penalty would still be a 20-year sentence.

J.B.'s argument in brief, then, would be that there was reason to believe that the 1975 law restricting capital punishment served as an incentive to kill. Standardizing it, we get:

**73**       **P1Ai:** Several recent murders were committed by criminals to avoid capture for other crimes.

> **P1Aiia:** The present law provides for a maximum 20-year penalty for murder.

> **P1Aiib:** Other crimes carry similar penalties.

> **P1Aii:** The penalty for murder is not much greater than penalties for certain other crimes.

> **P1A:** It is reasonable to believe that the criminals who murdered to avoid capture for other crimes did so because they could be no worse off as a result than if they were punished for the initial crimes.

**P1:** The law provides no disincentive to kill as a means of avoiding capture for crimes bearing heavy penalties.

**P2:** If the law provides no such disincentive, then it provides an incentive for murder in those cases.

**C:** The law as it stands provides an incentive for murder.

While this standardization may go into more explicit detail than you will need in order to interpret this sort of argument, it does serve to illustrate—particularly when contrasted with J.B.'s letter—how different a more literal statement of the argument can look when stripped of the rhetoric in which it was initially clothed.

The ability to field such rhetoric, to cut through to the meaning, is an important skill for the consumer of arguments to master. For, without this ability, the more important skill of evaluating arguments logically cannot be deployed.

# 2 Ambiguity

**5.8** The word "ambiguous" is defined in the Oxford Universal Dictionary as meaning: 1. "Doubtful; not clearly defined," and 2. "Open to more than one interpretation; equivocal." The fallacy we discuss in this section takes its name from the second meaning.

Incidentally, is the word "ambiguous" itself ambiguous, since it has two meanings? Loosely speaking, perhaps it is. More precisely, however, words or phrases are not in themselves ambiguous. The ambiguity occurs only when a word or phrase appears in a context in which it can be taken in more than one way. So it's words-in-context that are actually open to ambiguity.

Nothing is logically wrong with ambiguity *per se*. It may confuse, but that's a literary flaw. The logical fallacy of **ambiguity** is reserved for the manoeuvre *in argument* of trading on the potential of a word or phrase for more than one interpretation. This strategy results in blurring the focus of the argument, often resulting in the creation of a red herring or a straw man.

Look at how it can work in practice. The first example comes from a speech by then–Justice Minister Otto Lang to "The Continental Action Assembly of Christians and Jews" in June 1975 (reported in the Windsor *Star*). Mr. Lang touched on the abortion issue and defended his view that the 1969 legislation permitting abortion should be interpreted in a strict way so as to keep the number of abortions to a minimum—to cases in which the health "in the life and death sense" of the mother is in danger. In rebuttal of the counterclaim that such a strict interpretation of the law would lead to many unwanted children entering the world, Mr. Lang said that in Canada there is no such thing as an unwanted child.

It will help to have his argument standardized:

**74**    **P1:** There is no such thing as an unwanted child in Canada.
      **C:**  It is not true that a strict interpretation of the abortion legislation will result in unwanted children.

Mr. Lang went on to defend his premise, arguing, "There are many places where children are wanted. People are on waiting lists for years applying for adoption of a child."

It's clear from his defense that Mr. Lang meant **P1** in the sense that in Canada no children are not wanted by *somebody*—if not their natural parents, then by couples who want to adopt a child. But is that the sense in which the pro-abortionists (whose claim Lang was trying to refute) intend the proposition that fewer abortions will lead to more unwanted children? Not at all. What they mean is that there will be more children who are unwanted *by their natural parents*.

What went wrong with Mr. Lang's argument may be seen by noting that **P1** can be understood in two ways:

> **P1₁:** There is no child in Canada whose natural parents do not want to bear and raise it.

$P1_2$: There is no child in Canada who is wanted by no one at all.

$P1_1$ is the sense of **P1** that must be true if it is to lend support to Mr. Lang's criticism of the pro-abortionist position; $P1_2$ is irrelevant to that criticism, given the sense of "unwanted children" at issue. But Lang's argument employs $P1_2$. As a result, what he had to say never really made contact with the position he was trying to refute. He committed the fallacy of *ambiguity*. The culprit was the term "unwanted child."

For another example of *ambiguity*, consider the following argument:

**75**   The fact that there are laws of nature shows that God exists. For the existence of a law implies the existence of a law-giver, and God is the Supreme law-giver in the Universe. So, far from disproving the existence of God, science, in detecting the laws of nature, actually proves that God does exist.

Standardized, the argument may be set forth as follows:

**76**   **P1:**  Science discovers the laws of nature.
      **P2:**  Every law implies a law-giver.
      **P3:**  God is the Supreme law-giver.
      **C:**  Science proves that God exists.

The ambiguous word here is "law." This word has two quite different meanings. It may mean "an observed regularity in nature"; it may also mean "a prescription or mandate set forth by duly constituted authority." It has the former meaning in **P1**, but the latter meaning in **P2**. So although it looks like **P1** and **P2** work together to support **C**, they do not. **P2** is false if "law" means what it must mean in order for **P1** to be true; and **P1** is false if "law" means what it must mean in order for **P2** to be true. The fallacy of *ambiguity* occurs, and we may conclude that this argument fails to establish the truth of the conclusion.

Another example. In 1967 the Progressive Conservative Party of Canada held a "Thinkers' Conference" at Montmorency, Quebec, in order to begin to shape party policy for the next federal election. From this conference emerged a policy statement that asserted, in part, "that Canada is composed of the original inhabitants of this land and the *two founding nations* with historic rights, who have been and continue to be joined by people from many lands" (emphasis ours). When the 1968 federal election campaign began, the phrase "two nations" (a translation from the French, "*deux nations*") became a thorn in the PCs' side.

Liberal leader Trudeau asserted that there could be only one sovereign state in Canada, that sovereignty is indivisible, and that there could not be two nations and one nation at the same time. The Liberals attacked the Conservatives' position as a dangerous threat to Canadian unity. Their argument might be standardized along these lines:

77    **P1:** The Progressive Conservatives endorse the concept of two nations in Canada.

      **P2:** There can be two nations only if there are two political states.

      **C:** The PCs' policy of accepting the two nations idea is a threat to Canadian unity.

The Conservatives were furious with this argument. It traded, they charged, on the wrong meaning of the phrase "two nations." "Nation" can denote a politically sovereign state (a "nation state"), or it can refer to a cultural or ethnic group (as the English, Scots, and Welsh are three nations in the single state of Great Britain). What the PCs endorsed was the recognition of the two founding ethnic groups in Canada—the French and the British—as basic facts of national life. The Liberals were quite deliberately misrepresenting their position. Trudeau was right, they granted, that there can be only one sovereign Canadian state. But that was irrelevant as a criticism of the PCs' position. What the Liberals had to deny, to refute the PCs' policy, was that there should be no recognition of the two sociological groupings, French and English, in Canadian life. That, of course, they could not do.

We can make this point in terms of the argument as we've standardized it. **P2** is true if it is taken to mean:

      **P2₁:** There can be two politically sovereign states in Canada only if there are two politically sovereign states.

True—but trivially true. Moreover, it requires the willful misreading (according to the PCs) of the Conservative position. What they meant by "two nations" was "two socio-ethnic groups." Hence, if the term used in the Liberals' argument were correctly interpreted, **P2** would become:

      **P2₂:** There can be two socio-ethnic groups in Canada only if there are two politically sovereign states in Canada.

Both the Conservatives and the Liberals (unlike most separatists) take the position that **P2₂** is false. So the Liberals were able to employ their argument only by distorting the Conservative meaning of "two nations," taking it in a sense not intended by its advocates.

If this is a fair analysis of the Liberals' position, then they clearly did commit the fallacy of *ambiguity*. For their part, the Liberals defended their attacks on the two-nations policy on the ground that the Conservatives themselves vacillated between both senses of the phrase, and so were themselves the perpetrators of ambiguity. "In Quebec they are talking about two-nations and about special status, and in the rest of the country they are talking about one nation and no special status . . . ," Trudeau charged. (He thus accused the Conservatives of the fallacy of *inconsistency*, which we take up in Chapter 8.) There is still debate about who was right. Both sides agree that the "two nations" issue hurt the Conservatives in the 1968 election and contributed to Trudeau's victory.

**5.9** These are the conditions of the fallacy:

---

### AMBIGUITY

1. A premise, Q, in M's argument contains a term or phrase, T, that is open to different interpretations in different contexts;
2. the sense of T in Q (giving $Q_1$) is different from the sense of T (giving $Q_2$) relevant to defending M's conclusion or refuting M's opponent.

---

Typically, *ambiguity* is found in adversary contexts, and M's argument is a rejoinder to a position held by someone else. That was the case in two of our examples, 74 and 77. What those examples also illustrated was that usually the argument that results from M's interpretation of the term or phrase is a plausible one. That's what gives the exercise its credibility. But when the premise is interpreted in its *relevant* sense, the argument usually founders.

What you must do to prove *ambiguity* is locate the key term or phrase and identify the role its ambiguity plays in the argument. Standardizing the pertinent parts of the argument helps, as does identifying the two senses in which the ambiguous premise may be understood. You have then set down the necessary details for showing that the two conditions have been met.

**5.10** One last example to tie all the pieces together, from a letter to the Ottawa *Journal* (August 1974):

**78**    A small number of self-appointed loudmouths in Women's Lib, intoxicated with the exuberance of their own verbosity, have partially forced on the public a humorless demand that the word "man" shall be replaced by "person."

I offer a suggestion that would save thousands of dollars in printing . . . Drop "man" and "woman" and use the wartime slang word "bod" for everyone; e.g., "sales bod" instead of "salesperson" . . . "Boditoba" instead of "Personitoba" (Manitoba); "ebodcipation," "bodifesto" and "Bodilla"— the capital of the Philippines . . .

The bod who wrote this letter was having great fun playing on an ambiguity. Bod's implicit argument can be standardized as follows:

**79**    **P1:** Some persons in the Women's Liberation movement have suggested that the word "man" be replaced by the word "person."

**P2:** This suggestion would lead to such ridiculous consequences (which substituting the word "bod" where the Women's Liberation advocates would put "person" serves to dramatize) as: "Personitoba" for "Manitoba," "epersoncipation" for "emancipation," "personifesto" for "manifesto," and "Personilla" for "Manilla."

**C:** The suggestion to replace "man" with "person" should be ignored.

Of course, Bod's argument gets off the ground only if **P1** is understood in the sense of:

**P1$_1$:** Some persons in the Women's Liberation Movement have suggested that wherever the particular ordered sequence of letters "m-a-n" occurs it should be replaced by the particular ordered sequence of letters "p-e-r-s-o-n."

However, that certainly isn't the intention of the Women's Liberation's suggestion, which would render a very different sense of **P1**, namely:

**P1$_2$:** Some persons in the Women's Liberation Movement have suggested that where the word "man" is used to designate a male or female indifferently, it should be replaced by the word "person."

That's the sense in which **P1** is true, but then it has nothing to do with Bod's **P2** or **C**. We humourless logicians won't let a person get away with anything, even in jest; Bod is guilty of *ambiguity*. Also, since Bod's letter distorts and attacks the Women's Liberation position by using this ambiguity, we suggest that Bod be found guilty on a second count: *straw man*.

# 3 Vagueness

**5.11** The concept of vagueness deserves careful conceptual analysis. For our purposes, however, it will suffice to focus on one sort of vagueness that can plague arguments. We'll concentrate on propositions that are vague in the sense that you can't be sure what precisely they mean. You have no way of knowing what they include and what they rule out. This is the sort of vagueness often found in popular clichés. Here's a typical example:

**80**     You're the only one who knows what's right for you.

Sounds good, but what is it saying? "Right" in what sense? Morally right? The right size or fit? The right mix to suit your taste? It seems to rule out anyone else's knowing what is right for you, but that can't be, since others can know what size fits you, what flavours you like, and even what your moral duties are. Is it saying that no one else should tell you what you ought to do? Perhaps, yet that would rule out a parent or friend giving you well-meant advice. The guesses could continue; there are no doubt many other possible meanings of this cliché. Our point is that, taken as it stands, no one can know what they are committed to if they accept it, nor what they have denied if they reject it. Outside any context, it's incredibly vague; even when such clichés are encountered in actual use, the contextual furnishings merely reduce, but do not eliminate, their vagueness.

When such a proposition occupies the role of a premise in an argument, the support it provides for the conclusion will be diluted by its vagueness. When, on the other hand, the conclusion is vague, you cannot determine how well or poorly the premises back it up, since you can't be clear about what proposition they are intended to support.

We call **vagueness** a fallacy of sleight of hand because these indeterminate propositions don't *look* imprecise as they are slipped into the flow of everyday argumentation. Perhaps just because a variety of meanings can be read into them, we tend to gloss over

them, probably assuming our own interpretation as we go. And there
are those who have learned how to exploit vagueness for political
and social ends. It takes a *thinking* reader or listener to notice
vagueness; often it also takes a degree of courage to speak up (to
think out) and wonder—not whether the emperor has any clothes—
but whether there's anybody under the robes.

Consider now some actual examples of this fallacy. In September
1972 in an Ontario cabinet shuffle, J. D. McNie became Minister of
Education. In an editorial about the cabinet changes, the Toronto
*Globe and Mail* said:

**81**     Mr. McNie assumes his troublesome education post at a
time when "individual initiative and free enterprise" are
beginning to take on some of their old coloration, at least
for the Ontario Government and people. His immediate
charges—in college and university—may not yet have got
the message; but the Government and the public are united
in believing that there has to be a ceiling for education costs
somewhere up in those airy clouds. Mr. McNie's task will be
to see that not too many heads thrust through the ceiling
when he finds it. It will be interesting to see if he has the
strength to do it.

There seems to be an argument of sorts here, but the *Globe and Mail*
has managed an adroit editorial waffle so that it's hard to determine
precisely what the point of the argument is. Certainly one premise
has something to do with a ceiling for education costs, and the
conclusion has something to do with what Mr. McNie will do—or
should do—to impose such a ceiling. Can we get a clearer picture?
Is the second-last sentence a *prediction* ("Mr. McNie's task *will*
be . . .")? If it is, then how can the editorial in the next sentence
wonder if Mr. McNie will have "the strength to do it"? Does the
*Globe and Mail* mean that Mr. McNie *ought to* put a lid on education
spending? If so, why did it say "will be" instead of "should be"?
And look at the main premise, the contention that there has to be a
ceiling for education costs. We'll not quibble over the use of "has to
be" where obviously "should be" is what's intended. The problem is
that this contention, taken literally, is vacuous. What would it mean
to *deny* that there should be a limit to education costs? Would it
mean that schools and educators should get however much money
they ask for, even if it gobbled up the whole provincial budget or
required oppressive taxes? But who would take that stand? No,
obviously there ought to be a limit to the amount spent on education;
what is needed to assert anything significant is a statement of what
that limit ought to be.

At this point, the ambiguity of the term "ceiling" in its use here blocks precision. Does "a ceiling for education costs" mean a limit to the total *amount* spent on education in any given year, or does it mean a limit to the *percentage* of the provincial budget in any given year? (And if the former, what amount? If the latter, what percentage?)[2] Or again, does it mean stipulating an *absolute* limit beyond which education spending may not go?

In short, we don't know at all clearly what the editorial is recommending. We do not know what would count as accepting or rejecting its proposal. We don't have any clear idea what it is telling Mr. McNie to do (or predicting what Mr. McNie will do). We charge the *Globe and Mail* editorial here with *vagueness*.

In the fall of 1974, *Saturday Night* magazine, running into financial woes, announced it would have to cease publication unless it could find $100,000 on short notice.[3] The anticipated demise of this venerable Canadian monthly, first published in 1887, was cited by many as further evidence of the harmful influence of the special status of *Time* and *Reader's Digest* on Canadian periodical publishing, and lent further support to the lobbyists trying to get the federal government to revoke the exemption from the foreign periodicals' tax enjoyed by these two American magazines. N.H. took issue with this position in the following letter to the Edmonton *Journal* (October 1974):

**82**     As far as I'm concerned, *Saturday Night* could have quit many years ago. When *Maclean's* and *Chatelaine* give up the ghost I won't know the difference until I read of it in the obituaries. What in the world have these magazines done for Canadian citizens? They are dull, prejudiced, their subjects are nothing but political (by radicals), the cost is high, and a free-lancer can't get in once in a century.

As usual, Canadians, who are incompetent, inefficient, lazy, miserly, and jealous, cannot compete with the U.S.A. in anything—be it sports, food production, manufacturing, films, popular songs, TV writing, publishing, or just plain work. Consequently they always want U.S. products and performers banned so they can produce the usual poor product.

I think *Reader's Digest* is an excellent magazine . . . As for *Time*, not in 50 or even 100 years will Canada be able to produce anything comparable in coverage . . .

---

[2] Note that the ambiguity of "ceiling" here does not result in the fallacy of *ambiguity*. It merely contributes to the vagueness of the editorial's claim.

[3] SN did stop publication for a few months, but private capital was found to revive it, and as of this writing it is thriving.

We take part of N.H.'s argument to be that the basic reason Canadian periodicals have trouble competing against *Time* and *Reader's Digest* is that Canadians aren't competent to produce magazines as good as these, and therefore the claim that *Time* and *Reader's Digest* have an unfair advantage shouldn't be credited. Now let us assess the premise here: "Canadians are incompetent, inefficient, lazy, miserly, and jealous." Wait a minute! *Which* Canadians was N.H. referring to? You? Us? We aren't too ready to accept these characterizations, and no doubt you aren't either. Certainly not *all* Canadians exhibit these traits. Yet no doubt *some* possess some of them, and possibly even some (a much smaller number) possess all of them. Before we can take issue with N.H.'s allegation, we must know which claim he or she was making. The charge is too imprecise: N.H. committed *vagueness*.

We might note two other common domiciles of vagueness: clichés, as we've mentioned already, and advertising. As an example of the latter, recall the jingle:

**83**      So raise a glass of the beer that was brewed for the country . . .

"Brewed for the country"? "Country" as opposed to "city"? *This* country as distinct from others? So it means Molson's "Canadian" was brewed for Canada, not Britain or the United States? But then what does "brewed for Canada" mean? Does it mean that this beer is distributed only in Canada? That might make sense, but that can hardly be what "brewed for" means. And how can a beer be brewed for a country? It must mean that the beer is brewed for the people who live in the country. Is *that* all the jingle is saying? If so, how does that differentiate Molson's "Canadian" from other Molson's beers, and from other Canadian brewers' products: Labatt's, Uncle Bens', Moosehead's, Olands', Henningers', Carling's, etc. The evident conclusion is that the jingle is so vague as to be meaningless. Hence, it can hardly serve as a reason for purchasing the product. It's probably naive to expect that all advertising messages are intended to be taken literally as reasons for buying the product (although if some are, how do you distinguish them?). But we must defer further discussion of this point to Chapter 10.

**5.12** Generalizing from these examples, we can state the conditions of this fallacy:

---

**VAGUENESS**

1. An argument contains a premise, or a conclusion, Q, the meaning of which is indeterminate.
2. The indeterminateness of Q makes it impossible to assess Q's acceptability as a premise or its significance as a conclusion.

---

We can think of no rule for drawing attention to cases of *vagueness*. The examples we used illustrate a couple of common contributors, but there are many more. We have already met what might be called the "all-some" vagueness of N.H.'s letter in the sentence, "Canadians are . . ." Did N.H. mean *all* Canadians, or only *some*? And if the latter, who? Unmodified general nouns are often vague in this way. We also have seen the "must-ought" vagueness in the *Globe and Mail* editorial. When it said there "has to be a ceiling on education costs," was it saying that this is in some sense a *necessity* (something that somehow *must* be the case), or was it taking the view that such a ceiling is *desirable*? Other variants of this case are the "will-ought" and the "is-ought" vagueness. The *Globe and Mail* said that "Mr. McNie's task *will* be . . ." when pretty clearly what it meant was that "Mr. McNie *ought* to . . ." And you will have heard some teachers say, "A student's role *is* to . . ." when they mean, "Students *ought* to . . ." Of course, there is no vagueness when you can discern from the context which meaning is intended. But the looseness of these locutions can contribute vagueness when the context is not determinate.

**5.13** To conclude, we offer a passage that seems to us to contain at least two of the fallacies covered in this chapter. To see if you have mastered these fallacies, you might first read only the background material and the passage, and see if you can identify which fallacies have been committed. Then read our evaluation for another view.

By way of background, we should say that this is an excerpt from a flier circulated at the University of Windsor to announce a meeting to support ZANU—the Zimbabwe (Rhodesia) African National Union. The meeting was sponsored by the local branch of the Communist Party of Canada (Marxist-Leninist), and we do not know whether it or ZANU was responsible for writing the flier; we suspect it was the former. ZANU is one of the groups organizing armed resistance to the white regime in Rhodesia. Its spokesman was touring Canada in January and February 1976, soliciting political and financial support.

The flier read, in part:

**84**     The people of Zimbabwe have been waging a heroic armed
struggle ever since they were dispossessed of their land and
enslaved by the foreign exploiters. The racist and fascist Ian
Smith regime is on its last legs and victory is near at hand
for the people of Zimbabwe. However, the enemies of
Zimbabwe, especially the two superpowers, the U.S. and
the Soviet Union, are trying to liquidate the struggle for
national independence and freedom through their "detente"
fraud. It is important for the Canadian people to support the
resolute struggle of the Zimbabwe people against racism,
colonialism and imperialism . . . We call upon all progressive
and democratic people to give full financial and political
support to the just cause of the Zimbabwe people.

Here is our evaluation of the argument in this passage. First, we
should note that the argument seems to conclude that the ZANU
armed struggle against the Smith regime in Rhodesia is justified and
that it ought to receive our support. The defense of that conclusion
is (necessarily) a sketchy set of premises about how the people of
Rhodesia have been treated, and why the need for support is
especially acute at this time.

Starting from the top, we would challenge the use of "heroic" to
characterize the Zimbabwe struggle. This is a loaded term: a heroic
act is highly laudable. If we accept this description, we already go
some way towards accepting the conclusion. Hence, some documentation is necessary to support the claim.

The argument asserts that the people of Zimbabwe have been
"enslaved." That too is a loaded term. But what does it mean here?
We doubt that it refers to slavery literally. We would have heard
cries of outrage before now if whites in Rhodesia had been asserting
*ownership* of the Zimbabwe people. Much more likely, the word is
used metaphorically here. But then, "slavery" in what sense? Is
the contention that the people have been treated as the *equivalent*
of slaves; forced to work for subsistence pay, their freedom of
choice and movement restricted to nil, their lives totally controlled?
Or is the metaphor looser, referring instead to the fact that in
Rhodesia the whites control the positions of economic and political
power? Or again, should the term be understood as part of the
Marxist rhetoric of the flier, referring to the fact that the Rhodesian
economy is capitalist and hence its workers "enslaved" in the sense
that, according to Marxist theory, all workers are "exploited" under
capitalism? The use of "enslaved" here, despite its rhetorical punch,
is too vague to convey an assessable meaning. The fallacy is *vagueness*.

The next term that needs scrutiny is "foreign exploiters." Another loaded term, this one is ambiguous in the context: it may refer to international economic interests, such as multinational corporations; or it may refer to the white settlers in Rhodesia. Or it may refer to both. Since we can't be sure, we must charge *vagueness*.

There's more wrong with this phrase. If the reference is to multinationals, we need evidence that the pejorative label "exploiters" is justified. If it is, we are once again moved much closer to the conclusion. It may well be a valid charge, but we need some evidence. So we charge *questionable classification*. If, on the other hand, "foreign exploiters" is intended to refer to the white settlers in Rhodesia, we would have to charge *questionable classification* on different grounds. The use of "foreign" would then seem inappropriate. Certainly the whites were not native to Rhodesia, any more than people of European origin are native to Canada—in the sense that at some time in the past few hundred years, their forebears emigrated from Europe. But the whites have been in Rhodesia for several generations now, and it would be a misrepresentation to call them "foreign," just as it would be a misrepresentation to call a second- or third-generation Canadian "foreign."

We cannot see anything wrong with calling the Smith regime in Rhodesia "racist." Any challenge to that term would betray a woeful ignorance of long-available facts. But we do have qualms about "fascist." That term admittedly is difficult to define. However, roughly speaking a fascist is one who holds the following combination of beliefs: state absolutism (i.e., there are no limits on what the government is permitted to do), dictatorial leadership, organicism (i.e., people are organic parts of the state and exist only for, in, and through it), and irrationalism (i.e., myths and other irrational means may be used to enjoin popular sacrifice for the glory of the state). Smith would appear to fail on every count to qualify as a fascist. So this is a *questionable classification*.

Lastly, we think it is *questionable* to *classify* the situation of the Zimbabwe people as "colonialism," since the Smith regime has already severed colonial ties with Britain. To label the white domination of the blacks "colonialism" stretches the term out of its ordinary meaning and adds nothing to what has already quite accurately been called a struggle for independence and freedom. Further, it is not clear in what sense the ZANU's struggle is against "imperialism." Is the country economically controlled by foreign companies, supported by their governments? Or is this use of "imperialism" a reference to the ZANU's fears that Zimbabwe will be a pawn in the game of *détente* between the U.S. and the Soviet Union? Or both? Since we don't know what we are committed to if we accept this premise, we must reserve judgement, on grounds of *vagueness*.

As a result of all these complaints against the premises of the argument contained in the flier, it would be hasty to conclude, as we're invited to do, that ZANU should get our political and economic support. But we emphasize something we said about *questionable classification* that applies also to *vagueness*. These fallacies do not mark the death of the argument; rather, they simply point to where further elaboration, further support, is required. In all likelihood, those who attended the meeting announced by this flier could have raised the questions we have noted and perhaps have received clarification and further defense of these claims. Yet several students we talked to were turned off by the strident rhetoric of the notice, so they were not attracted to the meeting. This reaction underlines the observation we made in Section 1 of this chapter about how such loaded language tends to polarize debate and reinforce people in their prejudices. The result is particularly tragic when it turns people away from the violations of human rights of which Rhodesian blacks are certainly the victims.

---

## Exercises for Chapter 5

*Directions:* Determine which fallacies occur in the following passages. Remember that some may not contain arguments at all, some fallacies from earlier chapters may be present, some fallacies may not be classifiable in terms of the labels thus far introduced, and some of the arguments may be fallacy-free. As always, present reasons for your assessments.

1. *Background:* In a 1970 story about repression in the United States, American columnist John Roche stated:

> Every society is, of course, repressive to some extent—as Sigmund Freud pointed out, repression is the price we pay for civilization.[4]

2. *Background:* A social worker of our acquaintance reported the following argument to us, used by a caseworker in a review of a couple's qualifications to adopt a child:

> I found the husband extremely authoritarian. He made all the major decisions, and controlled all the spending in the family. I don't think that couple would make good adoptive parents.

---

[4] Cited in Kahane, *Logic and Contemporary Rhetoric* (Belmont, California: Wadsworth Publishing Company, 1971), p. 73.

3. *Background.* In 1971, the Ontario Government was reviewing its policy of restricting state aid to Roman Catholic separate schools, in the face of considerable pressure to extend that aid beyond Grade 10. The Toronto *Globe and Mail* editorialized (August 1971):

> . . . aid should not be extended to the Catholic secondary schools.
>
> The reasons for this stand are several. The first is that in Ontario, which has put behind it the Orange era of politico-religious wars, it would be a tragic backward step to re-introduce a system which divided children on the basis of religion, which balkanized them by sects during their most crucial years of adjusting to a free and non-discriminatory society. If we have forgotten how bitterly and irrationally religion can divide, we have only to look at Ireland . . .

4. *Background:* From another contribution to the abortion debate (Windsor *Star*, June 1975):

> Pro-abortion groups never refer to the true meaning of abortion. They use the phrase "termination of the pregnancy," they shy away from the term killing unborn babies. Perhaps the true meaning would not enhance their cause.

5. *Background:* The following is an excerpt from a letter to the Winnipeg *Free Press* (August 1974):

> Manitoba is no longer a freedom loving province. Not until such time as the New Democrats are ousted from power, will we, the freedom loving public, be able to breathe freely again and not have to worry that maybe tomorrow the government may step in and take away our free enterprise business and be dictators in the 1970s.

6. *Background:* In December of 1973, faced with mass resignations by high school teachers aiming to pressure school boards to negotiate favourable contracts, the Ontario government introduced a bill that would have outlawed such tactics during teachers' salary negotiations. (It was already illegal for Ontario teachers to strike) The teachers protested that their collective bargaining rights were being denied them, and some also argued along the following lines. This is an amalgam of several letters to editors across the province at the time:

> The government ought to withdraw the proposed legislation. The bill it has introduced takes away teachers' right to

resign. No government has the authority to force people to continue at a particular job if they wish to leave it. The bill interferes with a basic freedom of democracy: the right to choose your own job.

7. *Background:* In the fall of 1974, the Toronto *Globe and Mail* published a series of articles growing out of allegations by some citizens that Toronto police were guilty of brutality. One letter commented on these stories:

I am writing to express my deep regret at the publication of "Police Brutality" [the title of the series]. Sensational stories in your fine paper? Why have you turned to yellow journalism? You have done a great disservice not only to our superior police force but to the entire city.

8. *Background:* This is a letter to the Windsor *Star* (April 1976) concerning the petition by a group of francophones in the Windsor area for a French-language high school:

Regarding the petition which stated "the French were here first, so why can't they have their own high school?", well, the Indians were here first and they don't have their own anything. Since it took all nationalities to make Windsor what it is, I think all nationalities should have equal say in what Windsorites need, and not just what the French want.

You don't hear the French trying to speak English as readily as any other non-English, so that proves we don't need French high schools.[5]

[5] Our thanks to Mr. John Sleziak for bringing this example to our attention.

# 6 Fallacies of Prejudgement

## Introduction

**6.1** By "prejudgement" we mean not only making your mind up before the evidence is all in, but also having blinders on your thinking, so that it doesn't even occur to you that evidence might be needed or that a belief might be questionable. When prejudgement due to a limited point of view affects an argument, the fallacy is *provincialism*. When that restriction is due particularly to an unquestioning allegiance, the fallacy is *blind loyalty*. Finally, when prejudgement results in simply taking for granted a belief that may be challenged, the fallacy is *dubious assumption*.

## 1 Provincialism

**6.2** Here's one Canadian talking: "I am sick and tired of all the so-called Canadians who are saying the Russians are the greatest." (This was written during the 1972 Canada-Russia hockey series, after Canada had fallen behind.) Here's another Canadian, on a different subject: "Margaret Atwood, Margaret Lawrence—never heard of them, so they must be Canadian."

Look behind these statements to the *attitudes* of the two speakers. The first speaker is decidedly pro-Canadian, as if to say: "*How dare any Canadian even think that a Canadian hockey team could be* inferior to the Russians!" The second speaker has just the opposite attitude toward Canadian literature: *"How dare* any Canadian think that a Canadian writer could be good enough to be well known!" At the risk of generalizing, we distill from these two comments the following underlying attitudes: "If it's Canadian, it's got to be good" in one corner; and "If it's Canadian, it can't be any good" in the other.

The fallacies we are going to discuss in this and the next sections stem from a basic attitude with a number of more or less familiar manifestations, known variously under the labels of *racism, chauvinism, sexism, nationalism, colonialism,* and *ethnocentrism.* We propose to collect this host of attitudes under one roof and label the fallacy that results when any of them intrudes into an argument, **provincialism.** When understood in the sense of a "narrowness of view, thought, or interests" (Oxford Universal Dictionary), this label nicely captures the outlook behind the fallacy.

**6.3** A common denominator of many of these terms is that they suggest some form of *prejudice,* a concept worth having in mind as we proceed.[1] Like prejudice, the fallacy of *provincialism* is easier to spot when someone else is the guilty party. In late 1974, the federal government circulated a "Green Paper" on the subject of immigration into Canada. The Edmonton *Journal* condemned the proposed policy in an editorial (October 1974). In early November, G.S. responded:

**85**      As the *Journal* said on October 30, the new immigration law will be racist and discriminatory . . .
      *I am from India and am inclined to think that people from the Indian subcontinent have a very high percentage of well-educated, hard-working, sincere and well-mannered people—comparatively speaking—*and as immigrants, have tried to settle successfully by thrift and sobriety. (Emphasis ours.)

G.S. was arguing that the Green Paper's policy would have the result of limiting immigration to Canada from India, and that would be bad because Indians as a group have the traits highly desirable in immigrants. What we question is not the truth of G.S.'s claim, but the lack of any evidence to support this description.

There is some problem in deciding the sort of evidence that might lend credence to his claim: perhaps statistics comparing the educa-

---

[1] The etymology of "prejudice" is revealing. It derives from the Latin prefix "prae" which means "before" and the noun *"judicium"* meaning "judgement." Thus, the literal meaning is "before judgement"—i.e., an idea or belief arrived at prior to and without knowledge and examination of the facts.

tion of Indian immigrants with those from other lands; carefully compiled interviews with employers who had hired both Indian and other immigrants, asking about their respective industriousness and courtesy. But G.S. produced no such evidence. Instead, he said, "I am from India and am inclined to think . . ." That is, he seemed predisposed to think good things about his compatriots and to do so in advance of any evidence that might exist. A provincial attitude —a loyal identification with India—appears to have predetermined G.S.'s belief.

G.S. was guilty of *provincialism* not simply because his beliefs about people from India were unsupported, though that was a contributing factor. A second detail was also necessary: the most plausible explanation of why G.S. advanced his challengeable claim without any supporting evidence was his strong identification with his native land and consequent tendency to extol the virtues of its people.

**6.4** Here's another example, closer to home. A Little League official in Windsor, Ontario, wanted a cricket pitch removed from one of the city parks to make room for another baseball diamond. The press report of P.W.'s submission to a city parks and recreation services hearing (October 1975) read:

**86**     He said the cricket pitch is being used by people he doubts are Canadians, and who only play once a week while his league with a membership of 650 boys plays six days a week and could use more diamonds.
       Cricket is "an archaic sport . . . being thrust down the throats of residents in the area . . . It's just un-Canadian," he told the hearing.

The categorizing of cricket as "archaic" and "un-Canadian" is simply false, and so a *questionable classification*: the game is very much alive throughout the world and is widely played in Canada. Moreover, P.W. gave no evidence for these claims. It is fair to say that he wasn't very interested in evidence. From the point of view of someone who has a strong commitment to baseball, it may seem reasonable to believe that the game from which baseball spun off is obsolete. And from a particularly narrow point of view of what's "Canadian"—possibly one that excludes people with British or West Indian accents from doing anything "Canadian"—it may seem appropriate to call cricket un-Canadian. But these are restricted and parochial outlooks. P. W. committed *provincialism* in his attempt to persuade the parks commission to replace the cricket pitch with a baseball diamond.

We would be negligent not to include an example of *provincialism* arising from Canada's historic tension between francophones and anglophones.

In 1973, when the Queen was visiting Canada, Montreal *Le Devoir* editor Claude Ryan wrote an editorial giving his impression of the Quebec view of the monarchy. He said that the monarchy was a form of authority with which French Canadians "will never be reconciled," although most are willing to go along with it as the symbol of state authority for the present. In an editorial entitled, "A two-way tolerance," the Toronto *Globe and Mail* (August 1973) took issue with Ryan:

**87**  . . . he is definitely wrong in suggesting that Canada beyond Quebec should be asked by Quebeckers to relinquish . . . the monarchy.

English-speaking Canadians have not asked French-speaking Canadians to relinquish their visceral attachment to the French language and culture. Many of them have made valiant and successful efforts to become bilingual themselves. They have recognized that French-speaking Canadians should have their due place in the civil service, that business should recognize French across the country. They have contributed hundreds of millions to the extension of the French language and culture beyond Quebec, so that Quebeckers may feel at home in all of Canada.

The *Globe and Mail* editorialist's thinking seemed to be, "They're asking us anglophones to give up the monarchy! That would be equivalent to our asking them to give up their attachment to French language and culture. Not only have we not done that, we have worked very hard to respect and increase the status of French culture in Canada: witness 1 . . . 2 . . . 3 . . ."

Unlike the two examples of *provincialism* discussed previously, the writer in this editorial produces evidence to support the premises. A belief can be unreasonable even when accompanied by evidence, if the evidence is unduly *selective*. If only favourable evidence is selected from the total body of available data, and the selectivity stems from a provincial identification, *provincialism* has occurred.

In the *Globe and Mail* editorial the belief that must be assessed is that English-speaking Canada has done its part to promote Canada's bilingual and bicultural identity. The editorialist mentioned four pieces of evidence supporting this claim; however, in every case only part of the picture is presented. Let's examine each in turn.

1. "Many English speaking Canadians have made an effort to become bilingual." What percentage of Canadians would this group account for? How many more have made no effort at all to become bilingual?

2. "They have recognized that French-speaking Canadians should have their due place in the civil service." How do French-speaking Canadians fare in terms of career progress in the civil service? What has "their due place" turned out to be in practice? A professor of French at the University of Windsor recently stated, "When I go to talk about my taxes, sure they can usually find someone to speak French. But usually it is the janitor".[2]

3. "They have recognized that business should recognize French across the country." Can a francophone conduct business in French in Toronto? Vancouver? Calgary? Halifax?

4. "They have contributed hundreds of millions to the extension of French language and culture beyond Quebec." In what ways specifically was that money spent, and over how long a period of time? How receptive is the anglophone community in Canada to French plays and literature? How many read a French newspaper with any regularity, or make even a moderate attempt to learn about the culture and history of Quebec?

There exists, then, contrary evidence (and sometimes more than just the trickle we have hinted at) to each of the four points selected by the editorialist to advance the claim that English-speaking Canada has been active in promoting bilingualism and biculturalism. The editorial selected from the total body of evidence those portions that are favourable to its claim. A case for *hasty conclusion* is in order here, but that would fail to call attention to one very important component in the fallacy: the editorial's strong identification with English-speaking Canada and desire to have it appear in the best possible light. When *hasty conclusion* stems from a provincial attitude, the proper charge is *provincialism*.

**6.5** We can now present the defining conditions for this fallacy:

---

**PROVINCIALISM**

1. In the defense of some conclusion, M employs as a premise an unreasonable belief, Q; and
   (a) M's belief that Q is true is unreasonable because the belief has been formulated prior to and without the benefit of the total body of evidence; or

---

[2] Bill McGraw, "The Struggle to keep the Fleur-de-Lis blooming in the City of Roses," (*Detroit*, June 1, 1975), p. 11.

> (b) M's belief that Q is true is unreasonable because
>     the evidence presented by M for Q is selective.
> 2. The most plausible explanation for M's holding Q is
>    M's identification with some socio-cultural group to
>    which M belongs (e.g., country, culture, race, sex).

Arguments with such premises are fallacious because they fail to meet the requirement that beliefs submitted for public inspection and debate be reasonable (cf. 1.4). Provincial arguments propound beliefs as true that are often little more than an expression of a visceral attachment to one's country, culture, race, special interest, or sex. In some cases, it is difficult if not impossible to cite evidence which could conceivably count in their favour; for example, "My country is better than your country." In other cases, the beliefs may have evidence ("The people of my country are better educated than those in your country"), but the provincial eschew the difficult step of digging out and providing that evidence.

**6.6** A noteworthy factor disposing people to commit and be taken in by *provincialism* is the habit of thinking in **stereotypes**: Germans are industrious; North American Indians are lazy; Scots are stingy; the English are aloof; Newfoundlanders are simpletons. There are several ideas behind the concept of a stereotype. It's an attribute that is based on a surface or warped impression falsely taken to describe the "essence" of a group. Accepted uncritically, the stereotype systematically distorts one's perceptions of people classified as belonging to the group—an arbitrary classification itself. Once they take hold of the mind, they become self-reinforcing and confirming. The examples that fit the stereotype are rated as evidence. Those that do not fit the stereotype are dismissed as exceptions. The result will be unreasonable beliefs.

**6.7** Canada seems to be a mélange of attitudes about itself and "things Canadian." This fact brings us back to the opposite attitudes with which we began the section. On the one hand, Canadians are as capable as anyone else of nationalistic pride and sentiment. Witness the remark of Robert McCleave (MP for Halifax–East Hants) during a debate in Parliament over the CBC policy of withholding some of its TV programs from Canadian border cities in the hope of later selling them to American networks. McCleave was arguing that the U.S. networks needn't fear that Americans would have already watched the programs on neighbouring Canadian channels:

**88**    If we examine the statistics regarding viewer preference of

television stations, *the Americans, being much more parochial than Canadians and much more nationalistic-minded,*
probably will not be seduced over to a Canadian station in
any event. (Emphasis ours.)

Canadians, Mr. McCleave smugly implied, are above the parochial
and nationalistic feelings so characteristic of Americans. A beautiful
example of a provincial denial of *provincialism!*

On the other hand, Canadians are proficient at self-denigration,
which surfaces most often when comparisons are made with the
U.S. or Britain. Here, from an example we've used before, is a
comment made as part of an argument about Canadian magazine
publishing. N.H. wrote in the Edmonton *Journal:*

**89**    As usual, Canadians, who are incompetent, inefficient, lazy,
miserable, and jealous, cannot compete with the U.S.A. in
anything—be it sports, food production, manufacturing,
films, popular songs and singers, TV writing, publishing, or
just plain work. Consequently, they always want U.S. products and performers banned so they can produce the
usually poor product.

There are many examples of this sort of colonial attitude in Canada.
Numerous artists, musicians, and writers have had to achieve recognition elsewhere (usually in the U.S., Great Britain, or France) before
Canadian critics could find much to get excited about in their work.
We're not gainsaying the necessity of submitting artistic works to a
wide range of critical response, both within and without the country;
to go by local standards only is provincial. Yet to count exclusively
on the judgement of American and British critics is colonialism.
Times may be changing, but in Canada we still need to stand on
guard against colonialism.

# 2 Blind Loyalty

**6.8** It is natural to rush to the defense of something or someone you
love or value or identify with. Loyalty is a fine virtue. Unfortunately,
it can interfere with reasonable appraisal of criticism, blinding you
to fair and accurate challenges to what you cherish. Loyalty is not
necessarily a provincial attitude, but it becomes one when it
prevents you from even considering the evidence produced in an

attack on something you hold dear. When you respond to criticism of an object of your loyalty, either by discounting in advance the possibility of evidence for the critique, or else by refusing to acknowledge documentation that is plainly evident, you commit the variant of *provincialism* we call **blind loyalty**.

A classic example of this fallacy occurred during a controversy a few years ago surrounding an institution that's almost a litmus test of Canadian loyalty, the RCMP. In its July 1972 issue, *Maclean's* featured an article by ex-RCMP Corporal Jack Ramsay attacking the force for low morale, excessive image-burnishing, and rigid authoritarianism. Ramsay cited a fair amount of evidence for the conclusion that these faults were present in at least some parts of the force, and claimed that his examples were typical. In the September issue, *Maclean's* carried a letter from H.M., attacking Ramsay's allegations:

**90**   I am writing to tell you to cancel my subscription. I have never been so angry with an article. Ex-Corporal Ramsay's confessions are a disgrace to your magazine and I don't want another of your magazines in my house.

Our son has been with the RCMP for 25 years and we are proud of him. You really enjoyed yourselves trying to sabotage another Canadian tradition.

This writer did not reject Ramsay's charges on the ground that his evidence was mistaken or incomplete, as another writer did in that same issue, nor on the ground that his evidence was not typical of the situation in the RCMP, as did still another letter writer. The basis for H.M.'s rejection seems to have been simply that she was proud of her son who had been a Mountie for 25 years, and that the RCMP is an honoured part of Canadian tradition. Her blind, i.e. unquestioning, loyalty to her son and the RCMP interfered with an objective and impartial examination of Ramsay's evidence.[3]

H.M. committed *blind loyalty* by refusing to consider evidence that was literally staring her in the face: after all, she did read the article containing Ramsay's allegations. In the next example the fallacy is committed in a slightly different way, namely by ruling out in advance the very possibility of any warrant for the criticism. We go south of the border and back in time to the Watergate scandal. In July 1973, David and Julie Eisenhower—son-in-law and daughter of then-President Nixon—appeared on a late-night TV talk

[3] By the way, for a more sober assessment of the RCMP than you probably received in school, we recommend Lorne and Caroline Brown, *An Unauthorized History of the RCMP* (Toronto: James Lewis & Samuel, 1973), and Walter Stewart, *But Not in Canada!* (Toronto: Macmillan, 1976), Ch. 9, "Our Cops are Cops."

show. The U.S. Senate's Watergate hearings were taking place and conversation turned to them. Asked whom he thought the most important witnesses were, David Eisenhower replied:

**91**     The most important witnesses are the people who know most about it. The importance or non-importance of the witnesses is irrelevant if you believe as Julie and I believe that the president was not involved. They're all important, but the question is, can they be believed?

It's not hard to understand what had happened here. Naturally loyal to President Nixon, David and Julie Eisenhower had made up their minds *in advance of the evidence* (which special prosecutor Archibald Cox and the Senate Committee had only *begun* to accumulate) that Nixon was not involved. Nixon probably told them himself that he was not involved. Blindly loyal to the President, Julie and David were not prepared to accept the possibility of evidence indicating his involvement. This is the fallacy of *blind loyalty*.

**6.9** As we are treating it, *blind loyalty* is a version of *provincialism* that you should look out for, especially when deeply-rooted identifications are attacked: country, ethnic group, culture, family, for example. These conditions describe it:

---

**BLIND LOYALTY**

1. M rejects N's criticism of something M identifies with.
2. M's response is unreasonable because M either
   (a) refuses to credit the force of the available evidence, or
   (b) denies the possibility of evidence for N's criticism.
3. M's loyalty to the object of N's attack is the most plausible explanation of M's unreasonable response.

---

Notice that *blind loyalty* is by definition a fallacy of adversary contexts. We define it that way because typically the sorts of unreason itemized in Condition 2 occur in the rush to defend a valued object against attack. When they occur without provocation, even without the anticipation of criticism, the fallacy still falls under the broader umbrella of *provincialism*.

A final example of *blind loyalty* exhibits a typical blend of complacency tinged with a hint of racism. In August 1973, the Windsor *Star* ran an article about a local human rights officer and the evidence of racial discrimination (examples were given) she encountered daily through her work. That letter brought the following response from E.T.:

**92**     I have had much scope in knowing many, many white skinned people and never have I known one in Canada who felt superior to another because of skin color.

Often I have made a special effort to be friendly and kind to colored skinned people, and usually to find that they think it is condescension because many have an overwhelming inferiority complex which is revealed as a tremendous superiority complex, apparent disapproval and arrogance.

It is difficult for me to believe that any decent white skinned Canadian actually feels as this official indicates. All of us are judged in the working world according to character, ability, and potential and that goes for both colored and white skinned people . . .

I can't help resenting people preaching at white people against racial dislike when they know it is almost non-existent in Canada. If they don't know, they are out of touch with "reality" or distorting actual facts.

E.G. refuses to give any credence to the human-rights officer's evidence, and suggests that she may be out of touch with reality or else actually misrepresenting the facts. Yet it's that officer's job day in and day out to investigate complaints of racial discrimination! And why does E.T. insist that racism is "almost non-existent in Canada"—that the officer's examples cannot be representative of the attitudes of a significant (though not necessarily large) number of Canadians? Here we cannot be certain, since we must base our conclusion solely on E.T.'s letter. But the third paragraph of that letter evokes a rather smug image that many white Canadians have of themselves: "Racism is an American attitude; Canadians aren't racist". In our opinion, E.T.'s loyalty to that Canadian myth explains her response to the human rights officer's reports.[4]

**6.10** A factor deserving special mention as a cause of *blind loyalty* is friendship. Surely part of friendship is standing behind your friends when they are under criticism, lending them moral support.

The mistake people make is believing they must automatically take a friend's side in any dispute he or she gets involved in. What can happen is this: You accept your friend's description of the

---

[4] If you're not convinced that this *is* a myth, may we recommend again as a salutary purgative, Walter Stewart, *But Not in Canada!* Ch. 12, "We Love Our Niggers."

issues in the dispute and you see only his or her evidence that they are in the right and that the other party is wrong. Even if you get the other side's story, your sympathy and loyalty to your friend determine what sort of acceptance or non-acceptance you give to it. By getting involved in the controversy, you adopt your friend's orientation towards the situation, in terms of which you then filter and interpret the evidence. You give up your freedom to examine the issue reasonably, with an open mind.

A friendship that cannot brook criticism or tolerate disagreement is on shaky ground. True friendship requires the capacity to say, "Look, I'm your friend, but I think you're wrong this time."

# 3 Dubious Assumption

**6.11** To introduce this fallacy, let us explain what we mean by an **assumption.** The term can mean either something that's not proven and open to question, as in, "Wait a minute, you're making a big assumption when you say that . . ." or it can be used to refer simply to something taken for granted by or underlying an assertion or position, questionable or not, as in, "The assumptions of our policy are the following . . ." We are using it in the latter sense.

Clear examples of assumptions in our sense are provided by "double-bind" questions. Someone asks you, "Have you stopped doing dope?" or "Are you buying term papers again?" How do you answer if you've never done dope or never bought a term paper? If you say simply "Yes" or "No," you are ratifying the *assumptions* of the questions—that at one point you did dope, or that you used to buy term papers.

The following will serve as a rough definition of an assumption:

> A sentence or position, Q, depends upon an assumption, R, if the truth of R is a necessary condition of the *truth*, or *intelligibility*, or *appropriateness*, of Q.

In the double-bind questions, the *appropriateness* of the questions depended on the assumptions we indicated.

Our use of the word "assumption" rules out calling *problematic premises* assumptions, although it's tempting to do so, as the following example shows. G.T. wrote to the Ottawa *Journal* (November 1974), urging a reappraisal of our foreign aid program:

**93**   Canadians are continually being urged to give money to feed starving children in India. While it is distressing to think of their suffering, it has to be remembered that *as much as three-quarters of all aid sent goes into the pockets of corrupt politicians and black marketeers.* (Emphasis ours.)

You might want to respond, "G. T. doesn't prove that charge, and it's quite an assumption to make." But the assertion we put in italics does not stand behind any other claim he makes; it's an allegation that stands by itself. You would be right in saying that it is quite a remarkable charge to make and that it ought to have been defended. However, the correct identification of this weakness in G.T.'s argument, following our nomenclature, is *problematic premise*.

Our interest in assumptions stems from and focuses on their role in arguments. We shall be looking at how the premises of arguments can be freighted with questionable assumptions. In this connection, we find it helpful and natural to include *missing premises* as a species of assumption. Recall from the discussion in 3.7 how missing premises work. This argument:

**94**    Ellen is so irresponsible with money. Why, she spent her first month's salary from her new job on a dishwasher, of all things!

employs some such missing premise as this:

**95**    Anyone who buys a dishwasher before anything else is irresponsible with money.

The missing premise is an unstated link, needed to get from the stated premise to the conclusion, that is taken for granted. It is necessary for the *intelligibility* of the argument. As such, it may be called an assumption.

In summary, then, we'll be judging the reasonableness of (a) the assumptions underlying stated premises, or of (b) missing premises, when we watch for **dubious assumption.**

Here are the conditions of the fallacy:

---

**DUBIOUS ASSUMPTION**

1. M employs an assumption, Q, in an argument—either a proposition underlying a stated premise, or a missing premise.
2. Q is debatable or false.

---

**6.12** We can now review some examples. For the first one, we return to the exchange between *Le Devoir* editor Claude Ryan and the Toronto *Globe and Mail* over Quebec's view of the monarchy where we found an instance of *provincialism* in 6.4 (Example 87). The editorial said of Ryan's position:

96　　　. . . he is definitely wrong in suggesting that Canada beyond Quebec should be asked by Quebeckers to relinquish the monarchy.

　　　English-speaking Canadians have not asked French-speaking Canadians to relinquish their visceral attachment to the French language and culture . . . it must be a two-way street. If Quebec's most basic desires are to be honored and supported, even when not shared, then Quebec must honor and support some similar desires in the rest of Canada.

If we standardize the argument in this portion of the editorial, we get:

97　　　**P1:** Just as Quebec's most basic desires are to be honored and supported, similar desires in the rest of Canada are to be honored and supported.

　　　**P2:** English-speaking Canadians have not asked French-speaking Canadians to give up their language and culture.

　　　**C:** French-speaking Canadians should not ask English-speaking Canadians to give up the monarchy.

Grant **P1** and **P2** just for the sake of argument, and look at those two premises alone. Don't look at the conclusion. By themselves they in no way force that conclusion. There must be an unexpressed premise in the *Globe and Mail's* reasoning connecting the point made about basic desires in **P1**, the assertion about French-Canadian language and culture in **P2**, and the English-Canadian attachment to the monarchy mentioned in **C**: some such missing premise as the following:

98
**MP**　　**P3:** The English-speaking Canadian desire to retain the monarchy is as basic to them as the French-speaking Canadian desire to retain their language and culture.

In other words, the editorial's argument makes the assumption that asking francophones to abandon their language and culture is analogous to asking anglophones to part with the monarchy. But this assumption has gaping holes in it. Relinquishing the monarchy would certainly effect changes in the self-conception of many English-speaking Canadians: it would alter the way they see themselves in relation to their cultural roots and historical traditions. However, the language and culture of Quebec are not just a part of the French-speaking Canadian self-image; they are the whole sum and substance of *being* French-Canadian. Their abandonment would constitute cultural suicide. The *Globe and Mail* argument makes an assumption that is clearly *dubious*; in fact, it is a *faulty analogy*.

Here is another example. During the time of the U.S. Senate's Watergate hearings, John J. Wilson, a lawyer for a White House staff member, was heard to refer to the committee member from Hawaii, Sen. Daniel Inouye, as "that little Jap." This remark created a furor when it was widely reported in the media. Attempting to defend himself, Wilson wondered aloud what all the hoopla was about, saying:

**99**   I wouldn't mind being called a little American.

K.S. wrote to the Detroit *Free Press* and neatly exposed Wilson's *dubious assumption*:

**100**   What is Sen. Inouye but an American? It is quite apparent that Mr. Wilson still believes that American is spelled "W-A-S-P."

The following letter to the editor of the Halifax *Chronicle-Herald* (August 1974) contains several fallacies, but can you spot the *dubious assumption* in it?

**101**   I am surprised that English Canada seems so undisturbed about Premier Bourassa's Bill 22, making French the official language in Quebec after the federal government's spending millions of our tax money promoting bilingualism for the benefit of Quebec. Unless Prime Minister Trudeau declares Bill 22 null and void, of which I have grave doubts as about half his support is from Quebec, then the other nine provinces should make the English language the only official language. Bill 22 is also another step toward separation. Since 30% of Quebec has already voted for separation, it may come sooner than most believe.

This argument is tricky for two reasons. First, it contains a number of cases of *problematic premise* which it's tempting to identify as *dubious assumptions*. Second, you need some knowledge of recent

Quebec politics to spot the real culprit. You need to know that the statement, "30% of Quebec has already voted for separation," refers to the fact that the separatist *Parti Québécois* received 30% of the popular vote in Quebec in the 1973 provincial election there.

All that's recorded in the ballot count is how many people voted for each party, so all that is *known* is that 30% of the Quebec popular vote went to the *PQ*. Yet the writer asserts that 30% of Quebec voted for separation. He or she has a basis for the latter claim *only if* a vote for the *PQ* is automatically a vote for separation. In short, the writer is *assuming* that everyone who voted *PQ* favoured separatism.

However, a vote for a particular party is not necessarily an endorsement of all of its policies—and may not even signify approval of *any* of them, for you may prefer one party *on balance* over the others, considering the candidates running and the mix of policies. Also, a vote for one party may be a protest vote *against* another.

Both of these factors were said by observers to have been at work in the heavy *PQ* vote in Quebec. As well as being separatist, the *PQ* was the only democratic-socialist party available to Quebec voters in that election: the NDP ran no slate provincially. Voters with that preference had no other party to turn to. Also, the *PQ* had promised to make secession a question for a referendum, so a *PQ* vote was one step short of a vote for separation. Finally, observers believed no one thought the *PQ* had a chance of forming the government, so many voted for it as a way of lodging a protest against the ruling Liberal regime, without taking any risk of putting separatists in power. The letter-writer's ignorance of the political scene led to a *dubious assumption.*

**6.13** Frequently, questionable assumptions are built right into the stated premises of arguments. A premise can be a composite of two or more propositions. The charge of *dubious assumption* can be made more perspicuously if you are able to separate the claims. For that reason we need to introduce the following technique.

---

**DIVIDING COMPOUND PROPOSITIONS**   *Working from an example will best illustrate this technique. Here is a letter from the St. John's Evening Telegram (October 1974) on the subject of the increase of vandalism in the Newfoundland capital:*

**102**   The real problem was pointed out recently by assistant police chief Brown in the talk to the St. John's Kiwanis Club. He pointed out that the main cause of all this vandalism in the past 20 years is permissiveness in the families and in the schools.

*The assertion attributed to Brown is really a compound proposition because two propositions are wrapped up in one:*

>   Q: The vandalism of the past 20 years has a main cause.
>   R: That main cause of the vandalism of the past 20 years
>      is permissiveness in the families and in the schools.

*When these propositions are separated, it becomes clear that Mr. Brown was assuming that there is such a thing as a main cause of the vandalism. For R is meaningful only if Q is true. We think that Q lays the argument open to a charge of questionable cause, and if we are right, that certainly makes Q a dubious assumption.*

*The technique of dividing compound propositions is put to work to expose the dubious assumption in this next example. In the fall of 1974, the* Globe and Mail *published investigative reports on police brutality in Toronto. A reader responded:*

**103**    I am writing to express my deep regret at the publication of "Police Brutality." Sensational stories in your fine paper? Why have you turned to yellow journalism? You have done a great disservice not only to our superior police force, but to the entire city.

*The question, "Why have you turned to yellow journalism?" can and should be broken down as follows:*

>   Q: You have turned to yellow journalism.
>   R: Why have you done so?

*If the* Globe and Mail *articles had consisted of yellow journalism— which is irresponsibly sensational journalism—they would indeed have done the city and the police a disservice. But the assumption, Q, built into the double-bind question was moot at the time. Allegations had been made, but not authoritatively checked out. (Subsequently a provincial inquiry, initiated partly in response to the newspaper stories, confirmed the charges of police brutality.) Unpacking the question permits ready identification of the dubious assumption.*

---

The following excerpt comes from a letter objecting to school teachers' militant demands for higher salaries:

**104**    There's definitely a lack of commitment to education on the part of many people in our schools today. We seem to have lost the old crusading spirit which distinguished the profession years ago.

Can you identify the compound proposition that masks an assumption? As we see it, the second sentence is a compound proposition with the following ingredients:

Q: Years ago the teaching profession was distinguished by a crusading spirit.
R: The teaching profession has lost that crusading spirit which distinguished it years ago.

R assumes Q, but is Q acceptable? We find it hard to accept because we're not sure what it means. The term "crusading spirit" is pretty vague in this context. Does Q imply that years ago teachers were willing to work for incredibly exploitative salaries without thinking of going on strike? Or does it mean that teachers were more dedicated to the aims of education than they are at present? Our verdict is *dubious assumption* because of the *vagueness* of Q.

---

## Exercises for Chapter 6

*Directions:* Determine which fallacies occur in the following passages. As before, some may contain no argument, others may contain no fallacy, some fallacies from earlier chapters may occur here too, and some hitherto unclassified fallacies may be present. In each case, defend your verdict.

1. *Background:* The following is a UPI wire service story, titled "Women blamed," from Montes Claro, Brazil (August 1974):

> Saying that "in today's world it is the women and not the men who are doing all the seducing," Judge Emerson Pereia . . . acquitted Analindo da Silva of charges of seducing a minor, an 18-year-old girl.
> "Reality shows us that the real seducers are the daughters of Eve who sashay their way through God's world with their miniskirts, low-cut and see-through blouses and tight-tight pants, for the sole purpose of exhibiting their curvaceous

bodies to attract the attention and eyes of men," the judge's verdict read.

2. *Background:* In a letter to the Windsor *Star* (May 1975), P.B. was criticizing a column in which the publisher had argued against capital punishment:

> What Mr. O'Callaghan objects to is the state supervising this quasi-ceremonial execution of murderers. Yet when we state that "Canada cannot perpetrate murder," we are ego- tistically assuming that our society is perfect and that no crime which warrants death will ever be committed.

Has P.B. correctly identified a case of *dubious assumption* or not?

3. *Background:* From the *Temperance Education Journal:*

> Girls should never touch alcoholic liquors. The reasons are obvious. It is for them to steady the young men, and so maintain their dignity, their beauty, and their intelligence.

4. *Background:* Here's a passage from a Canadian history textbook which, while not an argument, is nevertheless per- suasive and needs scrutiny.

> A good number of the *coureurs-de-bois* married Indian women and abandoned all trace of civilization; some even lowered themselves to the level of savages and became as ferocious as the Redskins when they took to torturing or killing enemy captives.

5. *Background:* In his book, *My Lai 4: A Report on the Massacre and its Aftermath*, Seymour Hersh recounted some of the reactions of some Americans to the reports of the massacre in which U.S. troops killed over a hundred civilians. We para- phrase:

> Someone wrote to the Cleveland *Plain Dealer*, which had printed photos of the massacre:
> "I can't believe our boys' hearts are that bad. Your paper is rotten and anti-American."

6. *Background:* Charles Lynch, head of Southam News Ser- vices, wrote a column several years ago entitled, "Why Can- adians fought Hitler." In it he stated:

> The idea that Canada went to war because of Nazi atrocities against Jews is a widely accepted rationale, but the fact is that the main cause of the Second World War was German

expansionism, and the desire of other nations, principally Britain and France, to contain it.

The German invasion of Poland was the last straw, and Britain and France declared war. Canada followed a step behind, and made a mighty contribution in manpower and munitions over the next five years, as she had during the Great War of 1914-18. But for Canada, as one reader points out, the war could have dragged on many more years, or even have been lost. Today's youngsters might be marching to a Nazi drumbeat, instead of "contemplating life and its meaning through the euphoria of pot and the cacophony of over-amplified guitars."

7. *Background:* Here is part of a response to the letter by G.S. (see Example 85) on Canada's immigration policy:

Canada has never claimed to be a strictly white nation. Nor have we ever had, by comparison, a very restrictive immigration policy. We have always taken in unfortunate groups—Jews, Doukhobors, and black people from the U.S. before and during the Civil War.

The writer says most of our criminals are white—a reasonable assumption in proportion to the population. But statistics have it that a very large percentage of jail inmates are Indians. If they are not criminals, why are they in prison?

8. *Background:* An excerpt from an editorial in the Windsor *Star* (October 1972), which ran shortly after a newspaper report of a decline of sexual crime in Denmark following upon that country's legalization of pornography:

Latest crime statistics from Denmark provide a striking illustration of the beneficial effects of that nation's experiment in pornography, and will provide a powerful argument for those favouring the legalization and open availability of pornography here in Canada.

9. *Background:* from the same editorial mentioned above:

Whatever weight attaches to the moral or good-taste arguments against pornography, it seems doubtful that they will prevail, in the long run, over the increasingly liberal attitudes in modern society, particularly when the liberal position is buttressed by proof that legalized pornography leads to a decline of sexual crimes.

10. *Background:* The following is an excerpt from an article

by Ms. Jill Johnston, a feminist who is a strong and open advocate of lesbianism:

> You have to go to bed with me because you oppress me by sleeping with the enemy, meaning the man . . . most all women are socialized out of their feelings for other women . . . if the feminists won't join our marches, they can't keep us away from theirs. And when the lesbians take over it'll become a celebration.

11. *Background:* A letter to the Edmonton *Journal* in December 1974 referred to a negative attitude on the part of teachers in Alberta. A teacher responded:

> Far from being "holier than thou," I have found the majority of Alberta teachers to be open and dedicated. This dedication is measured in several ways.
> 1. A teacher in Edmonton with a four-year university degree and four years' experience is now making $11,900, whereas a construction laborer in Edmonton with no training and four years' experience earns an average $13,620 (based on UIC statistics).
> [Three other instances of teacher dedication were cited.]
> Surely these are signs of dedication. Or possibly lunacy . . .
> Perhaps if the public will support an increase in teacher salaries . . . I will rip up the resignation papers I have already filled out and education will not lose another good teacher.

12. *Background:* On the topic of Canada's immigration policy, an excerpt from a Windsor *Star* editorial of February 1975, entitled "Facing the Issue":

> Let's hope that Immigration Minister Robert Andras gets a resounding answer to his question about the immigration issue "that's there and that won't go away by itself"—the issue of race . . .
> Bringing the question into the open, as Mr. Andras did, was exactly the right course. Bigots speak slyly, quietly, in secret. When challenged to speak up in public, and perhaps challenged by their own consciences, they are not so free with their bigotry. Now challenged by Mr. Andras, the other side has a chance to speak up. The message, again, should be clear—Canada isn't a racist country. Canadians don't want racist immigration bars.

# 7 Fallacies of Intimidation

## Introduction

**7.1** The three fallacies we take up in this chapter are called "fallacies of intimidation" because they work by attempting to put pressure on us to accept a conclusion. **Improper appeal to authority**, for example, attempts to pressure us by appealing to our sense of respect for those more knowledgeable than we are. The fallacy of **popularity** caters to our tendencies to be steamrollered by public opinion and groupthink. The fallacy of **slippery slope** is an attempt to stampede us into the premature acceptance of a conclusion by making dire projections about the future.

## 1 Improper Appeal to Authority

**7.2** Originally, at least, many of the beliefs we adopt are based on the authority of others. From our earliest days as children, our thoughts are influenced and fashioned by the opinions of parents, teachers, and others who know more than we do. Ideally, as we mature we become less and less dependent on others for our beliefs and become independent investigators and evaluators. And to the degree that we become rational believers, we realize that our beliefs ought to be based where possible on a direct and personal examination of all relevant evidence. In practice, most of us fall far short of this ideal—something the famous psychologist and philosopher William James noted when he said, "As a matter of fact, we find ourselves believing, we hardly know how or why."[1]

Although the best strategy for forming opinions is thorough review of the evidence and a clear head, very few have the time or the intellectual resources to implement this strategy in anything more than isolated cases. What are we then to do? Suspend judgement on the subject? There are times when this is clearly the best course to pursue. But at other times we must adopt some belief or other, without having the opportunity to review all the evidence. In such a situation it is certainly reasonable to rely on the opinions of those who have reviewed the evidence, who know what they are talking about, who, in short, are **authorities** on the subject in question. When we cite experts to establish a point in an argument, we are making an **appeal to authority.** In this section we provide some rules of thumb for distinguishing between proper and improper appeals to authority.

**7.3** The mere mention of the word "authority" is enough to raise the hair on some people's necks. So let's be clear at the outset what we mean here by an "authority." We do not mean a person who is in a *position* of authority (priest, politician, teacher, boss) and who is therefore able to command others to act in certain ways, or to do certain things. We mean someone whose recognized knowledge about a subject makes her or his assertions *reliable*, more likely to be true than false. More about this in the next subsection.

Another misconception worth heading off is that any reference to the views of a knowledgeable person is necessarily an appeal to authority. That isn't so. Just above we quoted William James. But we weren't appealing to him as an authority. We weren't saying. "Believe this, because James—a famous philosopher and psychologist—said it." Our proposition was: "James has succinctly stated a point which we think you'll see on reflection is true." We quoted him because we liked his compact formulation of this basic truth. Standard practice calls for us to give credit for that statement to James himself. The mere mention of the views of an authority, then, does not necessarily constitute an appeal to authority. An appeal to authority only occurs when the purpose of such mention is to persuade you that the statement is true, or likely to be true, because an authority holds it to be such.

**7.4** With these preliminaries concluded, we can move on to the

---

[1] William James, *The Will to Believe* (New York: Dover Publications, 1956), p. 9.

important questions: What makes someone an authority? Under what conditions is an appeal to authority legitimate?

Basically, a person becomes an authority when her or his contributions to a particular field of learning gain widespread respect and recognition. A common mistake is to think that being an authority simply means knowing a lot about a subject. This is a necessary, though not a sufficient, condition.[2]

Two other conditions must be met. First, one's scholarship and research must be submitted to the appropriate community of inquirers for appraisal. Generally, this means publishing one's results in the appropriate vehicles. To get an article published in a scientific journal, for example, it must first be judged and found acceptable by a board of referees who must agree that the article merits publication. So this step toward becoming an authority involves some judgement of the value of one's thoughts. The second additional condition, dependent on publication, is that one's peers must find that work to be of significant value. What made Einstein an authority on theoretical physics was not just the amount of knowledge he had, but the reaction to and the assessment of that knowledge by his peers. Ultimately, then, authority is conferred on an individual by the collective judgement of her or his colleagues.[3]

Our resumé highlights the crucial concept in the notion of authority: *knowledge*. Knowledge and authority go together. In effect, this combination means that appeals to authority should be restricted to those disciplines or intellectual endeavours that can be characterized as pursuing and arriving at knowledge and truth. Such subjects as physics, chemistry, and history would qualify. What they all have in common is that the knowledge-claims made within them are subject to testing and validation. There are agreed-upon criteria of truth and falsity. Moreover, the personal preferences of the investigator are not relevant to statements in the domain of knowledge. Findings are confined by the world that is inexorably out there—for the investigator and for others.

In some disciplines the notions of knowledge, truth, and fact either have no clear application at all or have a drastically qualified or limited one. In philosophy, religion, and art, reasonable and competent specialists differ on fundamental questions and there may be

---

[2] Recall the discussion of necessary and sufficient conditions in our treatment of *questionable cause*, 4.20.

[3] If you find this account too brief, we recommend the following two books: Michael Polanyi, *Science, Faith, and Society* (Chicago: University of Chicago Press, 1964), and John M. Ziman, *Public Knowledge* (Cambridge: Cambridge University Press, 1968). Polanyi states: "Authority is not equally distributed among scientists. There is a hierarchy of influence; but exceptional authority is attached not so much to offices as to persons. A scientist is granted exceptional influence by the fact that his opinion is valued and asked for" (p. 48).

no way to adjudicate such fundamental disputes. The reason for such disputes is itself a controversial matter, but among the often-mentioned factors accounting for it are these: the absence of agreed-on methodology, a certain latitude for personal interpretation and preference, and a subject matter whose range and nature are them-selves somewhat dependent on the judgement of the individual thinker. In such areas, then, no appeal to authority can be legitimate.

We must add one more important qualification. Although appeals to authority are restricted to fields of public truth and knowledge, that does not mean everything a *bona fide* authority says about such a field is true. Authorities are not necessarily right all the time, and appealing to an authority does not presuppose that the authority is infallible. In fact, then, the correct schematic form of appeals to authority is *not*, "Q is *true*, because M (an authority) says so," but rather, "There is *good reason* to believe that Q is true, because M (an authority) says so."

**7.5** When is it permissible to appeal to someone as an authority? To answer this question, we are going to present five rules which specify the conditions of proper appeals to authority. If any one of these rules is violated, the fallacy of **improper appeal to authority** is committed.

> **Rule I:** If an authority is appealed to in support of a statement, Q, then Q must belong to some specifiable set of statements, S, which constitutes a domain of knowl-edge.

The force of this rule is to limit appeals to authority to those areas in which knowledge is achievable, in line with our analysis in 7.4. Consider some hypothetical cases. Suppose, for example, Q to be the statement: "Many chemical additives in food are more harmful than helpful to human health." In this case, Q belongs to S, the set of statements about the value of chemical additives, itself a subset of the science of nutrition. Such a statement could be the subject of an appeal to authority, therefore. Another example: suppose Q is: "Van Gogh painted *The Starry Night* at St. Rémy in 1889." Here Q belongs to S, the set of statements about Van Gogh, itself a subset of art history—which is a field of knowledge. Hence, it could be supported by an appeal to authority. Now suppose Q is this statement: "Van Gogh's *The Starry Night* is the finest painting ever done." What sort of statement is this? It is an aesthetic judgement, one which pre-sumes to rank the finest works of art. Such a statement may be defensible in that one might show what one admired in Van Gogh's painting, and explain why one preferred it to other great paintings. However, the attempt to get others to accept one's judgement by appealing to an authority betrays a misunderstanding about this sort of aesthetic statement. There are no recognized standards of truth here; at best, one can explain the basis for one's personal preferences. Hence, this kind of aesthetic judgement does not fall within the confines of any domain of knowledge. The force of *Rule I*, then, is to limit appeals to authority to the sorts of statement which can or do fall within some established domain of knowledge.

Let's put the rule to work on a real-life example, from a letter to the Windsor *Star* (February 1976) by R.H.:

**105**    The item in the *Star* noting the defection of General Electric engineers from the atomic energy program suggests that it might be profitable for some journalists to check up on what one of the pioneers in the field of atomic physics had to say about 20 years ago. Toward the end of his life, Prof. Milliken of the University of Chicago wrote his auto-biography which appeared about the time that atomic energy plants were being projected. He makes the flat statement that as a major source of power, atomic energy has no future—"it is out." He did not elaborate but he must have had solid reasons for this opinion which he must have stated elsewhere, probably in professional journals.

Note, first, that R.H.'s appeal to Milliken is guarded. He says that "it might be profitable" to consider Milliken's views. Reading this letter, we can't be sure just what R.H. wants to establish by the appeal. Does he want Milliken's views simply considered, or considered *true*? Read further. The tone of the letter seems to be that the defection of the engineers is symptomatic of a serious problem in the development of atomic energy as a power source, and R.H. goes on to surmise that Professor Milliken "must have had solid reasons" for his opinion that atomic energy "is out." Thus, R.H. seems to think that atomic energy has no future, takes this view as true because Milliken had adopted it, and invites us to do the same.

Interpreted this way, R.H. is guilty of *improper appeal to authority*. He does not even know why Milliken believed that atomic energy is out; sufficient for him was the fact that Milliken, an authority, held that view. We can see that the appeal is fallacious if we isolate Q and consider it. In this case, Q is, "Atomic energy has no future as a major source of power." What sort of statement is Q? To begin with, it is not a statement from the domain of theoretical physics, Milliken's own field of competence. That's a flaw which we will deal with in *Rule II*. Nor is Q a statement that would belong to some branch of technology or applied science. In fact, Q is a complicated statement that presupposes judgements about technology, business and industry, ecology, and lifestyles. If anything, it is a statement of social policy. As such it needs the support of various kinds of hard evidence, but as well will involve numerous reasoned value judgements of a social nature. Since in this case there is no guarantee of consensus, R.H. has violated *Rule I* and is guilty of an *improper appeal to authority.*

**7.6   Rule II:** If $M$ is appealed to as an authority on $Q$, then $Q$ must belong to a class of statements, $S$, on which $M$ is an authority.

Note first that this rule is violated if $M$ is not an authority on anything at all. We mention this point primarily because appeals to the "authority" of non-authorities are all too frequent. Think, for a moment, of the use of sports celebrities and entertainment figures in commercial endorsements.

The second thing which *Rule II* invalidates is the attempt to transfer authority, i.e. to use someone who is a legitimate authority in one field as an authority in some other field. Authority, however, is non-transferable, based as it is on the assessment of one's achievements by one's peers in one's field of knowledge. An authority on atomic physics may not be appealed to in order to support a biological claim (unless he or she is also an authority on biology). The Milliken example violated this rule, as well as *Rule I*, because the writer attempted to transfer Milliken's authority from atomic physics (where Milliken was an authority) to social policy on energy (where Milliken was not an authority—and indeed where no one is).

Don't misinterpret what we're saying here, and hang a *straw man* on us. In these times when many are busy debunking the Cult of the Expert, we don't want to be misread. Certainly there is nothing logically wrong or objectionable with considering and quoting the opinion of an authority on a matter which lies outside his or her area of competence, but such opinions do not carry the weight of authority. A scientist who airs his or her views on political questions, for example, deserves to have those views listened to with the same respect and courtesy afforded anyone else. And that is the point—the same respect that would be given *anyone* else. Outside the area of competence, an authority's views are only as compelling as the evidence presented for them.

In our next example, we see how the respect that people have for intelligence and achievement can too easily lead them astray. G.P., in the excerpt following, is responding to an earlier writer who had accused some Christians of being dogmatic and narrow-minded (Windsor *Star*, January 1975):

**106**     One naturally wonders how the writer would class the late
Sir Winston Churchill, whose word conveys what he thought
about Holy Scripture: . . . [G.P. then quoted Churchill as
stating that everything in the Bible is literally true.]

G.P.'s argument seems to have been that it is not dogmatic and
narrow-minded to claim literal truth for statements in the Bible,
because Churchill said that the Bible expresses the literal truth. This
appeal to Churchill's authority violates *Rule II*. First, it is not clear
that Churchill was an authority on anything. He was widely admired
as a statesman and influential as a politician; however, these are not
qualifications for authority in any domain of knowledge. Second,
even if we grant that Churchill was an authority on history (he did
publish several historical works), his field of specialization was the
English-speaking peoples and, more narrowly, World War II. He was
not a Bible historian. Moreover, many of the statements made in the
Bible belong to theology, not history—for example, that Christ is the
son of God—and Churchill was not a theologian. Hence, although
Churchill was an authority in one area of history, G.P.'s attempt to
transfer that authority to a different area is improper.

Violations of *Rule II* are usually found in tandem with violations
of *Rule I*, as we have seen in the Milliken example. Here is another.
A.N. wrote this letter to the Ottawa *Journal* (November 1974):

**107**     May I bring to your attention the following statement of Dr.
Joseph DeLee? He was one of the most eminent obstetricians
of this continent, who devoted his entire life to the improvement of obstetrical care. He said: "At the present time,
when rivers of blood and tears of innocent men, women and
children are flowing in most parts of the world, it seems
silly to be contending over the right of an annullable atom
of flesh in the uterus of a woman. No, it is not silly; on the
contrary, it is of transcendent importance that there be in
this chaotic world one high spot, however small, which is
against the deluge sweeping over us. If we of the medical
profession uphold the principle of the sacredness of human
life and the right of the individual, even though unborn, it
will prove that humanity is not yet lost and that we may
ultimately obtain salvation."

A.N., it would appear, is appealing to Dr. DeLee's authority as an
eminent obstetrician to support the view that abortion is wrong.
Dr. DeLee was undeniably an authority on obstetrics, as a check of
*Who was Who in America* will show.[4] He was, for example, the

4 Cf. Vol. II, 1943-1950, A. W. Marquis Company.

author of four books on obstetrics, one of which, *The Principles and Practice of Obstetrics*, was originally published in 1913 and went through seven editions through 1938. Dr. DeLee was an authority on obstetrics, but that does not qualify him as an authority on the subject of the morality of abortion, which belongs to the field of ethics. Thus, A.N. violated *Rule II*. Furthermore, it is not clear whether the proposition that abortion is wrong can be a matter of knowledge. Since it is hotly disputed whether there can be *any* moral knowledge, there is no justification for taking it for granted that there can be an appeal to authority on this topic. So A.N. has violated *Rule I* as well.

**7.7** The appeal to Prof. Milliken's authority used as an example in 7.5 is even more culpable than we've indicated to this point, for it violates yet another rule such appeals must honour:

> **Rule III:** If there is no consensus among authorities in S, to which Q belongs, then this lack of consensus must be noted in any appeal to authority about Q, and the conclusion qualified accordingly.

As we noted in our discussion of *Rule I*, when there is not even the possibility of a consensus, then no appeal to authority is valid. In areas where there is the possibility of consensus, but that consensus has not yet been reached, an appeal to authority is premature. The function of an appeal to authority is to provide a reason for believing the truth of some statement. When those who are in the best position to know have not yet reached a verdict, the appeal to any one authority rather than another cannot carry much weight. To refer to the Milliken example, then, even if the question of the use of atomic energy as a power source did belong to some particular domain of knowledge (which, we have already argued, is not the case), the appeal to Milliken would fail to abide by *Rule III*, for equally competent scientists do not share Milliken's views.

In a letter to the Windsor *Star* (August 1974), W.C. criticized an earlier article about Down's Syndrome:

**108**   I believe the *Star* is doing a great service to the mentally retarded in the Windsor area by their recent articles on the subject of retardation, however, I wonder why David Gibson was quoted in this most recent article. His statements are not supported by other researchers in North America, Great Britain or Europe.

In an Editor's note, the *Star* responded:

**109**     Dr. David Gibson is a Canadian expert in his field. He is president of the Canadian Psychological Association, professor of psychology at the University of Calgary, editor of the *Canadian Psychologist* and has spent more than 30 years in active work with the mentally retarded.

Having recited Gibson's impressive credentials, the *Star* then added:

**110**     *There are those equally learned in the same area who disagree with him*—an occurrence that is commonplace in most professions. (Emphasis ours.)

The crucial phrase in the *Star*'s attempt to defend its appeal to Gibson is in that last sentence. Since the *Star* had given no reason for citing Gibson's views rather than those of one of his "equally learned" colleagues, it violated *Rule III*. Where there are degrees of authority within an area, there is stronger justification for an appeal to a widely recognized authority than to one less well known. Where opinion among the best is divided, as was apparently the case here, no appeal to authority should have persuasive force.

**7.8** The rules listed thus far invalidate appeals to authority when the field in question is not a domain of knowledge (*Rule I*); or when it is, but the individual is not in fact an authority on that subject (*Rule II*); or when the domain is indeed one of knowledge and the individual properly equipped, but the appeal is vitiated by a lack of consensus (*Rule III*). Two additional rules are needed.

> **Rule IV:** The authority, M, whose judgement is appealed to, must not be in a situation of bias, or conflict of interest, about Q.

The very idea of appealing to an authority is that his or her judgement is likely to be true because it has been arrived at in a rational and competent way by someone familiar with the relevant evidence. Should there be reason to think that bias, rather than rational review of the evidence, could have dictated the judgement, then the appeal to that authority cannot be proper.

An example of such a violation occurs, apparently, in Gérard Pelletier's *The October Crisis*, quoted in Chapter 3 above. In reference to the *FLQ*, Pelletier writes:

**111**     When a marginal group tries, by using the most odious possible sort of blackmail (the threat to human life), to force the State to take actions contrary to principles on which it is founded, in most cases firmness is the only reasonable choice. (p. 95)

In a footnote, Pelletier quotes Quebec Justice Minister Jerome Choquette from a press conference of October 10, 1970, in which Choquette explained his reasons for refusing the demands of the *FLQ*. Choquette stated:

**112**   No society can consent to have the decisions of the judicial and government institutions challenged or set aside by the blackmail of a minority, for that signifies the end of all social order.

Is Pelletier appealing to Choquette as an authority here? Perhaps not, for he had already given his own reasons for thinking that political blackmail cannot be tolerated. There is, then, no need to appeal to Choquette. Still, the impressionable reader may think Choquette's office endows his judgement with authority. That would be a mistake. His office confers one sort of authority on him—the right to command people to act in certain ways. But it does not make him an authority on any domain of knowledge. Moreover—and to the point of our taking it up here—as Justice Minister, Choquette was himself involved in the kidnapping and the dramatic set of events which followed, so he was anything but a detached observer. His statement was, in fact, part of his attempt to justify the way his government responded to the crisis. So naturally he is disposed, or predisposed, to that viewpoint. Thus, Choquette, even if he were an authority, could hardly be impartial on this issue, and the appeal to his authority would violate *Rule IV*. Lastly, we're doubtful that this is an area that permits appeals to authority. Whether the State can both maintain itself in a position of public confidence and yield on occasion to blackmail by terrorist groups is, it seems to us, a judgement call rather than a matter of knowledge. If that is true, *Rule I* was violated here, too.

**7.9** G.P., whose appeal to Churchill's authority we saw as a violation of *Rule II* (Example 106), provided in that same letter an example of why our final rule is needed. G.P. wrote:

**113**   If the grounds of the writer's accusations [against Christians for dogmatism] are justified, then he must include in his list of those deserving the stigma inseparable from those words, prominent men in all walks of life, past and present—many of super intelligence, highly trained and educated in their particular fields and respected the world over who . . .

were and are immovable in their belief in the Bible as the inerrant word of God.

We might be willing to accept the testimony of these many alleged authorities—if we knew who they were and could assess their credentials! Since we don't we can't; and G.P.'s appeal to them remains bereft of persuasive force. This leads to a final rule.

**Rule V:** If M is appealed to as an authority on S, then M must be identified.

Should *Rule V* go further, and require that anyone using an authority list the pertinent qualifications? Or is it up to the person assessing the argument to do the legwork and check them out? We think the primary burden rests with the one who appeals to the authority. After all, that person is the one who is trying to persuade others. On the other hand, it's unfair to hold the arguer responsible when the authority appealed to is generally well known, and failure to recognize that authority is due to unusual ignorance. Furthermore, even where it's a just criticism of the argument that the authority's credentials are not given, the critic cannot dismiss the appeal on the grounds of *Rules II* or *IV* without doing the necessary checking. To reply, for example, "I've never heard of Dr. DeLee and don't know of any contribution he has made to obstetrics, so the appeal is improper," is not only the lazy way out: it is also to commit *hasty conclusion*, if not *irrelevant reason!* If you are going to do more than put a question mark beside an appeal to authority, if you are going to charge it with violating *Rules II* or *IV*, the burden shifts to you. It may require a bit of time in the library to determine M's qualifications.

Here's a borderline example. Does the appeal in the passage quoted below violate *Rule V*? The background is that in 1972 a group of researchers at the Massachusetts Institute of Technology did a computer projection of the world's population and resources, published as the famous Club of Rome Study called *The Limits to Growth*. They concluded that, "If the present growth trends in world population, industrialization, pollution, food production, and re- source depletion continue unchanged, the limits to growth on this planet will be reached sometime within the next one hundred years."[5] In an editorial entitled "Bad science, Good sense," the Windsor *Star* (November 1972) attacked the MIT projections by appealing to authority:

[5] Donella H. Meadows, Dennis L. Meadows, Jorgen Randers, William W. Behrens III, *The Limits to Growth* (New York: Universe Books, 1972), p. 23.

**114**    The latest criticisms of the MIT report were voiced in Windsor, by economist members of a panel discussion at the University of Windsor. One of the three speakers, himself an MIT professor, labelled the work "bad science," and two others agreed that the case had been grossly overstated. The criticisms should be welcomed by all those humans who are concerned about over-population and related problems . . .

The *Star* appealed especially to the unidentified professor of economics at MIT to defuse the conclusions reached by the Club of Rome. But who is this unnamed professor of economics? If we were intent on prosecuting this argument, it would be our job to do a bit of detective work, find out who was on the panel, then track down his or her credentials. We aren't as badly off here as we are in the advertisements which say "Doctors recommend . . ." Yet the *Star*'s appeal fails to persuade us precisely because it doesn't comply with the spirit of *Rule V*. (In this particular example, the appeal is flawed on another, more basic, count. What is it?)

Another point brought out by this example: just because someone is a professor does not mean that he or she is an authority on any subject at all. The prestige that goes with academic titles can be deceiving. A person can, for instance, enjoy a modest and worthwhile academic career, do a good job of teaching, advance through the ranks—all without making that sort of contribution to his or her area which would qualify that person as an authority.

Don't misunderstand. We are not suggesting that you dismiss what a professor says. What she or he is very often doing is *conveying* the findings of researchers, the positions and arguments of theorists, and the judgements of authorities. Part of that responsibility is to let you know what is authoritatively known and what is a matter of judgement and controversy. And part of this job will be to present the evidence on which opinions have been formed, so that you may develop independent judgement. You should accept a professor's competence as a conveyor of knowledge and as someone who knows the field well enough to recognize and distinguish between established truths and areas of contention. But unless your professor happens to be an authority in the subject, you should not accept what she or he says as true, merely because that professor says it.

Indeed, it is perhaps useful to distinguish various *degrees* of authority. In most areas where there is such a thing as authority, there is also a hierarchy of influence and recognition. Our analysis has been focused on the highest degree, attained only by the "top guns" in each field. Between the ultimate authority and the neophyte are the many competent specialists who have a great deal more knowledge than most, but whose contributions won't rank them with the best. Clearly, the more authority an individual has, the greater the weight attaching to an appeal to him or her. Sometimes, in verbal argument, a person will refer to someone (a friend, a local personality) as an authority. You should not dismiss that appeal outright, simply on the ground that the individual is not the ranking authority. On the other hand, the appeal cannot carry any greater weight than the degree of authority possessed by that individual. If you know the conditions required for the highest degree of authority, you can approbate appeals with that standard in mind, taking each case on its individual merits.

**7.10** To summarize briefly, an appeal to M as support for the truth of Q within S can go wrong in several ways. S must be a field of knowledge. If not, *Rule I* has been violated. There is no simple way to repair that sort of flaw. Remember, too, that M must be an authority on S: authority is not transferable from one field to another, and the attempt to do so violates *Rule II*. An argument violating this rule is not easily patched up. Keep in mind that authorities often disagree. When they do, an appeal to one rather than another is not persuasive unless there are reasons to think that that particular authority is more likely to be right. This is the caution implicit in *Rule III*. If there is any reason to think that an authority is not objective on the issue, then *Rule IV* is violated and the argument immensely weakened. The failure to name or identify an authority, a violation of *Rule V*, is not altogether serious, since it can be corrected by simply producing the identification.

The key to appraising any appeal to authority rests on your capacity to delineate carefully the general field or area, S, to which Q, the statement in question, belongs. You must then make a judgement about whether this is indeed an area of knowledge or not. Further, don't make the mistake of arguing against the truth of the claim which the so-called authority has been cited as support for. Here's an exchange which shows what we mean:

**115**    *Psych. Major:* Everything we do has some motivation, conscious or unconscious. Freud said so.
       *Logician:* That's an improper appeal to Freud's authority. Lots of behaviour, like tying your right shoe before your left one, is just happenstance or habit.

We're not endorsing the Psych. Major's appeal to Freud, but the Logician's rebuttal takes the wrong tack. When someone appeals to an authority in matters of belief, that person is giving a kind of reason for the claim. To say the appeal is improper is not to say that the claim is false—it's to say that the reason (that the "authority" said so) is not a good one in this instance. So the relevant critique is to show why it's not—which is where our five rules are intended to help out. The Logician should have said that the Psych. Major's appeal to Freud here was illegitimate because authorities in psychology disagree about whether all behaviour is motivated and they disagree about the truth of the theory of unconscious motivation. In our terms, *Rule III* is violated. So here's useful advice: when charging improper appeal to authority, *attack the appeal to the authority, not the truth of the claim.*

Appeals to authority are perilous. They are often arguments of last resort. As the 13th-century philosopher and theologian St. Thomas Aquinas aptly put it, "The argument from authority is the weakest of all arguments." Don't try to trip us up on the principles we've just listed, because (you guessed it), we aren't appealing to Aquinas's authority. You don't have to take his word for it—or ours, for that matter. With the five rules in hand, check out a few arguments from authority for yourself.

# 2 Popularity

**7.11** We had occasion to cite the philosopher William James in this chapter. We're going to do so again here, this time for an example of specious reasoning that comes preciously close to the fallacy we take up next: **popularity**. An anecdote from James' *Pragmatism* (Lecture 2; Cleveland: Meridian Books, 1955) serves to illustrate the kernel of this fallacy.

James and a group of his friends had gone camping in the mountains. While James was out for a walk, the members of the party got into a heated dispute. James tells us what he found upon his return:

**116**    In the unlimited leisure of the wilderness, discussion had been worn threadbare. Everyone had taken sides, and was obstinate; and the numbers on both sides were even. Each side, when I appeared, appealed to me to make it a majority.

James, of course, did what philosophers are famous for: he drew a distinction which he thought resolved the issue. But suppose he had sided with one group rather than the other, would that have made its view the correct one? If you think so, then beware the fallacy of *popularity*, which consists in thinking that if most people or the majority believe something, then it is true. For many, the popularity or widespread acceptance of an idea is an index of its truth, while lack of acceptance is often construed as an index of its falsity.

**7.12** In its purest and most blatant (and rarest) form, the fallacy of *popularity* occurs whenever an argument proceeds from the popularity of a view to its truth, thus:

**117**    **P:** Everyone believes Q.
       **C:** Q is true.

Instead of "everyone," the argument may refer to "almost everyone" or "most people" or "a majority." The flipside of the argument also occurs:

**118**    **P:** No one believes Q.
       **C:** Q is false.

Instead of "no one," the reference may be to "almost no one" or "very few" or "nobody I know of."

This move is so outrageous, when baldly stated, that *popularity* rarely occurs in this blatant formulation. You often have to dig below the surface to find it. For example, M expresses the belief that drugs are harmful and that people shouldn't rely on them. N counters, "Oh, come off it! Nobody believes that nowadays!" N has not actually said that because nobody believes it, it is false; but that is the clear implication. Or M says that women are inferior to men. N responds, "Surely you must be joking; that crazy idea went out with the '60s! Where have you been hibernating?" Again, N stops short of the explicit statement of the inference that because no one believes it, the view is false. The best way to counter such moves is to ask, point-blank, "Hold on, are you saying that because everyone (or no one) believes it, therefore it is true (or false)?"

Here's an example of the fallacy. It is from a letter to the St. John's *Evening Telegram* (October 1974) in which "Concerned" was arguing that laws should be more strictly enforced and that the courts should be handing out stiffer penalties:

**119**    *Every other person with whom one discusses this problem will say that the time has arrived when the lash will have to be re-introduced in our courts. (Emphasis ours.)*

"Concerned" stopped short of concluding that since this is what most people believe, it is true. But if that is the implication, the fallacy of *popularity* has been committed.

**7.13** To argue that a claim *is* true simply because a number of people *think* it's true is outrageous. However, we doubt that most people who commit *popularity* are following this line of argument. Instead, we expect they reason (implicitly) as follows: that many people believe Q is *a good reason* for thinking Q is true. That's because, so the thinking goes, there would not be popular acceptance of Q unless there were good reasons for thinking Q to be true. Hence, the popular belief that Q is true is evidence of good reasons for accepting Q. The key premise in this argument is that the widespread acceptance of Q entails the existence of good reasons for believing Q.

We are not about to propose that the popular acceptance of a belief is never any reason for thinking it is true. Suppose you find that everyone in a community you are visiting believes the fish in a nearby lake are contaminated. That would by itself be some reason for you to believe that the fish truly are contaminated. So popular belief is not always irrelevant as a basis for accepting a proposition.

However, we must insist that the mere acceptance by numbers of people of a belief is usually not a very good reason for you to believe it. If people were generally in the habit of arriving at their beliefs in a reasonable way (by considering all relevant evidence, weighing it, etc.), then a consensus would be as impressive in ordinary life as it is in, say, the case of science. But the evidence that people actually do this is scanty. Instead, people are persuaded by bad arguments; they are duped by fallacies; they judge first and think afterwards; they fail to search out and review the evidence; they face the limits of time and energy. If all this is true, the appeal to popular consensus, even as an indicator of what is probably true, is fraught with pitfalls. Moreover, rarely are the beliefs of others the only available basis for our own beliefs. Almost always we can check out other more generally reliable grounds.

Of course, in arguing against the reasonableness of popular opinion as a basis for belief, we are not for a minute supposing that the appeal to popularity is usually intended as a reasonable argument. Most of the time it's a tool of intimidation, an attempt to browbeat a person into accepting some claim. Still, it gets some of its influence by hiding behind the façade of good argument. So we need to be sure it is a façade, and not actually legitimate.

**7.14** In the absence of any strong connection between the quantity of people who hold a position and its truth or probability, the appeal to popular acceptance is a fallacy. The conditions for it are:

## POPULARITY

1. M claims or implies that Q is true (false) and offers as warrant that Q is widely accepted (not widely accepted).
2. The popularity of Q (or lack of it) is not an adequate reason for accepting Q.

For several reasons people find the appeal to popular acceptance attractive. In the first place, going against the grain of popular opinion is threatening to many people. (We haven't forgotten the "one in every crowd" sort who loves to disagree with everyone.) Peer pressure is difficult to resist.

But, second, two perfectly respectable principles provide perfect masquerades for *popularity:* "Majority Rule," and "Popular Sovereignty." A brief discussion of each of these may help you to detect *popularity* when it disguises itself in one or the other.

Majority Rule is the political principle that what the majority of members of a decision-making group agrees to is what should stand as the decision of the whole group. The principle does *not* imply that the decision thus arrived at is true, or right, or the best one, but only that this is an effective way to carry on the group's affairs. (It could be replaced by a principle that calls for 75% in favour, or unanimity, before motions are passed.) There is a difference between this political principle and the logical principle on which *popularity* is based. The Majority Rule principle is a *procedural* one prescribing a procedure for decision making; behind *popularity* lies a *criterial* principle—one offering as the criterion of a belief's truth or probability the fact that most people embrace it. When the distinction is not marked, people invoke the Majority Rule principle as justification for an appeal to popular opinion.

Related to Majority Rule (and sometimes used to help justify it) is the principle that what most of the electorate of a body politic desires and agrees to is what the legislature should do—the principle of Popular Sovereignty. The foundation of this thesis is the idea that the people are sovereign, and that the views and attitudes of the people should be reflected in the laws of the land. Up to a point this is a sensible principle, because if the laws of a country stray too far from widely shared public beliefs about the sort of behaviour that ought to be legally permissible or prohibited, then people will as a matter of fact begin to lose sympathy with and respect for the laws. (The principle cannot serve without qualification: popular opinion on some issues changes more rapidly than the law can or should; also, it allows no role for legislators to give leadership to popular opinion.) The principles of Popular Sovereignty is different from *popularity*. The former makes no claims for the wisdom of the people—for the worth of their preferences—but only for their right to influence policy, to have their interests served. *Popularity*, in contrast, takes the further step of supposing that what the majority (or any large number) believes is true.

Against this background, consider this brief excerpt from an article in the Halifax *Chronicle-Herald* (January 1975) entitled, "Trudeau cabinet's 'bleeding hearts,'" in which Robert Coates (Conservative MP for Cumberland-Colchester North) stated:

**120**   There are many bleeding hearts in this nation, but they are substantially outnumbered by those who appreciate that the death penalty is a deterrent.

Is this an instance of *popularity*, or is this a disguised appeal to the principle of Popular Sovereignty? If Coates is arguing that capital punishment should be restored because a substantial majority want it restored (because they think it is a deterrent to murder), then he is appealing to the sovereignty of the people. He's saying that Parliament should follow the will of the people in this case. On the other hand, if Coates is arguing that the death penalty would be a deterrent and his reason for holding that opinion is that most people think it is, then he is guilty of *popularity*, for whether the death penalty is or is not a deterrent is an extremely complicated question not to be decided by appealing to what most people believe, but by careful consideration of the evidence.

As a concluding note, we add that something like an appeal to popular acceptance is found in many advertisements.

**121**   You'll find Maple Leaf meats and cheese in more than a million kitchens across Canada, day in and day out. *They're that popular.*

**122**   More than 250,000 hairdressers the world over believe in what L'Oreal Hair Colouring can do for you. What more can we say?

A Quarter-Million Hairdressers can't be wrong! Here the assumption is that popularity is a criterion or index of the quality of a product, an assumption not far removed from taking popularity as an index of the truth of a belief. That assumption is questionable, although not necessarily false in these particular cases. (Chevrolet consistently outsells Rolls Royce. Which is the better-built car?) However, because advertisements have their own special logic, we will not multiply examples here, preferring to confront advertisements in Chapter 10.

# 3 Slippery Slope

**7.15** One way to assess a proposed policy or course of action is by predicting its probable consequences. If a proposal can be shown to lead to undesirable consequences, that's a strong reason for not going through with it. To project the effects of an action often involves telling a *causal story*. There are two typical forms of argument employing such causal forecasts. In one, the whole series of causal steps is included: "If we do/allow W, then X will follow; if X, then Y; if Y, then Z. But surely we don't want Z. Therefore we should not do/allow W".

**123**   If abortion were legalized, it would become more widespread; if it were to become more widespread, respect for human life would weaken; if respect for human life were weakened, our form of civilization would be jeopardized. But surely we don't want to weaken our form of civilization. Therefore abortion should not be legalized.

In the second form, just the first and last chapters of the causal story are included in the argument: "If we do/allow W, then Z will follow. But surely we don't want Z. Therefore we should not do/allow W."

**124**   The legalization of abortion will be the first step along the road that can only end with the weakening of our form of civilization. Surely we don't want to jeopardize our form of civilization. Therefore we must not permit abortion to be legalized.

When the causal story in either version goes wrong because one of the links in the causal chain is dubious and unsupported, the fallacy called **slippery slope** results.

The following examples illustrate both forms of the fallacy. First the long form. The example comes from an editorial in the St. John's *Evening Telegram* (October 1974):

**125**   The federal proposal to switch cannabis from the Narcotics Control Act to the Food and Drug Act will probably be the first step leading to the eventual legalization of this "soft" drug. Under the drug act the possession of marijuana or hashish will be punishable with a fine rather than with a jail sentence as called for in the narcotics act.

The penalties for trafficking, importing and cultivating the drug will still be stiff. However it is hardly likely that judges will take as serious a view of a drug as they do of a narcotic, and in time the penalty for trafficking or importing will probably be a light fine and a ticking off by the judge. Then, in turn, the fine for possession will likely be dropped and it will be legal to have cannabis for personal use.

From there the next step is controlled manufacture and sale along the same lines as alcoholic drinks. Then the emphasis on the nature of the crime will switch to smuggling and bootlegging with the intention that the Crown gets its legitimate revenue from the sale of the drug. By that time, cannabis will probably be called joy candy or fun smoke or by some other euphemism.

If we seem to be moving too fast, remember that this is the usual way of softening up the law. We hope that when Health Minister Lalonde makes the change he will understand that he is opening the door to putting pot in every pocket.

The editorialist is clearly opposed to the federal proposal. In his view, it's going to lead—by a nexus of events which the editorialist spells out—to a clearly undesirable end (as far as the editorialist is concerned): "pot in every pocket" and "pot being called joy candy or fun smoke." Therefore, the argument implicitly concludes, the proposal ought not to be implemented. The strength of this argument against the Lalonde proposal depends entirely upon the plausibility of this causal projection. To get a clear fix, then, we must trace the nexus through its various stages, identify each stage, and scrutinize the links. We begin by spelling out the steps in the nexus, one by one:

**126**   1. Marijuana put under Food and Drug Act;
2. Possession punished by fine rather than jail; trafficking, importing, and cultivating punished stiffly;
3. Judges take a less serious view of offenses against this law;
4. The penalty for trafficking and importing becomes less severe—a light fine;

5. Penalty for simple possession dropped; legal to possess marijuana;
6. The manufacture and sale of marijuana controlled by the government;
7. Emphasis changes from possession and trafficking to smuggling and bootlegging;
8. Marijuana legal and in common use.

Note that few of these links are defended. Some are fairly obvious. The transition from 1 to 2 seems incontestable, but that from 2 to 3 less so. If judges are already disposed to impose heavy penalties for trafficking and importing, why would a simple reclassification of marijuana change that disposition? Step 3 wouldn't necessarily follow on the heels of 2. The transition from 3 to 4 seems straightforward. And if judges were to take a lenient attitude towards trafficking, then it is likely that they would not penalize simple possession at all, so from 4 to 5 the link seems secure. If possession of marijuana did become legal, 5, then the government would probably set up controls on its manufacture and sale along the lines of liquor, to insure the quality of the substance and to increase its revenue base. If that did occur, 6, then the emphasis in enforcement would undoubtedly change to smuggling and bootlegging, 7, since possession would be legal, and trafficking would disappear. But does this mean that marijuana would be in common use? (8) That likelihood is unclear.

Weak links in this causal chain, then, appear in the inferences from 2 to 3 and from 7 to 8. There's reason to doubt both these steps, yet the editorialist asserts them without defense. Even *assuming* common use would be a bad thing, we cannot accept this as a clear consequence of the initial step—putting the regulation of cannabis under the Food and Drug Act. For these reasons, we think this is a case of *slippery slope*.

The next example illustrates the short form of the fallacy. In 1976, the province of Ontario made the use of automobile safety belts mandatory. Among the many who objected to this legislation was S.C., who wrote to the Windsor *Star* (February 1976):

**127**  If they can make us swallow this infringement of personal rights, what's next? A seat belt law for the bedroom, so we won't fall out of bed and hurt our little selves? Boy, when Big Brother watches us, he really watches us, doesn't he?

The argument here seems to be that the seat-belt requirement is the first step down an incline leading to a veritable 1984 ("Big Brother watching us"). But how precisely is this horror to come about? The intervening steps are not mentioned, except for the sarcastic reference to seat-belts in the bedroom. We are given the first and the last chapter but nothing in between. Most would agree that if the legislation were the first of a series of steps leading inevitably to the abdication of all individual rights, then that legislation is bad and ought to be repealed. But this outcome is far from obvious, and S.C. does nothing to persuade the reader of this chain of events.

Though it does not bear directly on the charge of *slippery slope*, we think worth pointing out the potential mischief of S.C.'s *classification* of the seat-belt law as "an infringement of personal rights." In one obvious sense, the law does take away a person's right: the right, if you will, to choose whether or not to use the seat-belt. On the other hand, it may be argued that no citizen has the right to take unnecessary risks when the consequences of that risk-taking must be borne by the rest of society. Since the evidence shows that the probability of severe injury and death is decreased when safety-belts are used, it could be argued that refusal to wear them constitutes an unnecessary risk. Second, the consequences of automobile injury and death—hospitalization, unemployment, compensation—have to be paid by other citizens. *If* this argument can be cemented, then the phrase "infringement of personal rights" is of dubious application here, and we have a case of *questionable classification* too.

Another example of the short form of *slippery slope* occurred when in 1972 the Trudeau government let it be known that it was considering the possibility of issuing work permits to Canadian workers in order to prevent foreigners from taking jobs away from Canadians. (The unions had been complaining that foreigners were coming into the country as visitors, and then, against immigration regulations, taking jobs.) Union leaders responded to the proposal with unanimous opposition. Dennis McDermott, Canadian director of the UAW, was quoted (in a story in the Windsor *Star*, September 1972) as responding:

**128**   They would run counter to our traditional freedoms and would be *the first step* toward a police state.

The implication is clear: No one wants a police state, so we should oppose any policy, such as issuing work permits, that would start us down the road to that repugnant outcome. One problem with McDermott's brief causal story is that we are given no idea what the intervening chapters are. However, it's not necessary to read McDermott's mind in order to throw doubt on his story, for work permits would not have to constitute any greater danger to our liberties than driving licenses or building permits do. Registration procedures and a system of inspection for work permits would seem to require no more police powers, no greater restriction of freedoms, than the sorts of bureaucracy that exist at present for getting and checking other permits and licenses. True, work permits *could* be introduced in such a way as to restrict freedom to change jobs. But there is no reason to believe that this would happen, if the purpose of issuing them were merely to reserve jobs in Canada for Canadians. Work permits in and of themselves would not start the ball rolling down the slope to a police state. By implying that they would, McDermott committed *slippery slope.*

**7.16** The conditions for the fallacy are:

---

### SLIPPERY SLOPE

1. M claims that if W is permitted, it will lead to X, X will lead to Y, and so on to Z.
2. M holds that Z is undesirable and therefore should not be permitted.
3. At least one of the steps in the causal chain is unsupported and open to challenge.

---

In the short form, Condition 1 will have just the step from W to Z (the last one); in the longer form, the intervening steps are given.

Not every argument that involves a projection into the future is a case of *slippery slope.* The following argument by John Hofsess (*Maclean's*, October 1973) seems reasonable:

**129** If you don't get into the habit of exercising regularly when you're young, you are less likely to keep exercising during your later 20s and your 30s, when career, home and family take up more and more time and interest. You'll then tend to become sedentary and physically unfit. That will set you up for various heart and lung diseases during middle age. No one wants to have a heart attack at 45 or 50, so to lessen that danger, you ought to get into the habit of regular exercise when you're young.

Notice how Hofsess hangs back from making categorical claims here, instead qualifying his steps by phrases such as "less likely" and "tend to."

**7.17** *Slippery slope* has to be distinguished from a form of legitimate argumentation which it resembles: the appeal to precedent. Decision-making bodies, especially in government, must take into account the effects of the policies they set. One of these is the setting of a precedent. Consistency and fairness require that if one case is treated in a certain way, similar cases must be similarly treated. For example, if your city council grants the Ukrainian community a parade permit for its national celebration, that sets a precedent. Other groups with similar requests will expect, and rightly so, to be granted the same permission.

Even the most judicious decisions can overlook important factors, so it is perfectly permissible to object to some plan or policy on the ground that it establishes an undesirable precedent. Such an argument will often be truncated, thus resembling *slippery slope*, but in full regalia it would be this:

**130**   **P1:** If you do/permit W, that will set a precedent which will justify doing/permitting X.

**P2:** X is undesirable.

**C:** Therefore you shouldn't do/permit X.

The acceptability of such an argument depends primarily upon whether X and W are similar in all relevant respects, for, if they are not, then **P1** is false and the argument fails. The fallacy in that case is not *slippery slope*, but *faulty analogy*. The problem is not a *causal* chain with a weak link. **P1** is false, instead, because the respects in which W and X are similar do not suffice to support the claim that if W is justified, then so too will X be. As we said, arguments from precedent are based on the requirement of consistency, that similar cases be treated similarly. These arguments break down when two allegedly similar cases are not similar in the relevant respect. Arguments harbouring *slippery slope* are based on empirical causal forces. They break down when a causal claim is unfounded.

Here's an argument using an appeal to precedent (and foundering due to a *faulty analogy*). At the end of June 1974, the spectacular Russian ballet dancer Mikhail Barichnikov, touring Canada with the Bolshoi, defected and was granted asylum in Canada. A.S. complained in a letter to the Ottawa *Journal* (July 1974):

**131**   I am amazed that the Russian dancer Barichnikov has been granted six months asylum in Canada.

The minister of external affairs is notorious for his preference and admiration for special immigration cases who are no-goods, American draft-dodgers and American army deserters who came here while there was any danger of them having to defend their country. *We shall probably soon have some Palestine terrorists.* (Emphasis ours.)

We don't think A.S. is arguing that giving asylum to Barichnikov is going to somehow *cause* Palestinian terrorists to seek and be granted entry into Canada. The point is that with the door opened for American draft dodgers and deserters and for Russians like Barichnikov, a precedent has been set that will allow *anyone* entry into Canada, including undesirables like Palestinian terrorists. The Minister of External Affairs made a bad decision in allowing Barichnikov's asylum, which only entrenched the undesirable precedent begun by letting in U.S. anti-war protesters during the Vietnam War.

A.S.'s argument is confused. These people do not belong to the same categories. American draft dodgers and deserters were allowed to immigrate to Canada only if they satisfied the qualifications any immigrant must pass, which do not require the listing of one's draft status in one's country of origin. Barichnikov, on the other hand, sought political asylum—an entirely different means of entry into Canada. The policy of recent Canadian governments has been to grant asylum in cases, like Barichnikov's, in which the petitioner would probably face prosecution at home were he or she turned back. Moreover, Barichnikov's defection was not intended as a political act. He stated publicly that he wanted to come to the West for personal artistic reasons. So on many counts the analogy breaks down; the precedent does not apply, and the appropriate charge here is *faulty analogy*.

To end, the point we have been making in this last subsection can be encapsulated in this slogan:

> Bad causal chain arguments commit *slippery slope*; bad arguments from precedent commit *faulty analogy*.

---

## Exercises for Chapter 7

*Directions:* Identify any fallacies committed in the following passages. Always fully defend your claim, whatever it may be: fallacy; no argument; argument, but no fallacy; hitherto unclassified fallacy.

1. *Background:* A letter from E.L. (August 1974) to the Halifax *Chronicle-Herald* prompted by the Justice Minister Otto Lang's opposition to further abortion law liberalization, quoted above in Exercise 4:

> Certain restrictions regarding curtailment of babies will soon be legislated in some countries. If it is not done at an

individual level, governments will have to act with certain measures. Otherwise, we will see nature revert to its first law, the one that was the sole arbiter before man came along: survival of the fittest.

2. *Background:* E.N. might have changed her mind by now, but in 1974 she wrote to the Windsor *Star* defending then President Nixon's performance in office. This is an excerpt from her letter:

> . . . Then on the home front, he isn't to blame either. On August 3 in the Windsor *Star*, Alan Greenspan wrote that 10 years ago, John Kennedy started the ball rolling towards inflation and we are suffering the consequences now. So why blame Nixon? As far as that goes, these conditions are in every country of the world, and more so in European countries.

3. *Background:* The subject once again is Canada's immigration policy. The source is Brian Kappler, the Ottawa correspondent for the Windsor *Star*, in a column entitled, "Strange things in the Green Paper" (February 1975):

> The only politician still blithely calling for virtually open borders is Andrew Brewin, the Toronto New Democrat. Brewin, 67, is a knee-jerk supporter of all left-wing causes and is commonly known in Ottawa as the Honorable Member for Hanoi.
>
> On immigration, he says that Canada is a big country with lots of room. As usual, Brewin is out of touch with public opinion. Recent Gallup Polls show that well more than half of Canadians think the country is the right size—in population—right now.

4. *Background:* In 1974, there were reports that the *FLQ* kidnappers of James Cross, who had been in Cuba, had left there for France. This move prompted the following letter to the Ottawa *Journal* from R.G. (July 1974):

> Any parliamentarian worth his salt realizes that the kidnappers could be returned to Canada by Mr. Trudeau asking France to extradite them due to their criminal acts. But it seems that Mr. Trudeau does not wish to open the *FLQ* can of worms. Mr. Trudeau shall now open the doors for other criminals to commit the same act and go the same route to gain their freedom. The kidnappers should be extradited to Canada from France and given a trial where justice can be served.

5. *Background:* The following is an adaptation of a letter to the Montreal *Gazette* (September 1974) on the topic of amnesty for those who resisted participation in the Vietnam War:

> A majority of the American people now believe that American participation in the Vietnam war was wrong. All Americans who resisted such participation were therefore patriotic and serving the American government, and all those who cooperated were unpatriotic and disserving the American government.

6. *Background:* An article in the Brandon *Sun* (August 1974) made reference to a decision by the Manitoba government which would force people to pay the tax on "free" car washes:

> For sales tax purposes, that scrubbing is assumed to be worth $1.50. And while you do not have to pay the price, you are required to cough up the tax bite. Which may be a small point. But think of the possibilities that are bound to come once the imaginative juices of the revenue boys really start to flow.
>
> How about a tax on savings, on the grounds that you would otherwise spend it on something taxable? Or how about assuming a value for tax purposes for do-it-yourself projects you sell to yourself? What about taxing the carwash you do in your driveway?
>
> Hell, why not go the distance and just assume a taxable value on dreams?

7. *Background:* The following is part of the copy of an advertisement for Kayak Pools which appeared in the Toronto *Globe and Mail* (November 1973):

> "I feel without any doubt the KAYAK Carefree Aluminum Pool is by far the finest above ground pool on the market today. As far as I'm concerned . . . KAYAK POOLS ARE THE BEST."
>
> *Dick Shatto*
>
> These words were actually spoken by former *Toronto Argonauts* great *Dick Shatto.*
>
> BUY WITH CONFIDENCE
>
> Dick Shatto swims in and endorses KAYAK POOLS because he feels they're the best.

8. *Background:* The following argument appeared in the *Canadian Public Safety* magazine some time ago:

(a) The average driver is not an expert.
(b) Racing drivers are experts.
(c) Racing drivers wear safety belts.
(d) Racing drivers agree that public highways are more dangerous than race tracks.
(e) You drive on public highways, therefore, why don't you wear safety belts?

# III The Rhetoric of Everyday Persuasion

# 8 Extended Arguments

## Introduction

**8.1** In 1.3 we demonstrated how to *standardize* an argument so that its logical structure is clear. For the past six chapters we have been discussing various fallacies that undercut or vitiate arguments. The purpose of the present chapter is to bring these two aspects of logical evaluation together and demonstrate how effective they can be in combination for purposes of critically appraising extended arguments.

Our customary procedure has been to extract one or two paragraphs from a longer piece of argumentation and say in effect, "There is a fallacy here. We will show you what it is and how to spot others like it." Although defensible for the purpose of learning the basic fallacies and the ins and outs of arguments, this procedure has severe limitations when it comes to handling the standard fare of ordinary discourse.

In the first place, the arguments found there are often situated in longer passages that contain an assortment of kinds of material as well—asides, explanations, humour, background information, etc. Second, in the cold print of the evening newspaper, a fallacious argument may look every bit as good as one that isn't. At the very least, there will be no built-in clues (as there have been in the Exercises) to guide you in deciding whether a fallacy is present and, if so, which one. Hence, to be able to confront arguments as they really are, it is necessary to outline a refined procedure for appraising them.

As we take aim now at the arguments typical of everyday discourse, we will refer to the entire passage containing an argument as the **text** of the argument. Examples of what we are calling a *text* would be a complete editorial in a newspaper or magazine, an entire letter to the editor, or the whole of a speech given in Parliament. This chapter consists of a demonstration of how to extricate an extended argument from its text, standardize it, and then appraise it logically.

# 1 Guidelines for Standardization

**8.2** Anyone who has taken a music or sports lesson knows how arduous it is to do the practise exercises. Their purpose is to help you master the skill by developing habitual responses, so that your moves become automatic, whether it's the fingering for the violin or guitar, or the service for tennis, or the swing for golf. Evaluating arguments is also a skill. It requires just as much training and practice as any physical skill. Here, too, a method or exercise is a boon for the beginner. In this section we shall outline a method for extracting extended arguments from their texts, and standardizing them for appraisal.

**8.3 Step 1.** Clearly the first thing to do is to read the text over carefully a couple of times. As you are doing this, you should be looking to see if it contains an argument and what the main points are.

**Step 2.** Before trying to standardize the argument in the text, it is useful to write out a **synopsis** of the argument: a brief outline of the *strategies* employed in defending the conclusion. Here are the four common strategies to watch for:

1. The basic strategy employed in most arguments is to **list the reasons or evidence that**, it is believed, **directly warrant acceptance of the conclusion** in the first place. For example, "Parliament erred in abolishing capital punishment because the death penalty is both a deterrent to murder and also just retribution for the crime."

2. An indirect strategy is to **anticipate possible objections** to the conclusion, and try to show that they are without foundation. This move is often signalled explicitly in the argument. For example, "Now there will be those who object to the restoration of capital punishment on the grounds that . . . however, such objections are not sound, because . . ."

3. Another indirect strategy is to **attack alternative positions** held

by others and to try to find a flaw in them. This move is often signalled by some such phrasing as, "Those who favour restoring the death penalty have overlooked the following arguments against that change . . ." (The strategy requires a statement of the alternative views, and hence the possibility of a distortion of opponents' positions. Thus, it opens the door for *straw man*. In fact, we already made reference to this move when presenting that fallacy, in 3.4.)

4. Still another indirect strategy, slightly different from 2 and 3, is to **examine the implications of alternatives** to the conclusion (whether or not anyone actually holds them), and to **show that these alternatives would lead to objectionable consequences.** We used this strategy in Chapter 2 when we argued that it is not necessary for every premise of an acceptable argument to be defended. We took the alternative—the position that every premise *must* be defended before an argument can be acceptable—and showed how it implied the absurd consequence that either no argument is acceptable or no argument is complete. (Recall the classical title for this version of Strategy 4: *reductio ad absurdum*, reduction to absurdity.)

These are the four main types of argumentative strategy you will encounter in longer arguments. Frequently they occur in combination.

Once you have identified the strategy or strategies employed, you are ready to write the synopsis in paragraph form. Use the paragraphing of the text as your principle of organization. However, remember that *the rhetorical organization of the text isn't necessarily going to be a reliable guide to the logical order and structure of the argument it contains.* There may be repetition—the same point stated in different ways for rhetorical effect. Sentences and even entire paragraphs may be devoted to *explaining* something or to providing *background information.* Parts of the text may contain digressions from the argument. In your synopsis you should note these pieces of **extraneous material** so that they do not find their way into the standardization, which is to be restricted to the logical bones of the argument: its premises and conclusion(s).

**Step 3.** With the synopsis completed, you are ready to begin drafting your standardization. This is partly a task of sorting the entanglements of sometimes disorganized reasoning, a goal you can achieve much more easily if you keep in mind the three basic **arrangements** in which premise-conclusion patterns can occur.[1]

The simplest of these is one premise supporting a conclusion:

---

[1] The diagrams of premise-conclusion patterns which follow were inspired by those of Michael Scrivens in *Reasoning*, cf. pp. 46-48.

**132**

The second consists of a series of two or more premises, each of which independently supports (or is *intended* to support) the conclusion:

**133**

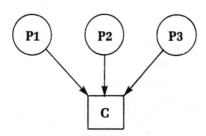

In the third arrangement, two or more premises function *jointly* to support the conclusion. The *conjunction* of the premises is considered *sufficient* to establish the conclusion:

**134**

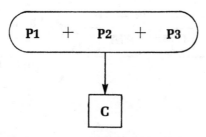

From these three basic arrangements, all the more complicated patterns of premises are spun. The complications arise in extended arguments because there the time is taken to support not only the main or overall conclusion, but some of the premises as well. Such arguments are compound, in the sense that they really contain *at least two* arguments, the argument supporting a premise, and the argument supporting the main conclusion. Here is a diagram of the simplest possible compound argument form:

**135**

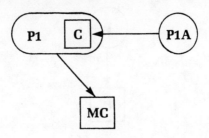

**P1** is at the same time both a conclusion supported by **P1A**, and the premise supporting **MC** (the main conclusion). A *very* complicated compound argument might have the following diagram:

**136**

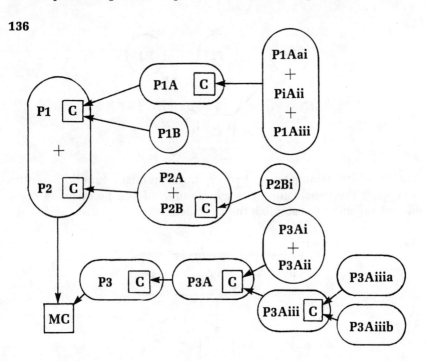

Here each circle or oval represents a premise or set of premises; each square, a conclusion. There are eight arguments in this representation and all lead eventually to one main conclusion. Each of the basic premise-conclusion arrangements occurs at least once. We mention this not to intimidate you, but to prepare you for what to expect: the above sample pattern is not untypical of the logical structure of extended arguments found in everyday discourse.

**8.4** To further assist you in learning how to standardize more complicated arguments here are some rules of thumb that we have found to be helpful:

1. Look first for the main argument—its conclusion and the premises directly supporting it. Only after you are roughly clear about it should you begin to fit together the pieces of the subordinate arguments.

2. Make sure all extraneous material is eliminated from your standardization.

3. When necessary for clarity, recast the actual wording of the text. Take care not to alter its meaning.

4. Generally, evaluation will be easier if only one proposition is contained in each premise of the standardization. This means you will sometimes have to divide one sentence of the original text into two or more sentences in your standardization.

5. Rarely can one premise alone provide sufficient warrant for a conclusion. If your examination of the text yields any argument with a solitary premise, consider the possibility of a missing implicit premise. Missing premises, marked as such, should be supplied in your standardization so that all of the reasoning is out in the open, but take pains to commit the arguer to nothing more than what's required to link the stated premises with the conclusion.

6. Treat subordinate arguments—arguments supporting premises—with as much consideration and care as the main argument.

7. Write up your tentative standardization as a rough draft. Check it for internal logical coherence and faithfulness to the text. Poor logic may be the fault of the original argument, but it may also be due to mistakes you make in transferring the argument into your standardization. Doublecheck against the text.

8. Write out a neat copy of your standardization, carefully numbering the premises to show their places in the argument and leaving plenty of space for jotting down notes to yourself about fallacies that may be present.

**Step 4.** Evaluate the logical adequacy of the argument. Locate any fallacies and be prepared to fully defend your judgements.

# 2 Begging the Question

**8.5** The last two fallacies on our roster, which we present in this and the next section, require for their detection all of the skills which you have been developing over the past chapters. They are typically found in the extended arguments and ongoing debates which are the focus of this chapter. Moreover, their defining characteristics do not place them in any of the natural groupings of earlier chapters.

**8.6** In Chapter 1 we listed the conditions governing good argument: the premises must be relevant, sufficient, and acceptable. Our next fallacy is linked to a criterion of acceptability. We have already talked about reasonableness as one such requirement. Here is another: a premise is acceptable only if it does *not* require prior acceptance of the conclusion. A corollary of this is that all premises must be different from the conclusion. The rationale of this criterion should be clear. Since an argument is an attempt to provide reasons which build up support for a conclusion, that conclusion cannot itself occur as one of the premises, nor may any of the premises be such as to require that we already accept the conclusion. If either of these occurs, then in effect the argument supposes that the conclusion is true. However, if that supposition is warranted, then there is no need for an argument to support it. Arguments that violate this stricture are said to contain the fallacy of **begging the question**.

**8.7** The essence of the fallacy is illustrated by the following tale. Two medieval Jews were engaged in a dispute about the spiritual gifts of their respective rabbis. To clinch his case, one of them said, "I'll give you proof positive that my rabbi is the most gifted in the world. Is there another rabbi who dances with the angels every night after he falls asleep?" His friend was skeptical. "How do you know that your rabbi really does dance every night with the angels?" he demanded. "Why," replied the first, "because he told me so himself!" The skeptic insisted: "But can you believe him?" "*What?*" exclaimed the first angrily, "would a rabbi who dances with the angels each night tell a lie?"

In trying to prove that his rabbi really did dance with the angels, the first chap was called upon to show that his rabbi's word could be trusted. In trying to do that, he used as a premise a compound proposition ("A rabbi who dances with the angels each night would not tell a lie") which contains as one of its components the conclusion he was trying to establish—that his rabbi danced with the angels. You can see why this form of *begging the question* is also called "arguing in a circle." So the argument offends against the acceptability requirement that the premises may not include the conclusion; that is, each premise must be *different from* the conclusion.

A premise can be the same as the conclusion without having exactly the same wording, as in the example just discussed. As long as the premise expresses the *same proposition* as the conclusion, the effect is the same. Here is a classic textbook example, from the

19th-century treatise, *Elements of Logic* (London, 1862), by Richard Whately:

**137**    To allow every man unbounded freedom of speech must always be, on the whole advantageous to the state; for it is highly conducive to the interests of the community that each individual should enjoy a liberty perfectly unlimited of expressing his sentiments.

The flowery phrasing of the argument serves to disguise that it begs the question. If we put the argument into standard form and use some common sense, we can see the flaw.

**138**    **P1:** It is (a) highly conducive to the interests of the community that (b) each individual should enjoy a liberty perfectly unlimited of expressing personal sentiments.
       **C:** (b₁) To allow everyone unbounded freedom of speech must always be, on the whole, (a₁) advantageous to the state.

   What does it mean for a practice to be (a₁) "advantageous to the state" if not that it is (a) "highly conducive to the interests of the community"? These two phrases express the very same notion but in different words. And what does it mean to (b₁) "allow everyone unbounded freedom of speech" if not (b) "that each individual should enjoy a liberty perfectly unlimited of expressing sentiments"? "Unbounded freedom of speech" and "a liberty perfectly unlimited of expressing sentiments" are synonymous. The premise says that "each individual should enjoy" such a freedom, while the conclusion states, in effect, that "everyone should be allowed" such a liberty. But these statements are merely semantic variations on the same theme. The premise and the conclusion are one and the same proposition expressed in different words. Thus, the argument *begs the question*.
   The first two examples offend against the requirement of acceptability that the premise must not be the same as the conclusion— either in the same words, or in the form of a logically equivalent proposition. The next example shows a violation of the more general stipulation that the acceptance of the premise must not require prior acceptance of the conclusion. You may remember this example: you've seen it already as Exercise 9 for Chapter 4, the excerpt from David Ogilvy's *Confessions of an Advertising Man.* Recall that Ogilvy was touting his own Rolls-Royce ad, in the *last* paragraph of which he had written: "People who feel diffident about driving a Rolls-Royce can buy a Bentley." He then went on to argue:

**139**    Judging from the number of motorists who *picked up* the word "diffident" and bandied it about, I concluded that the advertisement was thoroughly read. (Emphasis ours.)

We've standardized this much of Ogilvy's argument:

**140**    **P1:** Many motorists *picked up* the word "diffident" and bandied it about.

**P2:** The word "diffident" occurred near the end of Ogilvy's 700-word advertisement.

**P3:** Research shows that readership of advertisements falls off rapidly up to fifty words of copy, but drops very little between fifty and 500 words.

**C:** Many motorists thoroughly read Ogilvy's Rolls-Royce advertisement.

Focus on **P1**. Is it acceptable? That depends on where Ogilvy thinks the motorists "picked up" the word "diffident," and there's no doubt he thinks they were influenced to use the word by reading his advertisement. That supposition, however, *begs the question*. For if we are to accept **P1**—that the motorists picked up "diffident" from Ogilvy's ad—we must already have accepted the argument's conclusion, **C**—that many motorists read the Rolls-Royce ad thoroughly. Since the acceptability of **P1** depends on our already having accepted the conclusion, **P1** cannot be used to prove that conclusion.

When a candidate for political office in Florida claimed that Mickey Spillane's novel, *The Erection Set*, was pornographic and should be removed from the shelves of the local library, Spillane responded:

**141**    For the first thing, I wouldn't write pornography because it doesn't sell.

Look carefully at Spillane's abbreviated argument. His conclusion is that *The Erection Set* is not pornographic. His premise is that he (Spillane) doesn't write pornography. We can accept this premise, however, only if we have already accepted the conclusion, for if the book is pornographic, then the claim that Spillane doesn't write pornography (despite his own claim to the contrary) is not acceptable. Spillane's compact argument is guilty of *begging the question*.

Spillane's argument illustrates a kind of manoeuvre that often signals this fallacy. M makes a charge. N replies by asserting a more general claim which if true would rebut M's charge, but the claim cannot be accepted until we know on *other* grounds that M's charge is false. Spillane's claim that he doesn't write pornography would if true rebut the charge that *The Erection Set* is pornographic; for, if Spillane doesn't write pornography and did write *The Erection Set*, then it follows that the book is not pornographic. The problem is the allegation was made that the book *is* pornographic. The dispute about this particular book can't be resolved by Spillane's simply asserting a more general claim which, under the circumstances, is as much in question as the original one.

**8.8** We can now summarize *begging the question* and present its conditions. Two species are to be found. In one, the premises contain the conclusion, either expressed identically or else stated in a form that is logically equivalent to it. This first version of the fallacy is usually found in longer, compound arguments. The question-begging premise tends to occur in a subordinate argument; the conclusion it begs is one or more steps removed. In the second kind of *begging the question*, the guilty premise is plausible or reasonable only if one already accepts the conclusion. The acceptability of the premise depends on our first accepting the conclusion which it is being used to defend. In brief:

---

### BEGGING THE QUESTION

1. One of the premises of an argument is identical to the conclusion or logically equivalent to it; or
2. One of the premises of an argument is such that we could not accept it unless we had already accepted the conclusion.

---

Proving *begging the question* is impossible without identifying the culpable premise, so some degree of standardizing is necessary. Standardizing becomes particularly crucial in extended, compound arguments. The premise that begs the question can belong to a subordinate argument and the proposition it begs can be the main conclusion of the whole argument. The two may be considerably removed from each other in terms of the logical structure of the argument. Besides the ability to standardize, you will need your previously developed skills at cutting through rhetoric to recognize a proposition under different guises and at uncovering hidden assumptions.

# 3 Inconsistency

**8.9** What *is* consistency? Is it never changing your mind? Surely not, for conditions may alter, making a different decision appropriate. Is it never changing your beliefs? That would seem a confusion of consistency with pig-headedness or stupidity, for surely you should stop believing a proposition which has been refuted. Is it always acting the same way? Hardly, because that suggests someone who is completely set in his or her ways or morally dogmatic. In general, the simple identification of consistency and sameness is a mistake, but we're hard-pressed to produce a nutshell explanation of the concept. That is because we are dealing here with another of those fundamental concepts—like relevance (recall the analysis of relevance in 2.4)—that cannot be defined in terms of others more basic.

**8.10** We shall turn instead to some examples of *inconsistency* to evoke and sharpen your sense for consistency. One kind of inconsistency is holding two incompatible propositions to be true. Our best example of this is Vincent Teresa's brief panegyric to the Mafia, already quoted in *two wrongs*:

> 142   Not that mobsters are all bad. There are plenty of good things about them the public might be interested in. For instance, does the public know whether mob guys are patriotic or not. The truth is, most are. *We don't think about undermining the government. We corrupt politicians, but that's only so we can do business.* (Emphasis ours.)

The inconsistency here is hard to miss. What activity undermines the government more than corrupting politicians—regardless of one's motive? When people find out that politicians are being corrupted, being bought off by the Mafia, they lose confidence in those politicians; this loss of faith cannot help but undermine the government.

Another kind of inconsistency is not following your own advice. A high school advisor wrote to Ann Landers (August 1976) with this comment:

> 143   A question frequently asked by students is this: "My mom gets bombed every night, double-bombed on weekends, fills the house with smoke, then raises hell when I smoke and gets crazy if I have a drink. Does she have the right to keep

me from doing things she says are bad for me when she doesn't practice what she preaches?"

Kids who raise this question see the inconsistency between what people prescribe in the role of advisor or authority and how they conduct themselves in the role of agent.

A third typical sort of inconsistency is the one politicians are so often accused of: taking one position at one time (or in front of one audience) and a different position at a later time (or in front of a different interest group). In 1971, the RCMP came under attack for using teenagers as paid police informers in drug cases. Shortly after the story broke, then–Solicitor General Jean-Pierre Goyer denied that the RCMP ever used juvenile spies. Then, a week later, under questioning in the House, Goyer told the Commons that the RCMP would *no longer* pay juveniles for information, under any circumstances. You can see the assumption built into "no longer." "The RCMP will no longer pay juveniles for information" is a compound proposition which breaks down into the following two:

Q: The RCMP in the past used juveniles for information.
R: The RCMP will not in the future use juveniles for that purpose.

But Q conflicts with Goyer's prior denial; the two statements are inconsistent.

Of course, Mr. Goyer may have made the earlier denial in good faith, based on information then available, and only later discovered that information to have been mistaken. But since we have no way of knowing that, and since Goyer was in a political role in which he was trying to persuade the House and the public that his government, and he himself, were properly controlling the RCMP, the onus was on him to explain the incompatibility between his two statements.

**8.11** The fallacy of **inconsistency**, then, involves more than simply an inconsistency between statements, or between statements and actions. The additional dimension making such incompatibilities culpable is a *persuasive context*. When we are being asked to believe or do something, and the person doing the asking says inconsistent things in making the appeal, or sends inconsistent signals by his or her example, *then* the inconsistency short-circuits or cancels the force of the appeal.

Look back to Example 143 to see how this analysis of *inconsistency* works out there. If you have ever tried to stop smoking, you will understand the bind of the hooked smoker who opposes smoking, but finds it tough to break the habit. There is no logical failing when, against such a background, a mother says to her son or daughter, "I know I smoke, but I wish you wouldn't. It's not good for you. I'm doing my best to quit, but it's so hard to." However, the picture sketched in the youth advisor's letter to Ann Landers was quite different. The mother conjured up there doesn't offer any explanation of or excuse for the inconsistency between her own behaviour and the conduct she demands of her child. Her continuing to smoke and drink raises the question whether these things can be totally bad, so it implicitly conflicts with her demands. The persuasiveness of her prohibitions is undercut.

In Example 142, Teresa was trying to get his readers to accept the position that mobsters are not all bad and offered in evidence their patriotism. By asserting that mob guys don't try to undermine the government and also asserting that in effect they do, he pulled the rug out from under his own case for the Mafia's patriotism.

**8.12** The fallacy, then, appears to be characterized by the following conditions:

---

### INCONSISTENCY

1. M asserts Q, as well as R, which is incompatible with Q; or M asserts Q, but does X, which is incompatible with Q; or M does X, as well as Y, which is incompatible with X;
2. In the context, M's assertions and conduct are relevant to a persuasive appeal M is making. E.g., M may be seeking acceptance of a claim, approval of an action or policy, a resolve to act, obedience to a prescription, or emulation of an example.
3. The incompatibility of 1 undercuts the persuasive appeal of 2.

---

All parts are essential: (1) incompatibility (2) in the context of persuasion (3) that short-circuits the appeal.

So important is consistency, so much a part of our approach to evaluating views and arguments, that it can push us into committing fallacies. Recall that *two wrongs* is very often prompted by the drive for consistency; so also is *faulty analogy*.

Charges of *inconsistency* are probably the most common form of public logical criticism. It is a serious offense, since it completely undercuts any persuasive appeal. Moreover, it can be morally and politically grievous. Inconsistent parents can mess up their children's lives. Inconsistent politicians cannot be trusted. Since *inconsistency* is such a serious charge, making groundless accusations of *inconsistency* deserves reprimand too. The frequency of hasty or unsubstantiated charges of *inconsistency* prompts us to label them fallacies in their own right:

---

**FALSE CHARGE OF INCONSISTENCY**

1. N accuses M of *inconsistency*.
2. N's charge fails to meet all three conditions of *inconsistency*.

---

**8.13** Test your understanding of these fallacies on a few examples.

In 1971 the Windsor *Star* excised an entire story from an edition of *Weekend Magazine* and offered the following editorial justification:

**144**   The removal of a story from the issue of *Weekend Magazine* distributed with Saturday's *Star* was a matter of principle and not of censorship. There was nothing to censor in the story concerned. It was the first of three excerpts from a book written by Bill Trent about the case of Steven Truscott, who was the central figure in a sex crime 12 years ago. Publishing such a story, in the *Star's* opinion, would have been pandering to base tastes.

Do you see any *inconsistency* in the *Star's* argument? We do. The paper claimed its action was not censorship, but rather the removal of a story avoided "pandering to base tastes." But refusing to print material which "panders to base tastes" *is* censorship, by definition. (The *Star* ought to have said that it considered censorship legitimate in that kind of case. The "principle" referred to in the editorial and used by the *Star* elsewhere to justify cutting out the Truscott article was that convicted criminals should not profit from their notoriety by being paid for their stories.)

Here is an example of a *charge* of *inconsistency*. In October 1975, Canadian Press did a survey of responses to Ontario Attorney-General Roy McMurtry's announced crackdown on hockey violence. (The previous year William McMurtry, a brother of the Attorney-General, had prepared a report for the Ontario government on violence in amateur hockey, recommending that steps be taken to reduce it and citing violence in pro hockey as a contributing factor.)

Among those whose views were quoted in the CP story was John F. Bassett, president of the then Toronto Toros. Bassett was quoted as saying:

**145**  He [McMurtry] was the dirtiest hockey player who ever played, but now that he has the golden robes of office he has become the messiah for his little brother's cause.

Let's assume Bassett's quoted depiction of McMurtry's own hockey play is accurate. The question is, was McMurtry guilty of *inconsistency* because his policy as Attorney-General is incompatible with his own conduct as a player?

Clearly, one can change one's mind and come to disapprove of one's own earlier conduct. And hockey violence is only beginning to be challenged in a large-scale way. Perhaps McMurtry played the game the way it was played in his day (only more so), but later —maybe persuaded by his brother's report—came to disapprove of that style of hockey. So we can imagine a possible line of defense for McMurtry against Bassett.

There's a problem of burden of proof here. On whom rests the onus to produce the evidence? We think it lies with the person who initiates the criticism—in this case, Bassett. He made the charge of *inconsistency* (did you notice the *ad hominem* he committed in the process, by the way?); there is a reasonable explanation of how McMurtry's position is not guilty of *inconsistency*; it was up to Bassett to defend his charge. Since he did not—at least not in the remarks attributed to him—we find him, in the CP report of his accusation, guilty of *false charge of inconsistency*.

In political debate and commentary, charges of *inconsistency* fly thick and fast. Usually they are less easily resolved than the accusers suppose. One of the big examples in recent politics has been the charge that the Liberals, who may have won the 1974 election by opposing Conservative proposals for wage and price controls, were *inconsistent* in turning around and imposing those controls themselves in October 1975. Here is Richard Gwyn's version of the accusation, from a column in January 1976:

**146**  During the entire controls program, Trudeau has never once bothered, in public or in private, to apologize or to explain for completely reversing the anti-controls program he sold to the public during the 1974 election campaign. Consistency is for losers, and for professors and writers.

Gwyn at least committed *problematic premise* when he asserted that Mr. Trudeau never *privately* explained the turn-about, for how could Gwyn know that without complete access to Trudeau's private life? More to the point of Gwyn's charge, though, presumably the Liberal government would argue that conditions changed between the 1974 election and the fall of 1975, justifying its reversal on wage and price controls. Is that defense justified and would it exonerate the government? We must beg off from offering a verdict, since forming a fair one would require extensive study and documentation of the political and economic scene over a two- or three-year period. We refrain from any conclusion here, together with a note to ourselves to watch for more evidence. That, in many instances, is the only appropriate posture in the face of charges and counter-charges of *inconsistency*.

# 4 An Example

**8.14** In this section we shall give a sample analysis of a longer argument, proceeding step by step through the stages: synopsis, standardization, and finally evaluation. You've already encountered a segment of the extended argument that serves as our example here, in the section on *straw man* (Example 23). To refresh your memory, we add this bit of background. In December 1972, Dr. Lawrence LaFave, a professor of psychology at the University of Windsor, sent a long letter to the Windsor *Star* containing a number of arguments against capital punishment. His entire letter—too long to reproduce here—was typical of the extended pieces of reasoning and persuasion found in the public forum. Because of limited space, he had to compress his argument and omit details, although he touched on quite a few points in the space available to him. He wrote in colourful language, moving quickly from one point to the next to keep the attention of his reader. In this respect, the letter itself and the excerpt we deal with illustrates a factor that should be kept in mind here. Detail and depth of argument are often sacrificed for colourful style and language.

As we said, what you are about to read is an excerpt from a much longer letter. Care has been taken not to distort that entire argument, although we have selected those portions which will best serve our purposes.

**8.15** Here is our excerpt from Dr. LaFave's letter:

**147**       *a.* The federal report by University of Montreal criminologist Dr. Ezzat Abdel Farrah (*Star*, December 16) appears to represent an excellent public service. The statistics gathered seem to suggest that the death penalty *fails* to deter murder . . .

b. Such statistics as indicated above do not conclusively prove anything, based as they are on mere correlational (rather than experimentally controlled) data.

c. Nevertheless, experimentally controlled data in this area are non-existent; so we are stuck with these mere correlations. But such facts do definitely seem to throw cold water on any argument that legal murder (i.e., capital punishment) acts as a deterrent to illegal murder . . .

d. Criminologists inform us that most murders are hot-blooded, and between relatives, acquaintances, and close friends. It is psychologically obvious that hot-blooded murders are impulsive, rashly performed by a person so overwhelmed by emotion that he has lost control (rather than by a cold-blooded calculator of the advantages and penalties involved).

e. As famous Attorney Belli observed in one of his newspaper columns, of all the killers he has spoken with, none ever told him that just prior to committing the homicide he had stopped at the library to check on the penalty . . .

f. Who gets executed for murder is in fact probably much more closely associated with racial, sexual, and economic prejudice than with who actually commits murder.

g. In the United States the number of poor Negro men who have been executed for murder is legion; the number of rich, white, women victims of capital punishment can be counted on the fingers of one hand. (And it would be erroneous to conclude that the latter group did not commit a large share.)

h. The vast majority of Canadian policemen appear to favor capital punishment, especially when one of their colleagues is murdered in the line of duty. These policemen are entitled to their opinion.

i. However, the public should not take their views on this subject seriously . . .

j. The reason is that it is difficult to conceive of a group more incompetent on the subject of capital punishment than police organizations. Two basic reasons for their incompetence in this area exist: 1) Policemen are too emotionally involved in the issue to think about it with the detachment needed for sound judgement. 2) The interpretation of the statistical and other evidence as to whether capital punishment acts as a deterrent is far beyond the modest intellectual achievements of the typical policemen and their organizations.

**8.16** Let's begin by constructing a *synopsis* of the argument. To do that we must first see if there is any one overall conclusion and, if so, what it is. Although he never does state it in just this way, our interpretation is that everything LaFave says points to the proposition that *there is no good reason for having capital punishment in Canada* as the basic point or main conclusion. True, he gives much attention to the claim that the death penalty does not deter murderers, but he gives other reasons against capital punishment besides the no-deterrent argument (cf. paragraphs *f* and *g*). We think that the conclusion identified above is consistent with the text as it unfolds, and our synopsis reflects this interpretation.

In paragraphs *a-c*, LaFave *notes that there is evidence for the claim that the death penalty does not deter murder, and registers a reservation about the statistics which comprise that evidence:* "Since the statistics are based on mere correlational data, as opposed to experimentally controlled data, they do not conclusively prove anything."

In paragraphs *d* and *e* LaFave is clearly arguing that *capital punishment is not a deterrent to murder, in most cases*. In effect, he is *attempting to defeat one sort of argument proposed in support of the view that we ought to have capital punishment*. This is Strategy 3 that we noted in 8.2: attack your opponent's position.

In paragraphs *f* and *g* the argument takes a different turn. LaFave seems to be saying that *capital punishment has been and will continue to be prejudicially applied in practice*. In other words, he is *showing that one of the consequences of having capital punishment is unacceptable*. This is Strategy 4: show that the policy you oppose is likely to lead to undesirable consequences.

Once again a new tack is introduced in paragraphs *h-j*. LaFave argues there that *the opinions of police in Canada should not be taken seriously*. The Strategy is 2: anticipate and defuse a possible objection. In this case, the objection would go as follows: "But Canadian police seem to favour capital punishment, so that's a good reason for having it."

**8.17** The reason for doing a synopsis is to acquire an understanding of the organization of the text in order to prepare for the second stage: *standardizing the argument*. At this stage, the repetition, the overlap, the extraneous material all should be pared away, as you replace the rhetorical order by the logical order.

We begin with our conclusion clearly in mind (cf. 1 in 8.4):

**148**   **C:** There is no good reason for having capital punishment in Canada.

Next we search for the main premises (cf. 1 in 8.4). In the first three paragraphs, two references are made to the no-deterrent claim. Clearly enough, LaFave believes that capital punishment is not a deterrent to murder. Moreover, if true, this claim will lend support to his conclusion, since it negates one of the reasons frequently cited for having capital punishment. We will note and ticket it as:

**149**   **P1:** *Capital punishment is not a deterrent to murder.*

We have stated this proposition in our own words, slightly changing the wording in both *a* and *c*, but we haven't, we hope, altered the propositional content of LaFave's statements (cf. 3 in 8.4). Since at this stage we are attempting to identify the main premises only, we postpone standardizing the defense of **P1** that occurs in *d* and *e*.

We saw that paragraphs *f* and *g* make the point that capital punishment is unfairly applied. This relates to the conclusion, because, if a policy is prejudicially implemented, that's a reason for abandoning or not adopting it. So we get the second main premise:

**150**   **P2:** *Capital punishment would tend to be unfairly applied in Canada.*

Once again we point out that our formulation of **P2** does not match one to one with what LaFave actually stated. It does, however, appear to us to be the gist of his argument at this point. Again we defer standardizing the subordinate argument for **P2** for the moment.

Paragraphs *h-j*, we noted in our synopsis, serve to defuse one possible line of objection: that police appear to favour capital punishment. With an eye to the conclusion, we can formulate the point of these three paragraphs so as to connect them with that conclusion:

**151**   **P3:** *That police in Canada favour capital punishment is not a good reason for having it.*

True, these are not LaFave's precise words. What he said was that we should not take the views of Canadian police seriously. In the context of the argument, however, this point seems better rendered by **P3.**

We are ready now to display the structure of the main argument:

**152**   **P1:** Capital punishment is no deterrent to murder.

**P2:** Capital punishment tends to be unfairly applied in practice.

**P3:** That police in Canada favour capital punishment is not a good reason for having it.

**C:** There is no good reason for having capital punishment in Canada.

With the main argument standardized, we turn our attention next to the subordinate arguments.

**8.18** We must first see how the opening three paragraphs of the text logically connect with **P1.** In them LaFave mentions an earlier published report of statistics bearing on the effectiveness of capital punishment as a deterrent, and argues that these statistics provide some inconclusive evidence that capital punishment does not deter murder: (1) Dr. Farrah's evidence suggests capital punishment does not deter murder; (2) the statistics are not conclusive because (a) they are based on correlations and (b) we need experimentally controlled data; but (3) this is all the evidence we have to go on. Notice how (2) requires us to qualify our original formulation of this first main premise. Here is how the subordinate argument for **P1** looks when standardized:

153

**P1Ai:** Dr. Farrah's report gathers statistics that suggest capital punishment fails to deter murder.

**P1Aiia:** These statistics are based on correlational data only.

**P1Aiib:** Only statistics based on experimentally controlled data can prove anything conclusively.

**P1Aii:** Such statistics do not conclusively prove anything.

**P1Aiii:** Such statistics are all the statistical evidence that exists.

**P1A:** What relevant evidence exists gives some (less than conclusive) reason to believe that capital punishment fails to deter murder.

**P1:** Capital punishment is probably no deterrent to murder.

This is the first argument for **P1**, but it is not the only one. LaFave also argues in paragraphs *d* and *e* for this conclusion. The argument in those two paragraphs runs as follows: (1) most murders are hot-blooded (or so we are informed by criminologists): (2) hot-blooded murders are impulsive, rash, uncontrolled (that much is psychologically obvious); and (3) such murders are not committed in cold blood, with a view to the advantages and penalties involved. Let's put that much down:

**154**       **P1Bi:** Criminologists inform us that most murders are hot-blooded.
    **P1B:** Most murders are hot-blooded.
    **P1Ci:** It is psychologically obvious that hot-blooded murders are impulsive, rash, uncontrolled.
    **P1C:** Hot-blooded murders are impulsive, rash, uncontrolled.
    **P1D:** Impulsive, rash, uncontrolled murders aren't committed with a cold-blooded view to the advantages and penalties involved.

How do these premises show that capital punishment does not deter murder? They build up to the point that most murderers don't calmly consider the advantages and penalties of their action. That is a reason against the view that capital punishment would act as a deterrent to murder, because capital punishment can have this effect only if people contemplating murder consider beforehand the consequences of their act. We need to insert these obvious implicit links in the reasoning into our standardization (cf. 5 in 8.4). Doing so will also enable us to tie in the reference LaFave makes to Melvin Belli in paragraph e.

Belli's observation is offered as further evidence that murderers do not consider the consequences before they act. We should note here also the implicit premise that we may consider Belli's observations to be trustworthy: LaFave is using him as an authority to back up his claim. While we are mentioning implicit premises, notice that **P1Bi** links with **P1B** because of the implicit acceptance of the authority of those unnamed criminologists. That link should be brought out. What about **P1Ci**? Does it need to connect with some unstated but operative premise in order to lead to **P1C**? As we read it, no; if something is psychologically obvious, then that by itself is a reason for accepting it.

As a final emendation, we note that LaFave's argument speaks of "most murders"—not *all* of them. We ought not to allow the conclusion of this subargument (which is **P1**) to make a stronger claim than the evidence offered for it suggests.

In our revised standardization of the argument for **P1** in paragraphs d and e, we have to alter the premise numbers used in Example 149 in order to fit the implicit premises into their proper logical place in the argument. The italicized premises mark the new additions:

**155**

**MP**

**P1Bia:** Criminologists inform us that most murders are hot-blooded.

**P1Bib:** *The criminologists referred to are authorities on the behaviour of murders.*

**P1Bi:** Most murders are hot-blooded.

**P1Biia:** It is psychologically obvious that hot-blooded murders are impulsive, rash, uncontrolled.

**P1Bii:** Hot-blooded murders are impulsive, rash, uncontrolled.

**P1Biii:** Impulsive, rash, uncontrolled murders aren't committed with a cold-blooded view to the advantages and penalties involved.

**P1Biv:** *None of the killers the famous attorney, Melvin Belli, had spoken with ever checked the penalty before committing homicide.*

**MP**

**P1Bv:** *Belli's observations can be treated as authoritative.*

**P1B:** *In most cases, murderers do not consider the consequences before they act.*

**MP**

**P1C:** Capital punishment can serve as a deterrent to murder only if people consider the consequences before they act.

**P1:** *In most cases, capital punishment probably would not serve as a deterrent to murder.*

If you read from subordinate arguments furthest removed from the main argument—the arguments with **P1Bi** and with **P1Bii** as their conclusions—and work through to the main argument for **P1**, you will find that each is logically coherent. Also, if you check our standardization against the original text, paragraphs *d* and *e* (cf. 7 in 8.4), we believe you will find we have accurately captured the logical skeleton of LaFave's presentation.

We move on now to the argument for **P2** given in paragraphs *f* and *g* of LaFave's letter. His implicit claim that capital punishment would be unfairly applied in practice seems to be based on the allegation that it has been unfairly applied in practice in the United States. For this assertion to apply to Canada, we need to insert a missing premise (cf. 5 of 8.4), to the effect that if the American application of capital punishment has been inequitable, so would the Canadian. LaFave argues that capital punishment has been unfairly applied in the U.S. because, (i) "who gets executed for murder is . . . probably much more closely associated with racial, sexual, and economic prejudice than with who actually commits murder." The evidence for (i) that LaFave gives is twofold: (a) in the U.S., the number of poor black men who have been executed for murder is "legion," and (b) in the U.S. the number of rich white women victims of capital punishment can be counted on the fingers of one hand. LaFave adds, "It would be erroneous to assume that the latter group did not commit a large share." In other words, he is saying that (b) cannot itself be accounted for by the fact that rich white women commit very few murders. The force of this assertion is to suggest that while (a) and (b) have been stated in raw numbers ("legion" and "counted on the fingers of one hand"), the point really is that the *ratio* of poor black males executed for murder as against those eligible for capital punishment is far greater than the ratio of rich white women executed as against their numbers eligible for the death penalty. What this difference implies, in the context of LaFave's argument, is that the imbalance or inequality of ratios between the two groups is due to economic, racial, and sexual prejudice. Organizing the argument for **P2** according to this analysis, then, we get the following standardization:

**156**          **P2Aia1:** In the U.S. the number of poor, black men executed for murder is legion.

                       **P2Aia2:** In the U.S. the number of rich, white women executed for murder is few.

**MP**          **P2Aia:** In the U.S. the ratio of poor black men who have been executed for murder is far greater than the ratio of rich white women executed.

**MP**          **P2Aib:** This imbalance of ratios is clear evidence that economic, racial, and sexual prejudice affects the implementation of the death penalty.

        **P2Ai:** In the U.S. the correlation between those who commit murder and those who are actually executed gives clear evidence of economic, racial, and sexual prejudice.

     **P2A:** Capital punishment has been unfairly applied in the United States.

**MP**          **P2B:** If capital punishment has been unfairly applied in the U.S., then it would probably be unfairly applied in Canada.

       **P2:** Capital punishment would probably tend to be unfairly applied in Canada.

Next comes the argument for the third main premise, that police support of capital punishment is not a good reason for having it. The point about police being particularly in favour of capital punishment for the murderers of police officers we take to be an amplification that is not part of the argument (cf. 2 in 8.4). The acknowledgement that they are entitled to their opinion is an aside (cf. 2 in 8.4).

LaFave indicates clearly when he is getting to the point by announcing, "The reason is . . .": police and their organizations are not
competent to serve as authorities on the subject of capital punishment. He conveniently numbers two reasons for this latter judgement: (1) they are too emotionally involved to be detached and (2)
they are not qualified to interpret the evidence that bears on the
question. The subordinate argument shapes up like this:

**157**        **P3Ai:** Police are too emotionally involved in the issue
to think about it with the detachment needed for
sound judgement.

         **P3Aii:** The interpretation of the statistical and other
evidence bearing on the deterrent effect of
capital punishment is far beyond the modest intellectual achievements of typical police and
their organizations.

        **P3A:** Police and their organizations are not competent on
the subject of capital punishment.

      **P3:** That police in Canada favour capital punishment is not
a good reason for having it.

Note that **P3A** is the only premise listed for **P3**. Is there a missing
premise linking it to the conclusion? Clearly the argument employs
the following missing premise:

**158**

**MP**       **P3B:** If police and their organizations are not competent
on the subject of capital punishment, then their
favouring it is no good reason for having it.

Our standardization of Professor LaFave's argument is now
complete. Of course, it did not spring in its present, fully-developed
form straight from our heads onto the printed page. We made
several attempts to rough out the argument, some of which were
rejected, before we reached the one we were reasonably satisfied
with. To analyze and standardize such a fairly involved piece of
reasoning as this one requires much fussing with various interpretations, numerous revisions, and probably *several* rough drafts tossed
into the wastebasket, before a satisfactory version emerges. Of
course, the more practice you get, the more proficient you become.

Here, then, is a map of LaFave's argument:[3]

---

[3] Our map, which is really simply a method for displaying the pattern of
LaFave's argument, is similar to a device used by Scriven in *Reasoning*.

159

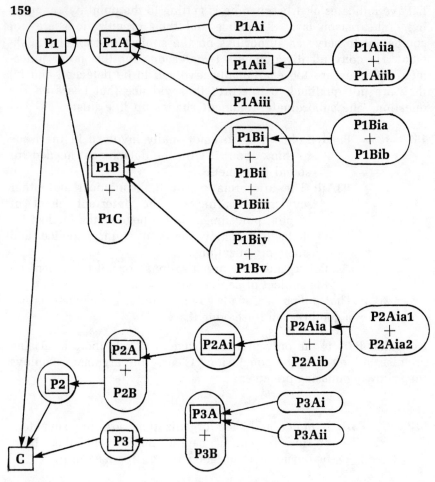

**8.19** We can now move to the last stage of the analysis of our example: the evaluation of the argument. We'll run through the arguments for the main premises first. The backing for **P1A**—the first main subordinate argument in support of **P1**—is an example of solid reasoning. LaFave supports his claim that what statistical evidence exists shows the non-deterrent effect of capital punishment by citing Dr. Farrah's report, at the same time making it clear how this sort of evidence is less than conclusive and giving us an idea of how these statistics relate to the kind of statistical evidence so far available. We can check out his claim for ourselves; we are warned not to jump to conclusions. Dr. LaFave's training in criminology serves as a warrant to accept **P1Aiia** and **P1Aiib**, and **P1Aiii**. In sum, this argument is well turned out.

The second argument for **P1** is not such clear sailing. **P1Bia** and **P1Bib** are the locus of an *improper appeal to authority*. *Rule V* has been violated. LaFave should have named the criminologists he referred to, so that their qualifications could have been verified, if necessary. Better still, he should have cited those qualifications himself. Perhaps in the interests of brevity, he did not do so. Still, we are given no reason for accepting the appeal to these authorities.

What about the reference to Belli in **P1Biv** and **P1Bv**? This reference seems to be an attempt to shore up the point that most murderers don't reflect beforehand on the consequences of their acts. Is there any reason to treat Belli's view as authoritative? No. In the first place, Belli's area of expertise is not criminal law. He is an internationally recognized authority on civil litigation, has written extensively in that area, and has edited two journals which specialize in civil litigation. Although he has handled criminal cases, this is not his area of expertise. Second, even if Belli were famous for his work in criminal law, that would not give his statement any exceptional weight, for the point at issue here is a psychological one; we have no reason to believe that Belli qualifies as an authority in this area. *Rule II* of the principles governing appeals to authority is violated; and, in **P1Biv** and **P1Bv**, there is an *improper appeal to authority*.

Premise **P1C** is a case of *dubious assumption*. Neither is it common knowledge nor obviously true that deterrence requires reflection prior to each occasion on which the act is considered. The threat of the penalty might serve to influence people to develop habits that comply with the law and yet, as is the case with habits, do not entail prior reflection each time they are performed. Since this premise is particularly crucial to LaFave's attack on the deterrence argument, he ought to have defended it.

There are two flaws in the argument for **P2**. Both might be corrected by further information and argument, but they seriously weaken the argument as it stands. First, **P2Aia** is a *hasty conclusion*. Its two premises refer to raw numbers, whereas the conclusion deals with ratios. We need to know the numbers of poor black men and rich white women, respectively, who have been eligible for capital punishment—e.g., those who committed capital crimes, or those who had their sentences commuted or reduced on appeal. The information in **P2Aia1** and **P2Aia2** is relevant, but by itself incomplete, to support **P2Aia**.

**P2B**, the missing premise, is acceptable only if one assumes that the situation regarding the application of capital punishment in Canada is analogous to that in the United States. That would be true if the social structure and practices—the economic, racial, and sexual biases—were sufficiently similar in the two countries. They *may* be; however, the point would have to be argued at some length.

It cannot be taken for granted, so it's a case of *dubious assumption*.

Somewhat more argumentation is required to complete the arguments supporting **P3**. The difficulties surround the argument for the claim that police and their organizations are incompetent on the subject of capital punishment. **P3Ai** is a *problematic premise*. Certainly the police are emotionally involved in the subject; they have more occasion than the rest of us to confront actual or potential murderers. But emotional involvement need not rule out sound judgement. Indeed, emotion may follow judgement: one may judge that something ought to be done, and then become indignant when it is not. In any event, what's in question here is whether police are *too* emotionally involved in the issue of capital punishment to be capable of sound judgement. The claim that they are needs support; LaFave has not provided any; we charge *problematic premise* here.

We think **P3Aii** is a *problematic premise* as well. We'd like to see some evidence to back up this claim, since more and more police forces are raising the standards the new recruits have to meet. But, even if LaFave were right here, the argument from **P3Ai** and **P3Aii** to **P3A** commits *hasty conclusion*. Nothing prevents police organizations from hiring consultants who *are* competent to assess the evidence and statistics that relate to the deterrent effect of capital punishment. For one example, most police forces negotiate contracts for their members with the municipalities they serve, and such negotiations require the use of people competent to handle all sorts of statistical information. So it is hasty to conclude that police and their organizations lack the statistical competence necessary on the subject of capital punishment, even if it were true that police themselves are too emotionally involved.

Our appraisal of LaFave's argument has turned up a medley of fallacies. We emphasize two things about this analysis. First, at no point can we claim to have decisively refuted his argument, and we've certainly not demonstrated that the main conclusion is false. Second, at least as we have tried to employ it, the charge of fallacy serves to extend the argument, not to cut off debate. Uncovering the fallacies we have found in LaFave's argument invites the search for more information, additional evidence, amplification. Our verdict is that *as it stands* the argument doesn't succeed in establishing its conclusion.

**8.20** This section has been offered as a model for handling the analysis and evaluation of the kinds of extended reasoning found in everyday persuasive contexts. If you master and use this technique or develop a parallel or better method of your own, you should be well equipped to defend yourself against the bad logic of longer attempts at reasoned argument.

Everyday persuasion comes in a variety of non-rational approaches as well. In the next two chapters, we give brief attention to two of the most prominent: the news media and advertising.

---

## Exercises for Chapter 8

### I

*Directions:* This first exercise is to give you some practice detecting the three new fallacies we dealt with in this chapter: *begging the question, inconsistency,* and *false charge of inconsistency.* As usual, determine which of these fallacies is committed and support your judgement by showing that the conditions are satisfied.

1. *Background:* This letter to the Ottawa *Journal* (April 1975) objected to Canada's abstention from a United Nations vote on whether to allow the Palestinian Liberation Organization to participate in a debate about the Middle East:

> Four years ago, Prime Minister Trudeau and his government suspended civil liberties in Canada in order to deal with a perceived terrorist threat. The media printed stories and showed pictures of *FLQ* members being trained with and by Palestinian terrorists. Four years ago the *PLO* was as much an anathema to most Canadians who thought about it as the *FLQ*.
>
> Recently, Prime Minister Trudeau and his government changed their minds about terrorists. Suddenly an organization that proudly boasts such atrocities as the Munich and Lod massacres . . . and numerous other outrages against world justice and order, became legitimate—with the quiet consent of Canada.
>
> Not objecting to evil is tantamount to condoning it. Canada's abstention on the United Nations vote to allow the *PLO* to participate in a General Assembly debate on the Middle East is tantamount to condoning all terrorism, wherever it occurs. What a disgraceful action for a country that claims to work for world peace!

2. *Background:* In 1971, a commission was established to investigate allegations of corruption in the New York City police force. One of the witnesses was a police officer who, having

once himself been guilty of taking payoffs, turned undercover agent. He was a key witness before the commission, claiming that all plainclothes detectives took regular payoffs and that "there's no way one man can go in a division and remain straight." Following his testimony, the police commissioner told newsmen:

> That is an absurd charge. I know for a fact that there are plainclothesmen who are not "on the pad."

3. *Background*: The Detroit *Free Press* has a daily question to which it invites its readers to phone in their answers and comments. The results are tabulated and printed the following day, along with a capsule of some of the comments. This letter is about the response to one "Sound Off" question:

> We feel that people are entitled to express their opinions on your Sound Off poll, but it is not necessary for the *Free Press* to publish remarks to the effect that Jews are responsible for the oil shortage. Printing that comment was not worthy of your paper nor was it in the interest of our national security.

4. *Background*: Howard Cosell is an American sports commentator, currently famous for his role in Monday Night Football. In 1974, on the eve of the championship fight between Joe Frazier and Muhammad Ali, Cosell received a transcontinental call from Ali in Zaire, Africa. Terribly excited that Ali would take the trouble to call him, Cosell quickly reported the contents of the call to his audience. It later turned out that the call was a prank, perpetrated by a student at the University of Western Ontario. Naturally, Cosell's vanity was stung when he learned of the joke. He said: "If he did that, he ought to be in jail instead of being glorified by the press." The Windsor *Star* editorialized (November 1974):

> Sorry, Howard. But it just seems like you're suffering from the same ailment you have constantly derided and deflated the old-line, oldtime sports owners and reporters for: you're taking yourself much too seriously.

5. *Background:* In July 1976, the Detroit *Free Press* editorialized against Canada's decision to refuse to allow the athletes from Taiwan to participate in the Olympics as representative of the Republic of China. A Canadian reader objected to that editorial:

> There is only one flag, one government, one anthem per

nation. As mainland China is recognized as that nation, no other action need be considered.

If one of our provinces were to secede from our country, it would not be allowed the Canadian flag or anthem. Would one of your separatist states be allowed your flag or anthem?

6. *Background*: This letter appeared in the Toronto *Globe and Mail* in October 1972:

I note that Dr. Wilder Penfield may not visit Moscow or the next meeting of the Soviet Academy of Sciences because to do so might be construed as approval of the behaviour of Team Canada.

Do his previous visits there imply approval of the Russian invasion of Hungary and Czechoslovakia? Or of its treatment of intellectuals, e.g., refusal to allow Alexander Solzhenitsyn to visit Stockholm to accept has Nobel prize?

7. *Background*: A letter to the Windsor *Star* (September 1972) defending abortion:

The controversy seems to be over when a fetus becomes a human. There is no way it can happen at conception. Sure, there is life at conception, but there is a great difference between that life and human life. Abortion is just another form of birth control, and if it is not used, the population explosion will be on us before we know it.

## II

*Directions*: Evaluate the following extended arguments. Your evaluation should include a synopsis, a standardization, and then an inspection of the argument for fallacies. The first two examples are shorter and more straightforward than the last two.

1. This is a letter to the Regina *Leader Post*, October 1974:

Why pick on dogs? What about other nuisances on city property? The suggestion made by the parks board that owners who allow their dogs to relieve themselves in the park pay a fine is ridiculous.

Have they forgotten that the dog is an animal and as such cannot ask its master to "go to the washroom"? What is the owner to do? The owner pays a license fee for the privilege of keeping a dog. He also observes the law that forbids him to let his dog run loose.

In taking his dog for a walk on a leash, he is within the law. The fact that the dog might have to perform a natural function is automatically included under the law, because of the dog's status as an animal.

2. A letter to the Vancouver *Sun* about pesticides, October 1974:

It seems to me that people are going too far when they claim that it is not safe to eat apples and pears because pesticide sprays have been used.

What they do not seem to know is that sprays against fruit pests, the codling moth and pear psylla, for instance, have been used in the Okanagan for 50 years at least. If sprays are dangerous, this surely would have shown up by now in Okanagan medical records. I was born in the Okanagan and lived there for 30 years but I, my daughter and granddaughter seem quite healthy and I see no evidence of genetic damage.

If sprays had not been used during all those years the insects would have taken over and there would now be no apples and pears, or else wormy ones. The entomologists are trying to find alternate ways of controlling insect pests but entomologists are hard to come by.

I should like to suggest that an orchardist using spray is no more dangerous to the human race than the automobile which is not only air polluting but uses a vital resource which is fast disappearing.

3. An editorial in the Windsor *Star* (October 1972), which was entitled "A Powerful Argument":

Latest crime statistics from Denmark provide a striking illustration of the beneficial effects of that nation's experiment in pornography, and will provide a powerful argument for those favoring the legalization and open availability of pornography here in Canada.

According to the figures, sexual offences against females in Copenhagen, the heart of the "dirty picture" business, dropped 59 per cent from 1965 to 1970. During the same five years, cases of exhibitionism or indecent exposure dropped 58 per cent; peeping, down 85 per cent; child molestation, down 56 per cent; and verbal indecency incidents decreased 83 per cent. There was no noticeable effect on cases of rape and intercourse with minors.

According to one expert, the availability of pornographic material provides the psycho-sexual stimulation for those people who would otherwise take illegal means to seek such stimulation.

Whatever weight attaches to the moral or good-taste arguments against pornography, it seems doubtful they will prevail, in the long run, over the increasingly liberal attitudes in modern society, particularly when the liberal position is buttressed by proof that legalized pornography leads to a decline of sexual crimes.

In Canada, pornography and the issue of legalizing it are probably still too emotion-laden to be subjected to dispassionate debate. As a result, the confusing situation with respect to pornography will probably continue, which is unfortunate.

It is unfortunate because the necessarily haphazard way of enforcing pornography legislation cannot help but make the law and the process of its enforcement look ridiculous, thus undermining the respect for law on which every civilized nation depends.

4. This letter to the Windsor *Star* is a response to Prof. LaFave's letter analyzed in this chapter:

The logic of the professor's argument escapes me completely and being a "man of modest intellectual achievements, a typical policeman" I defer to his superior intelligence.

The first portion of Professor LaFave's letter indicates his knowledge of the United States and its customs; his lack of knowledge of Canadian policemen is apparent in the latter part of his letter and is exceeded only by his colossal vanity. After permitting the policemen the luxury of having an opinion, he then instructs the public and the news media to ignore these opinions—The Lord giveth and the Lord taketh away.

Admittedly risking the ire of Professor LaFave, I nevertheless would like to correct several of his mistaken assumptions regarding policemen (with whom it is glaringly evident that he has had no social contact) and their views toward capital punishment. No rational person expects any punishment to halt murder—particularly the "hot blooded" type "between relatives, acquaintances and close friends." However, any experienced policeman knows that capital punishment is a definite deterrent to murder committed during the course of another offence–robbery, rape, etc.

How do I know this? From more than 20 years of association with criminals who have little, if any, knowledge of psychology but who realize that once capital punishment has been utilized, they have no hope of a life sentence, which today means a parole after seven to 10 years, including weekend passes to fill the interim.

The murders that concern most policemen are the murders committed for profit or to eliminate witnesses, committed by cold blooded professional criminals and these are the murders . . . that are increasing and will continue to increase until, Heaven forbid, our country can then be statistically compared to the U.S.A.

I can't offer a remedy for this situation but possibly the professor, with his educational background, can. In fact he may have in his letter but if he did, it was hidden in his verbiage. Like most psychologists he is familiar with the human mind as portrayed in his textbooks but he fails to realize that there are, in every community, persons to whom the life of another means absolutely nothing, to whom several years in prison also means nothing and whose only interest is in furthering their own ends.

The value of capital punishment as a deterrent may be arguable but there is no argument that today's "life sentences" is any deterrent. Our main concern is the safety of the public in our country and we ask only that punishment of some deterrent value be incorporated into our laws.

While Professor LaFave could not "conceive of a group more incompetent on the subject of capital punishment than police organizations," I've had no difficulty at all and suggest an organization composed of psychology professors of Lawrence LaFave calibre.

# 9 Defense against the Media

## Introduction

**9.1** Much of the information we use when we assess the persuasive appeals constantly directed at us comes from the information media: TV, radio, newspapers, magazines. Yet the media shape the message. In order to interpret this information intelligently, you ought to have a general understanding of how information is picked up by and filtered through the different news sources, as well as up-to-date knowledge of the practices and policies of the particular outlets from which you get your information: your local newspaper(s), radio and TV stations, national CBC and CTV news and current affairs programs, *Maclean's*, and probably several American sources. It is important, for logical self-defense, to be knowledgeable and intelligently critical about the information media, so we offer this chapter to raise consciousness and stimulate your own further research.

With this purpose in mind, we provide two items here. The first is a **checklist** of questions that everyone ought to be in the habit of asking when reading the newspaper or listening to or watching the news. The second is a list of **projects** intended to lead you closer to the understanding we just spoke of.

## 1 News Checklist

**9.2** In the list that follows, we present a cluster of questions under each heading, and after the questions, a brief explanation of why they should be asked. You should be able to answer these questions after a careful reading or viewing of any news report. Unless you can, you have a good chance of digesting misinformation. Hence, your needs as a media consumer—your need for an accurate and complete picture of ongoing events—won't be met. There is then the danger that you'll base your assessment of persuasive rhetoric on this false understanding of events.

## A. All Media

### 1. Billing

(a) Does the headline (or title) accurately and fully indicate the contents of the story or article?
(b) Do picture captions suggest interpretations of photographs with other plausible interpretations?

RATIONALE
(a) Headlines can give a slant to a story not warranted by the text. By referring to only one of several parts or aspects of the story, they can give it undue prominence.
(b) Photo captions can give a totally inaccurate interpretation of the event pictured.

### 2. Completeness

(a) Is the account full, clear, and coherent? Are there inconsistencies, puzzling assertions, questions left unanswered?
(b) Are there technical (or pseudo-technical) terms or statistical data that you don't fully understand?
(c) Are the details too skimpy to form a clear picture of the event?

RATIONALE
(a) News reports are usually gathered and written in a hurry to make deadlines. Coherence and completeness are casualties of the rush. Events may still be unfolding when the reporter must write the story. Parts of the report may be second hand; sources may give conflicting accounts.
(b) Reporters, like the rest of us, are sometimes smitten by meaningless jargon; stories may omit technical explanations as too cumbersome; newswriters may assume more knowledge in their audience than it possesses, or may not themselves understand what they are reporting.
(c) Readers and viewers tend to kid themselves about how much they really learn from news reports. Do you have a complete picture of the events? If so, could you describe and explain them to someone else?

## 3. Sources

(a) Where did the story come from? Is it a report of a press release? A rewrite of a public relations handout? A news conference? A leak? A "background" interview with an official who refuses to be identified? Is the story the result of the reporter's observations, research, interviews?

(b) Does it come from a wire service (CP, AP, UPI, Reuters, AFP)? From a news service (Southam, FP, Financial Times; some American news service)?

(c) How *could* the writer whose story you are reading, listening to, or watching, have obtained the information he or she is presenting?

RATIONALE

(a) Every large corporation, union, government department, institution (e.g., university) has a public relations officer who writes "news" releases publicizing the outfit and putting its interests in the most favourable light. Often these releases get into the media unverified, or only slightly rewritten. News conferences can be stage-managed to overdramatize, divert attention, obfuscate. Leaks and backgrounders can be self-serving. (b) Wire services tend to avoid controversy and overrepresent "establishment" news sources; foreign wire services (all but CP, and UPI in Canada) plus CP reports of foreign events from elsewhere than London, Paris, or New York (where CP has its own bureaus, and doesn't depend on AP stories), write for their own national points of view—American, British, French—not with Canadian interests and outlooks in mind.

(c) Some events are not accessible and reports can be based on rumour, stereotypes, or political prejudice. Reports from some locations (e.g. wars) may be censored. Study the habits of accuracy and the personal biases of local reporters and columnists on whom you frequently rely for information. Some reporters cover a "beat" (e.g., city hall, labour, education) for years and acquire great knowledge of its inner workings and politics, but some also establish a cozy working relationship that may result in self-censorship or biased reporting.

## 4. Background

(a) What is the historical context into which the story fits? Is it about an event that connects with other recent or less recent events? Is it a development of earlier events? Is it a response or reaction to them? How did it come about?

(b) Why is it being reported? Why is it being reported *now*?

(c) Is it an "update" report on an ongoing event, or a fuller account of events earlier reported in less detail?

RATIONALE

(a) Most, if not all, events make sense only when understood against the past background from which they have emerged. (The "past" may be as recent as the previous day, or go back over a period of years.)

(b) The "reporting" may itself be part of the event—what makes it news; hence, what occasions the report may help explain the significance of the events reported.

(c) Often news reports presuppose that readers or viewers are familiar with prior accounts or earlier developments.

## 5. Balance

(a) Does the story report the views of all the individuals or groups who have an interest in a dispute?

(b) Does the story present events or issues from one perspective when others are available? Can you identify that perspective? What other perspectives are there? How might those same events be reported from those other perspectives? Does the report try to get you to draw a conclusion or share a judgement? Is its angle justified?

RATIONALE

(a) Each adversary in a dispute tends to picture his or her side in the right and the other in the wrong. A fair judgement requires that all claims be considered.

(b) Tom Wicker, an American columnist, has noted that the practice of objectivity is an act favouring the status quo.[1] Every report has some angle, if only the angle that no interpretation, no background, no judgement should be given (thus contributing to the image of a world of unrelated, "neutral" events, on which we bring our "personal" and "subjective" judgements to bear). Most language is evaluative, judgemental, by virtue of the words used (and those not used). You can either unconsciously accept the reporter's outlook, or identify it and thereby gain the option of rejecting it.

## 6. Connections

(a) Will the events reported affect you directly? Might they touch you indirectly? What should you do as a result of the information: Watch for further developments? Change your mind about a previous opinion? Behave differently in some respect in the future?

(b) Do the events connect with other, similar, events and form a pattern? What is their significance? What do they mean? What do they portend?

---

[1] As reported in Robert Cirino, Power to Persuade: Mass Media and the News (Toronto and New York: Bantam, 1974), p. 202.

RATIONALE

(a) Forewarned is forearmed. You can put the information you receive from the media to good use if you're thinking while you ingest it.

(b) This is perhaps the most significant question on the list. The mosaic of information from the media to some extent creates or reinforces an overall picture of the world. It reflects a theory, or interpretation, or understanding, about the nature of society—its function and purpose, its possibilities and its confines. (This is not done intentionally; it's not controlled: we aren't suggesting manipulation.) Either you accept that theory by default, or you develop and bring your own theory into play, using it to place and connect and exhibit the significance of events reported in the media.

## 7. Importance

(a) How important is the event reported compared to other stories elsewhere in the news the same day? Does it merit its prominence (front page, big headline; top of the news—or second-last page, small headline, short account; etc.)? What is its importance relative to other recent and current events?

(b) Was the event staged or created exclusively for the media?

RATIONALE

(a) *Some* stories have to be on the front page or at the top of the news; *some* have to go on the second-last page; some stories that are written or filmed are just not printed or shown; most events aren't even reported. Editors make these decisions, but you don't have to agree with them. Also, there have to be stories on the front page even when there are no "front page" stories. You, the reader or viewer, are the only one to judge the relative importance of day-to-day events.

(b) Many events—some press conferences, even street violence—are pseudo-events in the sense that they are put on *just* for media coverage.

## B. TV News

In television news, obviously the big difference is the visual ingredient. Film not only seems to bring you closer to events; it also is an enormously more powerful medium than words for creating an *impression* about the events reported. Remember, however, that TV newsfilm is always *edited*. Film footage is chopped up and then pieced together by an editor who must make judgements about what to show, what to leave out, what shots to juxtapose, what order to present events in, where to interpose still photos, how to pace the story, how much time to allot to it. Each filmed news item is a work of journalistic art; that means it's part *creation*. (We're *not* saying the film is faked.)

## 8. Narration

Does the voiceover suggest an interpretation that the film does not by itself bear out?

RATIONALE
Same as for photo captions: narration can convince you to "see" what is not there in the film.

## 9. Film

(a) Does the film use props? Is it posed? Is the film actually shot from the events reported, or is it old film from the station's or network's library?
(b) Does the film emphasize certain aspects of the events (e.g., action: violence), giving them undue prominence?
(c) Is the story on the news *only* because of its visual interest?
(d) What bias or perspective did the editing of the story produce? What *impression* did you get about the events you were viewing? On reflection, is that impression warranted?

RATIONALE
(a) Given the power of visual impressions, it's mandatory to know whether the image you're left with really captures the event reported.
(b) Film of a single fight at a demonstration can be used to give the impression the whole demonstration was violent (*even when* the announcer's or reporter's voiceover states otherwise).
(c) Other things being equal, of two equally important stories the one with interesting film will get into the news and the one without film will be cut. A corollary of this TV truism is that TV news stories tend to come from urban centres where camera crews are stationed.
(d) See the general comments under the heading "TV News," above. We might add here that editing can not only influence your interpretation of the meaning of what you see and your value judgements about it, but it can also actually affect your impression of the *facts* you witnessed.

This checklist and the accompanying rationales for the items on it suffer at least two defects: they are abstract and they are opinionated. We must leave it to you to apply questions to concrete examples—to a particular day's newspaper or news broadcast or, better still, to a series of both. See what particular questions our necessarily abstract ones generate. Also, check whether our outlook towards the information media bears up under examination.

These questions are not intended as veiled criticisms of the media, nor as recommendations for changes in its policies or practices. Neither are we saying they should *not* change in various ways; on that issue, we pass. Our perspective is that of the news and information *consumer*, not that of the journalist. The goal is short term: the intelligent use of the media as they now operate.

# 2 Projects

**9.3** The questions on our *checklist* came from a certain limited acquaintance with how the media function and from a point of view that is skeptical of the capacity of the mass media to provide a totally adequate diet of information. The limitations and bias of the checklist are not serious failings in a device designed to pique your curiosity rather than sell you a bill of goods. However, asking yourself those questions is at best only half-enough. To be able to use the media intelligently, you have to investigate two general topics: (1) how the various media actually operate, day in and day out; (2) the ideological role of the media.

## 1. Finding Out How the Media Operate

(a) The first thing to do is to read everything you can get your hands on about the media. Much more information about American media is available than about Canadian media, and the situations in the two countries is very different. Laws governing the media differ— e.g., advertising in them, coverage of the courts—and in the broadcast media there is nothing remotely like the CBC in the U.S. Hence, much that is written about the media for U.S. readers is irrelevant to us in Canada. Here are four good paperback books about the Canadian media we've come across.

Donald R. Gordon, *Language, Logic and the Mass Media* (Toronto: Holt, Rinehart and Winston of Canada, 1966). An informative basic account of the workings of Canadian newspapers, radio and TV news.

Benjamin Singer (ed.), *Communications in Canadian Society*, 2nd rev. ed. (Toronto: Copp Clark, 1975). A collection of articles and excerpts from books, mostly about the information media. Has a good bibliography.

Dick MacDonald (ed.), *The Media Game* (Montreal: Content Pub-

214 THE RHETORIC OF EVERYDAY PERSUASION

lishing, 1972). A collection of articles about Canadian news media from the journalists' magazine, *Content*. Much information and many interesting criticisms of the media by journalists.

C. Stuart Adam (ed.), *Journalism, Communication and the Law* (Scarborough: Prentice-Hall of Canada, 1976). A collection of excellent informative and critical articles written for the book by practising and academic journalists. Excellent bibliography, especially for Canadian material.

Note that the last three of these books are written mainly for journalists or students of journalism. Only Gordon explicitly adopts the consumer's viewpoint.

**(b)** Once you know how the media operate in general in Canada, you should try to find out about the outlets that you come into contact with personally: local newspaper(s), radio and TV stations. Invite the editor or managing editor of the paper, and the station manager or news manager of the radio and TV stations, to talk to your group. (Usually they're delighted to come.) He or she will probably prefer to give at most a short talk, then answer your questions, so prepare them in advance. (You should ask questions about the ideological role of the medium at this time too. See 2, below.) In addition, you might visit the newspaper, radio, and TV newsrooms. Talk to reporters, editors, newswriters. (You might have to assign small groups to different tasks.) See if you can follow a reporter or a camera crew around for a few days. All of this will produce fascinating insights into the whole news operation—though it will also tend to distract you from the basic question for the defensive consumer: In what ways does all this affect the information I get as I sit reading the paper or watching TV?

**(c)** A third way to learn about the media is to systematically study newspapers and newscasts over an extended period of time: at the very least a week. Compare stories within each medium. Get an out-of-town newspaper or two during the same period. Watch different channels and listen to different radio stations. Also, compare different media. Study TV, radio, and newspaper treatments of the same story. Such observation of the media in action is useful for reality-testing the descriptions of the ideal you might get from articles—cf. (a) above—or even informal talks and question-and-answer sessions—cf. (b) above. We have observed that many (not all) newspeople tend to be unreflective about their working assumptions.

## 2. Discovering the Ideological Role of the Media

By the "ideological role" of the media we don't mean only or primarily the political views influencing the information packaging by the media. We are referring more generally to the *overall* world-view the media propagate, usually unintentionally. Here are three of many possible avenues of discovery.

(a) Investigate the "working categories" of the media. These are the conceptual groupings into which they sort the realities they report, and consequently into which the information we consumers receive about those realities is parcelled. We'll list a few such categories as examples; your own research will uncover others.

Newspapers try to keep a strict separation between *factual* information, which goes into the news columns, and *opinions* about that information, which goes into editorials, or news analysis or opinion columns. Is such a distinction between fact and opinion supportable? What are the defining features of each? What is the effect of working in terms of this division of reality upon the picture of the world the newspaper conveys?

An obvious working category is the concept of "news." What is or should count as news? What are the defining characteristics of events that are news or newsworthy? What definitions of news are *operative*? (Do they differ from medium to medium? E.g., does film make a difference so far as what is "news" for TV goes?) What assumptions or other factors might affect editors' judgements about what is newsworthy? What is the effect of the news media's operating with this category called "news" on the picture of the world received by the consumer?

The newspaper divides its information according to an explicit conventional set of categories: news, editorial material, features, entertainment, business, sports, family, to list the main ones. Do the events in the world actually sort themselves out in this way? What effect does this organization have on the image of reality we consumers receive by reading the paper each day?

(b) A second way to become aware of the media's ideological impact is to look for their own conception of their role and the standards they try to meet in filling it. For example, many editors, producers, and reporters see themselves as having a responsibility to "mirror" society. Your research should quickly uncover expressions of or reactions to this belief. What are the practical consequences of the idea that the function of the news is to mirror events in the world? What is the cash value so far as influencing the content and form of information the media carry? Is it really *possible* for the media to "mirror" society in any intelligible way? If not, as some have argued—if this mirror metaphor is a *myth*—then what is the effect of journalists' working in terms of this myth on the information they produce?

A value taken very seriously by media people in both rhetoric and practice is "objectivity." The idea is that the media should not doctor the information they convey or serve as apologists for any political point of view. But what is a workable definition or set of conditions for objectivity in the media? Can the media be "objective" in any realistic sense? If not, how does their belief that they should try (and that they usually succeed) affect the information received by the consumer?

Or again, what should a reporter's role be? We've heard it argued that a reporter should be: (i) an impartial *reporter*; (ii) an *adversary* of those in positions of power, a protector of the common people's interests; (iii) an *advocate* of a publicly acknowledged point of view. Which view prevails? Are there differences between the media here? Are there differences between individual reporters whose work you read, hear, or see? And, as always, what is the effect on the message?

(c) The third factor that might affect the picture of the world emanating from the media consists of what we call—without begging any questions—"hard determinants." We are thinking here of things such as financial resources, technological restrictions and other effects of technology, concentration of media ownership, the economic interests of media owners, the education and training of reporters and editors, to mention a few factors. Each of these, and others this list might suggest, should be studied for its effect on the overall outlook shaping the information processed by the media. We urge you to look for concrete connections here, not generalizations before the facts. It's easy to *say*, for example, that because the owners of private media outlets are business people, the news is therefore likely to be slanted to favour the business point of view. But is that true? How, in *detail*, do the owners have any influence on the information or editorial slant of their media? Indeed, do they have any influence at all? What influence specifically? You'll have to pose questions like these if you hope to learn anything about the influence of these "hard determinants" on the flow of information.

**9.4** We have tried to produce, in 1 and 2, both suggestions for research and examples of the sorts of questions to ask in order to learn about the media. Many more such questions than the ones we've listed here need to be answered. If our *checklist* and *project* ideas stimulate you to investigate, but, more importantly, to think about the significance while you seek information, then they will have served the purpose of making you a more reflective consumer of media information.

# 10 Advertising: Games You Can Play

## 1 The Logic of Advertising

**10.1** If you're like most people, you probably find it hard to keep your cool when the topic of advertising comes up. Ads are annoying, repetitious, offensive, degrading, deceptive, and sometimes patently false. That's a generalization, to be sure, and by now you know the dangers of such statements.

Not all ads have the odious traits just cited. Think, for a moment, of that record you just bought on sale. How did you find out about the sale? Advertising, of course. Where did you first learn about the products and services you're satisfied with? Again, advertising. In an economy like ours, with new products entering the marketplace almost daily and old ones being improved, advertising often performs the much-needed task of informing the consumer of the available products and services so that he or she can make a rational choice.

**10.2** It would be extremely naive to think, however, that the sole purpose of advertising is to provide information and rational persuasion. If that were the case, we could comb them for fallacies, just as we would any argument. It's true that many ads have a superficial resemblance to arguments, so they encourage us to approach them in this way. Think of ads which use the line, "Here are the reasons this product is the best." But this line is usually nothing more than a façade or window dressing, for, although advertising is an attempt to persuade, the type of persuasion generally used is not *rational*. Instead, advertising attempts to persuade us by appealing to our emotions (our hopes, fears, dreams), to the vulnerable spots in our egos (our desire for status and recognition), by applying pressure to the tender areas of our psyches.

This assault on consciousness is accomplished by what is known in the trade as "creative strategy," or what we will more accurately call, a **gimmick.** A gimmick is an attention-getting device with a persuasive hook, designed to attract the consumer's attention and create a favourable climate for the product. The gimmick may be a straight-out emotional appeal; it may be an unstated implication or suggestion; or it may involve getting you to make an unwarranted assumption.

In sum, *advertising has a logic of its own.* Thus, learning how to evaluate ads from the standard logical point of view becomes a gratuitous exercise. We propose instead to say something about the logic of advertising, about the various gimmicks and ploys it uses. We'll be reviewing some of them and giving examples; we also have some pointers on what to look out for. Armed with these clues, you will be in a better position to defend yourself against these gimmicks; or at least you'll know what's coming.

But watch out for the *boomerang* effect. That is, in order to heighten your consciousness about the gimmicks used in ads, you must pay close attention to them. Yet that is exactly what advertisers want. So, in a sense, you'll be playing right into their hands. But the alternatives are even less attractive. You can attempt to ignore advertising, which is virtually impossible; or you can pretend that you are ignoring it, not really susceptible to its influence, which is most unlikely. Under the assumption that advertising is here to stay, we advise you make the best of the situation, learn the games they play, and what some of their tactics are so that, if nothing else, you can have some fun trying to detect the gimmicks being used.

**10.3** Advertising is a fascinating subject and many books have been written about it. We'll simply mention the four that we have found particularly helpful:

Carl Wrighter, *I Can Sell You Anything* (New York: Ballantine Books, 1972). This is perhaps the single most valuable (and entertaining) sourcebook for learning the tricks of the trade, particularly about television advertising. It is replete with examples. Unfortunately, Wrighter discusses ads from U.S. network television of some five years vintage. So you may not have seen them or may not remember them.

Jerry Goodis, *Have I Ever Lied to You Before?* (Toronto: McClelland and Stewart, 1972). Goodis has some worthwhile things to say about advertising in this country, and about advertising generally:

**160**  Let me just say it again: the difference between good advertising and bad advertising is simply (1) ingenuity, (2) taste, (3) truth, (4) humanity. And the all-purpose, magic-formula secret ingredient is a little love for the consumer. And just a modicum of respect for his or her intelligence. (p. 133)

Sam Sinclair Baker, *The Permissible Lie* (Cleveland and New York: World Publishing Company, 1968). Baker's book is somewhat outdated and also focuses on the U.S. scene. But it has many useful nuggets of information and history.

Ellen Roseman, *Consumer, Beware!* rev. ed. (Don Mills: New Press, 1974). An invaluable source for anyone who wants to develop an aggressive, consumer-oriented approach toward advertising. It tells of the legal avenues open to anyone who wants to combat deceptive, misleading, or false advertising.


# 2 Advertising Claims: How to Defuse Them

**10.4** At the heart of all advertising lies *the claim*. Whether supplemented by visuals or made more palatable by a catchy tune, the claim is the anchor for all gimmicks in each ad. The claim's function is to capture your attention and to present you with the product's (or service's) *reason for being*. It tells you what the product is going to do for you and why you should buy it rather than some other brand. Consequently, the claim should also furnish you with your *reason to believe*, which is why you so often hear or see the phrase "Here's why" in ads.[1] It signals the advertiser's attempt to put across the product's reason for being, and your reason for believing. Effective commercials—those which increase the product's sales and share of the market, or at least create a favourable selling climate—are based on the all-important claim. TV commercials, for instance, typically use a claim as a springboard for a story line or demonstration. For these reasons, settling on the right claim is usually the most strenuous part of building an advertising campaign. An example of a claim is one currently in use for Coca-Cola: "Coke adds life." Stop and ask yourself: What does this mean? How can Coke add life? What does it add life to?

An obvious point: A great deal of thought is given to the creation

[1] The terms "reason for being" and "reason to believe" are Wrighter's. Cf. *I Can Sell You Anything*, p. 44.

and the formulation of every advertising claim. We make that point because when you are confronted with it in print or on TV, the advertising claim appears to be casually formulated, almost nonchalant. This is especially the case with a medium like TV, where verisimilitude suggests spontaneity. However, there is nothing capricious, haphazard, casual, or nonchalant about any advertising claim. It has been ruthlessly scrutinized before it ever reaches your eyes or ears. If you are willing to analyze advertising claims, you'll begin to notice some interesting things.

As we said, most advertising claims employ a gimmick. To spot it, you must know what to look for and what to listen for. You must know how to question the advertising copy. You have to be able to figure out exactly what has been said and why. Just as important, you have to be ready to figure out what has *not* been said, and why it hasn't. You must also learn to watch for nuance, implication, suggestion—all species of utterance which purposely fall short of forthright assertion.

In the next few paragraphs, we'll give you some pointers about what to watch for.

## 10.5

### A.  Learn to Distinguish between Fact and Opinion

When advertisers make *factual* claims, they must be able to support them if challenged. If they assert that, for example, their automobile "has the smoothest ride of any," then they must be able to support that claim. If, on the other hand, they put that same statement in the form of an opinion by saying, "We think you'll find that our car has the smoothest ride of any," they're home free. They have simply given you their opinion. Or perhaps they will solicit someone else's opinion (a celebrity's) and pay that person for it; or take an ordinary-looking person and let him or her state the opinion. Remember this point: Factual claims must be supportable and are challengeable; they can be held in court to be misleading, deceptive, or false, and those responsible can be fined if convicted. On the other hand, there are very few restrictions on the expression of opinion, which is why you should ask: Who is offering this opinion and why?

Here's an example:

**161**    Carrington. It's special. And in our opinion, like no other whisky in the world.

Here we find a claim labelled opinion in black and white. But what about the claim, "It's special"? Is that fact? Opinion? What?

What it is, is *vague*. What does "special" mean? Do you know?

More important, do you know what it means in this context? This brings us to our next point.

## B. Read Ads with a Dictionary Handy

Words in ads have a way of not quite meaning what you think they mean. "Special," for example, has several meanings: "1. distinctive, peculiar, unique; 2. unusual, uncommon, exceptional, extraordinary . . ." Which of these is meant in the Carrington ad? Better have a careful look at the copy which leads up to the claim in question:

**162**     Carrington is distilled in small batches, aged and mellowed in seasoned oak casks; it's light in look and smooth in taste.

Possibly the basis for the claim that Carrington is special lies in the fact that it is batch-distilled. Since most whisky manufacturers these days use a process known as continuous distillation, that would make Carrington "special," i.e. uncommon. If you are cynical another possibility might suggest itself: the graphics accompanying the copy show that Carrington comes in a bottle which has an unusual, unique shape. So Carrington could claim to be "special" because of that. However, neither of these facts provides a reason to believe that the whisky in that peculiar bottle or that is made in small batches is any better than any other whisky.

Generally, then, we think it is educational to practise reading ads with a dictionary close at hand: advertisers have mastered the art of exploiting the difference between what words actually mean and what you are likely to think they mean. Think, for instance, of the word "strength," as in the claim, "That's why there's Javex Bleach for the Unbleachables. Javex *strength*. Javex *power*. To get out the dirt and stains detergent alone can't." You hear the word "strength" here, and it suggests a product that is muscular—more muscular than its competition. But look it up. "Strength" means "the power or capability of generating a reaction or an effect." "Whisk puts its *strength* where the dirt is". How does it read when we make this substitution? "Whisk puts its 'capacity to generate an effect' where the dirt is." There'd be no problem substantiating that claim, would there? Whisk contains chemicals. When those chemicals are immersed in water, they will generate an effect. But what kind of effect?

Here's another word to watch for: "quality." "At Zenith, the quality goes in before the name goes on." "Quality" can mean "superiority," but could Zenith substantiate that their products are superior? Perhaps. But there is another sense of the word: "the essential nature or character of a thing." So the question is: Does Zenith's claim mean anything more than: "At Zenith, we put the essence of the television (i.e., picture tube, chassis, circuits, etc.) into our product before we put our name on it"? While putting in all the essential components is no doubt a sound practice, it does not furnish the buyer with any reason to believe.

## C. Watch for Implications and Suggestions

One rule of thumb to follow in unpacking factual and quasi-factual claims is this: If advertisers can make a strong statement about the product, they will. If, therefore, an ad makes only an indirect statement (an implication, a suggestion, or a hedge), it is probably because the advertisers want you to think what they cannot come right out and declare. Suppose, for example, there was hard proof that Flash is the best toothpaste on the market. The ad will come right out and state that. If, however, Flash is one of many equally good toothpastes, the advertisers cannot make that strong statement. Instead, they must be content to suggest or imply. They will word the claim in such a way as to encourage you to (mistakenly) draw the inference they want. They might then say, "Nothing works better than Flash in fighting cavities." All this claim does is rule out the possibility that another product is better than Flash, while leaving open the possibility that many others are just as good. A less than forthright claim, then, one that implies, suggests, or tempts you to make the statement, is something to be leery of.

## D. Watch for Pre-emptive Claims

There is a reason that advertisers have to resort to gimmicks. To understand their problem, consider the words of a legendary figure in the annals of advertising, Rosser Reeves:

**163**    Our problem is—a client comes into my office and throws two newly-minted half-dollars on my desk and says, "Mine is the one on the left. You prove it's better."[2]

The point of Reeves' remark is this. Most brands are similar. The differences between them are marginal and/or subjective. The problem advertisers must confront is how to make their product appear to be better than the others, how to place it in a favourable light, and implant the name of the product in the consumer's mind.

That is the problem. For one solution, we turn to the words of yet another legendary figure, Claude Hopkins:

[2] As recounted by Martin Mayer, *Madison Avenue U.S.A.* (New York: Harper and Brothers, 1958), p. 53.

**164**    Another early adman, Claude Hopkins, had no trouble proving that Schlitz beer was better than all others. He visited
the factory, watched the beer being made, and came up with
the slogan, "Washed with live steam." When told that this
was standard procedure in the beer industry, Hopkins wasn't
worried. "The vital fact was not what the industry did, but
what the individual brewers said they did, and the steam
bath had never been advertised," he explained.[3]

Hopkins introduced a basic strategy which advertisers have been
copying ever since: Take a basic ingredient or a standard feature
common to all products of a given type and price, and construct the
advertisement around it. Of course, you have to be the first to use
this strategy, but if you are the dividends are many. First, the claim
will be the truth. Of course, it will not be the whole truth. In the
case of Schlitz, the whole truth would have been: "Washed in live
steam, as is every other beer." Second, in the context of advertising,
the pre-emptive strategy ratifies an *assumption* which the consumer
finds it natural to make; i.e., the natural assumption that the feature
around which the claim is built is unique to that product. Thus, it
would be only natural for consumers to have assumed that Schlitz
was the only beer washed in live steam. Why? Because it seems
preposterous to sound the trumpets for a feature or ingredient which
is common to all products, and thus does not serve to differentiate.
Who could get excited by an ad for a television set which said
simply: "Our set has a picture tube"? Unless advertisers explicitly
claim uniqueness for some feature or ingredient of their product,
then, don't *assume* it; that is, don't do the work for them.

**10.6** To get around the fact that the difference between most products of a given type are only marginal and subjective, advertisers
have developed a number of other strategies. Here are some things
to watch for.

### E. Watch for the Word "Different"

Beware of the use of "different" and its implications. One product
may be different from all others and yet not be any better. The
crucial question to ask is: Is the difference marginal or functional?
And remember that when advertisers use the word "different," it's
because they want you to *think* "better."

### F. Watch for Comparisons

Comparisons are usually tricky. The question to ask yourself is:

---

[3] As recounted by Ellen Roseman, *Consumer, Beware!*, p. 127.

*What is being compared to what and why?* The strongest possible comparison would be: "My product is better in every way than anyone else's." But you will probably never see such a strongly worded comparison, because then the advertiser and manufacturer would have to back that claim up with proof, if they were challenged, and few products have such superiority.

A recent whisky ad runs, "Introducing *Town & Country.* A better whisky." That's a perfectly vague and innocuous comparison, isn't it? Better than what? The ad doesn't say. Better than no whisky at all? Better in what way? Again, it doesn't say. The ad continues, "*Town & Country* spent longer in the barrel than most Canadian whiskies." Does the fact that it was in the barrel longer than most mean that it is better than most? Not necessarily. Whisky improves with age, but only up to a point. Just what point that is, is a matter of considerable debate. It also depends on the process of distilling and on *taste.* And don't forget the price factor, too. Wiser's Deluxe uses this claim, "Four years older than Canada's two best known whiskies. But priced the same." Does that mean that Wiser's is better simply because it is older? Not necessarily. Again, with whisky as with anything we eat or drink, the subjective factor of taste is an important consideration.

In any comparison, cost is an important but often unmentioned factor. One pain reliever may have "twice as much of the pain reliever doctors recommend," (i.e., acetylsalicylic acid), but it may cost twice as much, too. It may get into the bloodstream *faster,* but by how much? And how much of a difference will that really make in relieving a headache?

With any comparison, it is important always to establish what is being compared to what and why.

## G. Watch for Semantic Claims

These claims are not really so much about the product as they are about the product's name or label. This is often a variation on the *Pre-emptive Claim.* For example, Colgate is currently using the following claim: "Only Colgate has MFP." MFP is their mysterious-sounding abbreviation for a flouride ingredient. Is Colgate the only toothpaste with flouride? No. Then how can it be claimed that "Only Colgate has MFP"? Because they are the only ones who *call* flouride "MFP" and they own the trademark on the letters! That is the reason for the claim of uniqueness here; that's why they can get away with saying that "Only Colgate has MFP." But in effect this is not a claim about the product. It is a claim about *their name* for one of its ingredients. It is a *Semantic Claim.*

Gasoline ads frequently employ the "Mystery Ingredient" version of the Semantic Claim, for they often construct their ads around an additive with a set of initials: "HTA," "TCP," etc. The classic example of this is a Shell TV ad of several years back. The ad compared the mpg (km/l) of a car using Shell without Platformate to the mpg of that same car with Platformate. The ads never said exactly what Platformate was, content simply to describe it as a "mileage ingredient" (an ingredient for increasing distance per tankful of gasoline). The *implication* of the ad was that other gasolines were like Shell without Platformate, so Shell had some terrific new discovery. In fact, Platformate turned out to have been simply Shell's name for an ingredient contained in almost every premium brand of gasoline. A comparison here was based on nothing more than a Semantic Claim.

Another way of working the Semantic Claim involves use of "the." Several years ago, Uniroyal gave the label "The Rain Tire" to one of its products. This label is very suggestive. The implication is that the tire was designed specifically for maximum performance on wet roads. An added implication is that if it does so well on wet roads, it will be even better on dry ones. All of this has been suggested and implied by the title, "The Rain Tire." None of it has been *stated*. No real claim has been made.

So don't be hooked by names, titles, labels, and mysterious ingredients.

## H.  Watch for "Weasel" Words

These words *help* the advertiser say something which sounds much stronger than the facts will allow. First on the list of weasels is "help(s)." "To help" means "to aid or assist." So "Crest helps prevent cavities" means simply "Crest aids or assists in preventing cavities." That claim is undoubtedly true. The problem is that we've become so accustomed to hearing this great *qualifier* that we hardly hear it at all; we tend rather to hear what comes after it. So if we take their claim to mean that Crest prevents cavities, well, that's not strictly speaking what they said, is it? No toothpaste can positively prevent cavities. Yet every parent devoutly wishes that keeping children cavity-free could be as easy as buying that tube of toothpaste.

A recent ad for 2nd Debut Liquid Make-up claims, "Built IN Moisturiser Helps Keep Skin From Drying . . ." Right, because nothing will keep skin from drying. Later in that same ad, we read:

**165**    "That's because 2nd Debut Liquid Make-up contains CEF . . . Cellular Expansion Factor. CEF *compels* the dry skin to again drink in fresh, pure moisture . . . *helps* plump up the skin from underneath, makes it soft with the precious dewy look of youth." (Emphasis ours)

Note the use of "helps" again; and we cannot help but wonder just what CEF is, nor can we help but wonder how it can *compel* the skin to drink.

Second by a nose to "help" is the weasel "like." "Like" is what is known as a transfer word, and here is the way Wrighter explains it:

**166**   "Like" is a qualifier, and is used in much the same way as "help." But "like" is also a comparative, with a very specific purpose; we use "like" to get you to stop thinking about the product per se, and to get you thinking about something that is bigger or better or different than the product we're selling.[4]

Here's an example of the transfer effect, an ad for Black & White Scotch from the November 1974 edition of *Maclean's*:

**167**   Discovering Black & White Scotch is like:
       1. Finding out the penny stock you bought and forgot about is worth five bucks a share.
       2. The blind date you dreaded, turns out to be a long-stemmed beauty called Rose . . .
       6. The gorgeous creature who just moved in across the hall loves Mozart and her favourite drink is Black & White too. Girl's got taste.

Just how discovering Black & White is similar to any of these items is unclear. But the transfer effect is surely noticeable. (Could the similarity be that all of these are instances of "discovering" something—and the similarity begins and ends there?)

The classic case involving this weasel was a campaign for Ajax Liquid Cleaner some years ago which centred around the claim that "Ajax cleans *like* a white tornado." On the surface, this claim violates the transfer effect because there is nothing particularly pleasant about a tornado: they're devastating killers in a great many cases. But ordinarily they're grey or black, or appear to be. Ajax, however, is a *white* tornado and lives in a bottle. So it's as though they had tamed Nature, brought Nature's raw power under control, and put it in the bottle. None of this is stated, of course.

**10.7** Television advertising is a realm unto itself, and much too complicated to be dealt with fully in the short space available here.

[4] Wrighter, *I Can Sell You Anything*, p. 26.

What TV ads have going for them is the visual effect, the impression of reality, immediacy. There are basically two types of television ad: (1) the demonstration and (2) the dramatization. We'll make just brief comments on each in turn.

## 1. Demonstrations

In a demonstration, we supposedly see the product in use and some benefit of the product is shown. The thing to ask here: Exactly what is being demonstrated? To this end, you may find it useful to turn off the sound and simply watch, so that what you see cannot be influenced by the voiceover. Several years ago, STP used an ad which showed very clearly that the human hand cannot hold onto the tip of a screwdriver which had been immersed in STP. That is all that was demonstrated. While it was being *shown*, here is part of what the viewer was *told*: "STP reduces friction in your engine." The "demonstration" did not lend any substance to the claim. After all, skin and metal are very different. Unless you keep the show (demonstration) separate from the tell (voiceover), the two may blend together effortlessly in your mind, creating an impression that the claim has actually been demonstrated.

A classic in this genre is one of Bounty towels ("The Quicker Picker-Upper") that featured the following demonstration. Two glasses with equal amounts of liquid are shown. A sheet of Bounty is immersed in one glass, a sheet of "another leading paper towel" into the other. Then the two glasses are turned upside down. We see that the Bounty towel has apparently absorbed all of the liquid, because nothing drips out; but some liquid comes out of the other glass, so the other hasn't absorbed everything. What has been demonstrated? Here's Wrighter's commentary:

**168**    If you believe the pictures, then they have just proved that Bounty towels absorbs more liquid than the other paper paper towel. But what did they actually say? "Bounty. The quicker picker-upper." They say that Bounty picks up *faster* than the other. They have shown you one thing, but they have said something else. Don't misinterpret what I'm saying. Bounty knows exactly what it's doing. They are presenting you with a new idea in paper towels: Speed in absorption. But it's very hard to prove that two inanimate objects move at different speeds, so the demo they use is the closest they could come to it. They use the words to get you to see what they want you to see.[5]

[5] Wrighter, *I Can Sell You Anything*, p. 81.

Notice again how the ad was designed so that the "show" and the "tell" would coalesce. That Bounty towels absorb liquid more rapidly than "another leading paper towel" is not necessarily enough to make them better. Perhaps they absorb *less* liquid, but do so more quickly.

In viewing TV commercials in which a demonstration of the product in use is featured, be sure that you understand exactly what is being demonstrated. And don't allow the words (the "tell") to influence what you're seeing (the "show").

## 2. Dramatizations

Dramatizations are just that: little pieces of drama with a cast of characters, actors and actresses, a script, a director, a budget, a shooting schedule. Of course, they're made to look as spontaneous and life-like as possible. Advertisers use them when they have a product that cannot easily be shown in action. For example, advertisers for detergents and bleaches find this approach a natural because it's hard to get a close-up picture of the enzymes and additives "eating stains" in your clothes while they're tumbling around inside a washer. So they set up a situation which calls for their product, cut to a close-up of the box or package, then back to the situation to show the resolution. It's the "Before" and "After" routine.

Typical of such TV commercials was one aired several years ago for Alberto VO-5 Shampoo. In outline, it began by showing a woman (she's an actress, remember) before she had washed her hair. Then we see her sudsing away, with lots of lather. Then, presto! Her hair looks fantastic after that one shampoo with Alberto VO-5. The *impression* created by this sequence is that the shampoo was responsible for her beautiful-looking hair. No doubt she did shampoo with the product. But that doesn't mean that washing with VO-5 is the only thing that happened between the "Before" and the "After." Never mind that the actress or model chosen has lovely hair to begin with, she has probably also had her hair professionally set, dried, and combed. But none of this is alluded to. This visual impression was reinforced by the claim, "She's got hair she can wash and wear." Taken one way, this claim was totally meaningless. Could someone wash their hair and not wear it? Taken a different way, this claim was probably meant to connect up with the wash-and-wear revolution in fabrics. Most consumers consider these fabrics a real godsend because they eliminate the need for ironing clothes. The fabric is ready to wear after washing. The *implication* of "wash-and-wear hair," then, is that you'll be able to bypass some steps. This could not be stated, of course. If you wash your hair, with Alberto VO-5 or any other shampoo, you'll still have to dry it *and* brush it *and* comb it *and* perhaps put hair spray on it. But we never see this process. For, in such commercials, just as in plays, more of the action takes place off stage. The problem is that we have no way of knowing what has happened offstage. Even if we did, the immediacy of TV tends to lure us into forgetfulness of the off-stage activity.

Dramatizations are particularly effective in hammering away at our emotional foibles. The advertiser can zero in on some weakness in our self-images, such as our fears of being offensive (ads for dandruff removers, mouthwashes, and deodorants) or of being behind the times ("You mean you haven't heard about new, softer, more absorbent Toilet-tish?") How ecstatic must have been the advertiser who stumbled across the word "halitosis" in the dictionary! And think of the ad for Whisk: "Ring around the collar." We see the embarrassed wife, suffering what seems to be the ultimate ignominy—public revelation of her inadequacy at the washing machine! "What will people think? They'll think I don't take good care of my husband, that I don't really love him." Comes the answer to this severe trauma: "Whisk!" In such commercials, persuasion is accomplished, but not by dispensing reasons for a conclusion. Instead, the advertiser attacks your fears and desires and hopes you'll look to that product for help.

As you watch these dramas unfold, remember what we said at the beginning. The people are actors working from a script, and the entire production is under the advertiser's control. While it is carefully designed to look spontaneous and lifelike, you won't see anything they don't want you to see. You won't see the people they interview with hidden cameras who do not praise the product to the hilt. That footage winds up on the cutting room floor.

**10.8** It seems appropriate to conclude this chapter, and the book as well, with a few reflections on a most profound comment about advertising. The owner of Revlon is reported to have once said, "I don't sell cosmetics; I sell dreams." Think about this statement in connection with these lines from Graham Nash's song, "Teach Your Children": "And feed them on your dreams/the one they pick's/the one you'll know by."

We've been a bit harsh on advertisers. They often sell us fantasies wrapped in fancy semantic clothes and designed to catch us where we dream. But those dreams are, after all, our dreams that make it all possible. So, whether we turn our attention to arguments, editorials, and political rhetoric, or to the news media, or to advertising, we are perhaps too willing to settle for shoddy goods. We don't say this to exonerate the media and advertising, but rather to add a bit of perspective, and to locate some of the responsibility for this situation where it really belongs—on all of our shoulders.

The index of success we have in mind for this book, therefore, is not really whether it has taught you how to spot fallacies of logic, misleading headlines, or advertising gimmicks, for, being able to pick them out, while certainly not unimportant, is just a means to an end. If, on the other hand, this text has caused you to become more aware of your own level of acceptance in these vital areas, has sparked you to become less willing to accept bad arguments, poor news reports, deceptive advertising, then it has achieved everything that we can reasonably have expected.

# Index